Mobile Media In and Outside of the Art Classroom

"Mobile media are changing teaching and learning. Impressive are the ways that the contributors to this volume use Design-based Research (DBR) to propose educational interventions that assist students in the critical use of mobile media to advance social and civic engagement. *Mobile Media In and Outside of the Art Classroom: Attending to Identity, Spatiality, and Materiality* is a must-read primer on a topic that could not be more timely."
—Doug Blandy, *Professor of School of Planning, Public Policy, and Management, University of Oregon, USA*

"Castro and his collaborators' vivid account of teaching and researching teen artists has everything, and gets it right. For art teachers and teacher educators, there's the real-time enactment of a conceptually rich photography curriculum that deftly merges teens' expressive interests, contemporary image-making skills, and the mobility of social media. For readers interested in research design and pedagogical findings on adolescent artmaking, the book's theoretical framing and qualitative analysis are compelling and insightful. A must-read for all art educators and pedagogical researchers."
—Mary Hafeli, *Professor of Art and Art Education, Teachers College, Columbia University, USA, and Author of* Exploring Studio Materials: Teaching Creative Artmaking to Children *and co-editor (with Judith Burton) of* Conversations in Art: The Dialectics of Teaching and Learning

"In this important anthology, art educator Juan Carlos Castro brings research expertise and practical classroom experience together. This book generates questions and strategies for engaging students in their visual communities while challenging assumptions about curriculum. Both creative and critical, Castro's team of art education researchers focus on the centre of a complex of emerging challenges: how students can learn 'with' mobile media and why educators should grow past simply being 'for' or 'against' those technologies."
—Michael J. Emme, *Associate Professor of Art Education in the Department of Curriculum and Instruction, University of Victoria, Canada, and Editor of* Arts-based Approaches to Collaborative Research with Children and Youth

"Increasingly youths are engaging in ubiquitous smartphone usage shared through mobile social networks. In this text, the authors describe compelling, longitudinal research about effective and creative ways in which to use influential, highly engaging digital technologies in today's classrooms. The authors question traditional pedagogical approaches, provide useful information about curricula development, and reframe changing student and teacher roles. This is an extremely important, provocative book for educators, administrators, and researchers confronting the ubiquity of smartphone and social media usage in today's fast-paced, transforming world."

—Joanna Black, *Professor in the Faculty of Education, University of Manitoba, Canada*

Juan Carlos Castro
Editor

Mobile Media In and Outside of the Art Classroom

Attending to Identity, Spatiality, and Materiality

Editor
Juan Carlos Castro
Concordia University
Montreal, QC, Canada

ISBN 978-3-030-25315-8   ISBN 978-3-030-25316-5 (eBook)
https://doi.org/10.1007/978-3-030-25316-5

© The Editor(s) (if applicable) and The Author(s), under exclusive license to Springer Nature Switzerland AG 2019
This work is subject to copyright. All rights are solely and exclusively licensed by the Publisher, whether the whole or part of the material is concerned, specifically the rights of translation, reprinting, reuse of illustrations, recitation, broadcasting, reproduction on microfilms or in any other physical way, and transmission or information storage and retrieval, electronic adaptation, computer software, or by similar or dissimilar methodology now known or hereafter developed.
The use of general descriptive names, registered names, trademarks, service marks, etc. in this publication does not imply, even in the absence of a specific statement, that such names are exempt from the relevant protective laws and regulations and therefore free for general use.
The publisher, the authors and the editors are safe to assume that the advice and information in this book are believed to be true and accurate at the date of publication. Neither the publisher nor the authors or the editors give a warranty, expressed or implied, with respect to the material contained herein or for any errors or omissions that may have been made. The publisher remains neutral with regard to jurisdictional claims in published maps and institutional affiliations.

Cover illustration: © Alex Linch shutterstock.com

This Palgrave Macmillan imprint is published by the registered company Springer Nature Switzerland AG
The registered company address is: Gewerbestrasse 11, 6330 Cham, Switzerland

For Frances and Gabriel

Acknowledgements

I gratefully acknowledge the financial support of the Canadian Social Science and Humanities Research Council (SSHRC) and the Quebec Fonds de recherche Société et culture (FRQSC) who supported this research through two grants: a SSHRC Insight Grant, "MonCoin: Investigating Mobile Learning Networks to Foster Educational Engagement with At-Risk Youth" (Juan Carlos Castro, principal investigator; David Pariser, co-investigator), and a FRQSC, Établissement de Nouveaux professeurs-chercheurs grant entitled "L'enseignement des arts visuels et médiatiques en contexte d'apprentissage mobile pour le renforcement de l'engagement social et de la motivation scolaire des adolescents" (Juan Carlos Castro, principal investigator).

I want to thank David Pariser, who has been a tremendous research partner, collaborator, mentor, and a McNulty to my Bunk. My research and this book would not have been possible without the immense contributions and support of Martin Lalonde, Ehsan Akbari, Lina Moreno, Bettina Forget, and G. H. Greer. As contributors to this book, graduate students, research assistants, and colleagues, they have taught me more than I could ever have taught them. I would also like to thank Melissa Ledo, Matthew Thomson, and Marie-Pier Viens, whose research support on the MonCoin Project was instrumental in its success.

Thank you to the cooperating teachers and students of the MonCoin project who taught us how teaching and learning happens. A big thank you to two of our cooperating teachers, Anne Pilon and Sabrina Bejba, for their valuable contributions to this book.

Thank you to Léah Snider, whose smarts, can-do attitude, and organizational masterwork helped bring this book together.

Projects like these are always supported by those who help carry you through the day-to-day realities of life. A big thank you to Lorrie Blair, Stan Charbonneau, and Larissa Yousoubova for their support.

Finally, my deepest gratitude to Aileen Pugliese Castro for her unconditional love and confidence in me—I would not have accomplished what I have done without her.

CONTENTS

1   Introduction: The MonCoin Project   1
    Juan Carlos Castro

2   The Connected Image in Mobile and Social Media:
    The Visual Instances of Adolescents Becoming   27
    Martin Lalonde

3   The Social Organization of Students in Class Versus
    in an Online Social Network: Freedom and Constraint
    in Two Different Settings   47
    David Pariser and Bettina Forget

4   Girls and Their Smartphones: Emergent Learning
    Through Apps That Enable   77
    Bettina Forget

5   Spatiality of Engagement   103
    Ehsan Akbari

6   Spatial Missions: My Surroundings,
    My Neighbourhood, My School   127
    Ehsan Akbari

7 Integrating Traditional Art Making Processes and
   New Technology in the High School Curriculum   151
   Anne Pilon

8 The New Point and Shoot: Photography Lessons
   Using Phones and Scanners   165
   Sabrina Bejba

9 Visual Mapping Workshop: Materializing Networks
   of Meaning   183
   Lina Maria Moreno

10 Conclusion: Heeding Enchantments and Disconnecting
   Dots—A Sociomaterialist Pedagogy of Things   193
   G. H. Greer

Index   221

List of Contributors

Ehsan Akbari Concordia University, Montreal, QC, Canada

Sabrina Bejba Educational Consultant, Mik^w Chiyâm Arts Concentration Program, Montreal, QC, Canada

Juan Carlos Castro Concordia University, Montreal, QC, Canada

Bettina Forget Concordia University, Montreal, QC, Canada

G. H. Greer Concordia University, Montreal, QC, Canada

Martin Lalonde Université du Québec à Montréal, Montreal, QC, Canada

Lina Maria Moreno Research and Development, Mik^w Chiyâm Arts Concentration Program, Montreal, QC, Canada

David Pariser Concordia University, Montreal, QC, Canada

Anne Pilon Villa Maria High School, Montreal, QC, Canada

List of Figures

Fig. 1.1	The missions and micro-missions of MonCoin	13
Fig. 3.1	4×4 Matrix of posted images exploring identity	51
Fig. 3.2	Seating chart of the classroom showing affinity groupings	56
Fig. 3.3	Comprehensive sociogram showing major student connections in the online MonCoin class social network	57
Fig. 3.4	Online sociogram for a student with many social connections in the classroom	61
Fig. 3.5	Online sociogram for a student with few social connections in the classroom	62
Fig. 3.6	4×4 Matrix of posted images exploring identity	64
Fig. 3.7	Gamer Boys' sociogram	66
Fig. 3.8	Alternative Girls' sociogram	68
Fig. 4.1	Apps by type	88
Fig. 4.2	Apps by function	92
Fig. 5.1	These images were taken during the school and neighborhood walks. They are organized top to bottom, left to right, from a to f. a Samnantha La Rose—comfortable/uncomfortable. b xpapichulox1—My School. c illogic_13—Nature. d Ehsan Akbari—Neighborhood walk documentation. e Artistic_101–MyNeighborhood. f liliespinosa2000—MyNeighborhood	119
Fig. 6.1	- Inspiremydesire's responses to spatial missions (from top left to bottom right): #Micromission_Nature, #Micromission_Unique, #Micromission_notice, #Micromision_pathsItake, #Mission_myneighbourhood, #micromission_notice	135
Fig. 7.1	Amalia Iliacopoulos and Alysson Valery-Archambault: Paper sculpture and forced perspective	158

Fig. 7.2	Myah Argento: One-point perspective drawing and selfie	159
Fig. 7.3	Adrianna Paris Fumai: Monument to mother nature (**a**), Sofia Tiseo: Monument to mark the last year our school would be an all-girls school (**b**), Sofia Melatti: Gargoyle (**c**)	160
Fig. 7.4	Kristina Nahas: Hybrid chair advertisement	161
Fig. 9.1	Students create a map and look at each other's connections	184
Fig. 9.2	Students map the formal, emotional, and conceptual connections they find between the pictures	186
Fig. 9.3	The first connections are observations on the pictures' formal qualities with notes like "Gold" or "String + Flower"	188
Fig. 9.4	Links become more complex as students look at each other's interpretations. The link "they are blue" that the students made between a blue rubber watch and a bed with a blue duvet became "blue I wake up"	189
Fig. 9.5	Each map's configuration reflects the peer-thinking and learning that is at work when students see each other's images	191

List of Tables

Table 3.1 Showing each student ranked according to 3 criteria: (1) The raw number of images they posted; (2) The number of "likes" their classmates gave them; (3) Each student's "like-to-post" ratios   58

Table 4.1 Overview of the top ten most popular apps mentioned by the girls in my study   89

CHAPTER 1

Introduction: The MonCoin Project

Juan Carlos Castro

Spend any time in schools in North America, and you are likely to observe young people using their smartphones to take pictures, record sounds, make music, or videos. From selfies to sexting, digital images—created and shared through mobile, social networks—play a significant role in the daily lives of teens and young adults. Typically, educators, parents, and school administrators react with trepidation or outright prohibition to the presence of image producing and broadcasting tools—the smartphone—in school. As a former high school art teacher and now a university educator preparing the next generation of art educators, I have witnessed the simultaneously radical and yet subtle shifts mobile media has prompted in classrooms. In the art room, the smartphone is, for the most part, an indispensable image research tool for students. Yet, much to the lament of art teachers, students are becoming too reliant on Google Image search. Students can make professional quality images and distribute them all over the world. Conversely, they can also make harmful images that can devastate the lives of their peers (e.g., bullying, sexting, and revenge pornography). What are art educators to do with these devices that contain such creative and destructive power? This question is the rationale for this book and the eight years of research it represents.

J. C. Castro (✉)
Concordia University, Montreal, QC, Canada
e-mail: juancarlos.castro@concordia.ca

The motivation of this book and research started for me when I began researching how young people can use social and mobile media as a creative learning tool. In 2006, after I left my high school art classroom to undertake a Ph.D., I received an invitation from my former students to join a group hosted on an online platform called Facebook. At the time, I had heard little about Facebook, and I assumed it was just another variation of MySpace or its earlier predecessors, a bulletin board system (BBS). However, I was captivated after a few months of watching what my former students did on Facebook. On the Art Group page, students from the beginning to the end of my time as a high school art teacher were sharing their artwork and interacting. What made Facebook and social media different was the ease in which users could upload images and other media content.

The shift in Internet computing—going from having to code HTML to build a Web site to quickly posting images—was so compelling that I decided to devote my doctoral research to its potential for art classrooms (Castro, 2010). I found that peer-learning, or peer-networked learning, has tremendous potential in art education. I also discovered that media forms—specifically images and text—that are peer-generated are potent teachers (Castro, 2015). As I was conducting my dissertation research with art students and their teachers on a closed social network in 2007, the first Apple iPhone was released. Although the iPhone was not the first smartphone on the market, it did seamlessly converge multiple media tools into one device. The iPhone untethered access to the Internet from desktop computers. The speed, amplification, and ubiquity of information sharing increased radically. By the time I completed my dissertation, I knew the future was mobile.

In 2012, with my colleague David Pariser and Art Education graduate student Martin Lalonde, we piloted MonCoin, an experimental art curriculum that used mobile media to foster civic engagement with at-risk youth. MonCoin, French for "my corner" or "my area," is based on research that contended if at-risk youth were engaged with their civic environments using digital tools, they would be more engaged with their education (Bennett, Wells, & Rank, 2009). Our pilot research worked with young people who either dropped out or were at risk of dropping out, aged 16–18 years old, in Montreal. They attended a specialized school that was designed to reintegrate students into the school system or help them obtain a high school equivalency. For 18 months, we tested a curriculum based on missions that were sent to student participants' mobile devices through a semi-private image-based social network—Instagram. The curriculum was designed to have students examine themselves in the context of their immediate surroundings and move outward to explore their larger civic environment. We implemented the curriculum in four- to six-week cycles, getting valuable feedback from our participants along the way, and then redesigned the missions and sequence for the next group of students.

Our data analysis from this pilot phase yielded insights into the potentials and pitfalls of using mobile media in schools that both affirmed and challenged our initial assumptions. In terms of civic engagement, we found that young people were initially more interested in learning how to make "good-looking" images, before looking critically at their civic environments (Pariser, Castro, & Lalonde, 2016). When we asked students to photograph and share areas of their public spaces that needed change, we barely had any response from participants. We found that young people, especially at-risk youth, felt disempowered, so much so, they had no interest in pursuing the question of how to change their neighborhoods for the better. Within the past decade, the field of art education has come to understand the vital role of social and civic engagement as an essential part of contemporary art (Tavin & Ballengee Morris, 2012). What our participants told us was that they did not feel as if they had any power to make a meaningful change. They instead wanted to learn how to make good-looking photographs, which we did teach them in follow-up workshops. In future iterations of the MonCoin curriculum, we strove to integrate the teaching of design and photographic techniques, and we affirmed that this was empowering for young people. Students were learning the grammar of visual culture and as a result, were then more inclined to address questions of civic concern. Mobile media is a powerful tool for image making, but it is still just a tool. Users still need proper instruction on making engaging pictures. These skills are empowering currency on social media for young people.

We also found that young people are invested in constructing their identity online through the multimodal documentation of the physical and temporal spaces of their everyday lives (Lalonde, Castro, & Pariser, 2016). Much of mobile and social media use for young people is motivated by building one's identity, presentation, and dissemination. To protect the student's identity in the project, we required them to refrain from posting images of themselves or others directly. This restriction coupled with projects that asked students to explore aspects of the self produced an abundance of pictures of participants' material world—their favorite objects and collections that expressed their affinities and ideas about themselves. The material world is rich with meaning for teens and adolescents and often ends up as essential signifiers of social status and identity. Material culture is also a rich source of pedagogical material for art educators (Blandy & Bolin, 2018). The smartphone has become a necessity in how young people construct and share their identities through the material world around them—it is just as crucial to their identity as selfies.

Further, the use of mobile media was initially hypothesized as a means for engaging at-risk youth outside of school. However, we found when participants had the choice of where they could move and meet, participants expressly sought out opportunities to be together in school (Castro, Lalonde, & Pariser, 2016). MonCoin was an opportunity to give at-risk youth, who had a high rate of absenteeism, a way to engage with school using the networked capability of mobile devices, a social network, and a curriculum premised on exploring civic environments. We thought we could deliver the MonCoin curriculum, through their own mobile device or one we lent them, to students regardless if they were physically in school. What we observed were students who usually did not want to come to school, gathering after the school day to meet up with the instructor and fellow students to discuss the projects or self-organize walking field trips to explore their neighborhood. In our final interviews with students, we discussed their willingness to come together at the school or in the neighborhood during the MonCoin project. They expressed an affinity toward the sense of agency they were granted, which stemmed from the movement afforded by the curriculum and technology. The increased mobility provided to these students was in marked contrast to their typical experience of school—whereas for at-risk students their mobility was considerably restricted. Mobile media coupled with a curriculum predicated on exploring space created the conditions in which the freedom to move empowered students to engage more with their education and peers inside and outside of school.

This book picks up where our pilot research ended and the MonCoin project expanded into the formal curriculum of a variety of types of secondary schools in the Montreal area. There is no shortage of mobile media projects to use with students. Yet, social and mobile media are often construed as a distraction in schools, and educators are at a loss for how to address this social phenomenon. This edited volume will provide an in-depth and considered examination of the MonCoin curriculum and the associated and varied conditions (e.g., social, technological, spatial) in which we conducted our research. Overall, the book takes a worked-example approach (Gee, 2009)—our designed curriculum that was iteratively adapted and refined to local contexts and with collaborating art educators—to explore the theoretical and practice-based concerns of using mobile media in educational settings. While worked examples are used mainly in fields such as mathematics and science to explain a problem and provide a solution, James Gee (2009) suggested adapting the model for contributing new knowledge to the field of Digital Media Learning. Since MonCoin is a large-scale research project, a worked-example model provides a certain amount of conceptual cohesion while also offering a wide array of insights into the varied learning experiences that arose from integrating mobile media into the visual arts curriculum in schools. Meaning, the specific theoretical examples used in this book will be rooted in practice.

Drawing on hours of interviews with students and teachers, ethnographic field notes, and thousands of images made by students with associated data such as likes, comments, and geo-tagging, this project provides a rich source of real-world data to articulate considerations for theorizing curricular design that uses mobile and social media inside and outside of the art classroom. In the remainder of this chapter, I will give a brief and relevant literature review of the sociocultural conditions involved in how young people use their mobile media devices, smartphones in education, and new technologies in art education. I will then provide a brief summary of the overarching theoretical framework—complexity theory, network theory, and mobilities. This summary is followed by an introduction of the MonCoin curriculum, followed by a summary of our methodology, and an overview of the book.

Mobile Media, Young People, and Schools

In America, a vast majority of teens and young adults have regular access to or own a smartphone (Lenhart, Smith, Anderson, Duggan, & Perri, 2015). In Quebec (CEFRIO, 2017), over 80% of young adults own a smartphone. Besides texting (sending short messages), the taking and sharing of photographs through their phones are essential social activities for teens (Duggan & Rainie, 2012). In Canada (Steeves, 2014) and the United States (Lenhart et al., 2015), more than half of smartphone users take digital photographs and video to share on social networks like Instagram. The smartphone is a ubiquitous device in the social lives of teens and communication through image production, and dissemination is now a key part of life in North America. Since the early 2000s, digital tools and content have merged, creating a culture of media convergence (Jenkins, 2006). The convergence of digital photography and mobile phones has spurred a "technology of everyday life" (Goggin, 2006, p. 145).

Now, photographs of everyday events and objects are judged worthy of sharing—for those reading this book who used to use film cameras, can you ever remember taking pictures of your meals and then sharing it with all of your friends? While some scholars argue that this practice of social interaction through mobile media leads to isolation and mental health issues (Turkle, 2011; Twenge, 2017), other researchers like danah boyd (2014) argued that teens are often able to negotiate the complex social relationships online to build healthy ones offline. Further, Gerard Goggin and Larissa Hjorth (2014) asserted that the creative capacity of the smartphone makes it a tool for creativity, which in turn can lead to self-actualization.

When it comes to what teens do in digital networks, Mimi Ito (2008) categorized two forms of sociality—friendship and interest-driven activity. While social media is mostly used for maintaining relationships established in offline environments (boyd, 2014), there is also the small, but growing use of social media to explore and develop new knowledge around specific interests. This can include participating in specialized groups, which may include (but is not limited to) visual arts such as anime and comic art, video editing, photography, creative writing, and fandom groups based on reality television shows. Engagement in such activities has been described as typical of a participatory culture (Jenkins, Purushotma, Weigel, Clinton, & Robison, 2009). Participatory culture is exemplified in situations where teens and adults, whose interests converge, interact online by sharing information, teaching, and learning from each other. These practices of informal learni ng are of particular interest to art educators as a source for informing curriculum and pedagogy.

In the book, *Youth Practices in Digital Arts and New Media: Learning in Formal and Informal Settings* (Black, Castro, & Lin, 2015), we examined research on informal and formal learning settings stemming from previous research by Joanna Black (Model New Media: Video Programs in Art Education Case Study Research, 2010–2012) and Kit

Grauer, Juan Carlos Castro, Ruth Beer, and Ching-Chiu Lin (Citizens of Tomorrow: Investigating the Impact of Community Media Arts Practice on Marginalized Urban Youth, 2012–2015). In our analysis, we confirmed Julian Sefton-Green's (2014) assertion that the informal and formal divide is misleading. The innovation found in informal sites of learning and formal sites of learning was dependent on several factors, one of which was the incorporation of young people's cultural practices into the creative practices shared by teachers. For example, at one of the community arts programs studied in Quebec, we found that instructors who integrated the informal creative practices of their students into their teaching practices resulted in a higher level of student engagement and learning (Lalonde & Castro, 2015).

Over fifteen years ago, Brian Goldfarb (2002) argued that most literature on media education focused on youth media consumption, neglecting youth media production in education. The focus has now shifted as is demonstrated in research such as the study of model new media/video programs (Black, 2014), and community-based new media arts programs (Grauer, Castro, & Lin, 2012). Researchers into Visual Culture Learning Communities—the informal group of young people and their creative practices—are mapping the networks and cognitive traits of learning in the arts to apply to curriculum design in the visual art classroom (Freedman, Heijnen, Kallio-Tavin, Kárpáti, & Papp, 2013; Karpati, Freedman, Castro, Kallio-Tavin, & Heijnen, 2017). What the MonCoin project contributes to these studies is a consideration of how the smartphone has transformed how young people learn about themselves and their world. MonCoin builds on the salient qualities of mobile media to build bridges between the physical, social, and cultural worlds that teens and adolescents navigate daily.

LEARNING THROUGH NETWORKS, MATERIALS, AND MOVEMENT

The standard definition of learning is that it is a process of acquiring knowledge. Most teaching in schools today is based on this assumption of knowledge as a kind of object that can be packaged and delivered. This definition of knowledge is conflated with the meaning of information. Information is a fact, while knowledge is grounded in interpretation of something and the subsequent action that comes in response (Maturana & Varela, 1992). When knowing something, a knower will reference their experience. It is these previous experiences that guide a learner's movement through the world. Knowledge also resides in the body and is both a mental process and physically structured (Davis & Sumara, 2006; Maturana & Varela, 1992). Learning is the ability to adapt to new experiences and contexts—it is a process of change in the formation and structure of knowledge. What this means for educators is that teaching is not solely the act of delivering information, it is also about creating experiences that learners both can understand based on their prior knowledge, but also moves them to adapt to new experiences.

Now, the individual learner is not the only one that changes. A learner, along with other learners, teachers, and the material world are co-specifying (Varela, Thompson, & Rosch, 1991), that is to say, that as groups of students learn, so does the teacher and the environment. To better understand the qualities of movement, space, and the relationships that form the conditions for learning, we use sociomaterial frameworks, which are "how systems and practices and knowledge become more or less connected, performing comparable (if often distinctly different) activities across space—time" (Fenwick, Edwards, & Sawchuk, 2011, p. 5). What this means is that learning is contingent on a network of relationships with peers, teachers, curriculum, materials, technology, and more. Sociomaterial frameworks encompass theories such as actor-network theory (ANT), complexity, and mobility.

We use an ANT (Fenwick & Edwards, 2010) approach nested within complexity thinking (Davis & Sumara, 2006; Fenwick et al., 2011), to better understand the role of images and the interface of the mobile phone—the production, circulation, and consumption of images and how they relate to learning through social media. Further, understandings from mobility studies help us to understand the continual movement of learners through space, the circulation of images, and the subsequent power dynamics that regulate such movement, especially in schools (Adey, 2010).

Scholars who use ANT argue that it is not really an explanatory theory; instead, it is better understood as an orientation that attends to the non-human and its effects on the human and vice versa (Latour, 2005). The network of associations that arise between the human and non-human is critical for understanding how images are consumed and interpreted, all the while being delivered through a complex array of software and hardware across time and space. Using an ANT approach is critical for tracing the paths of the movement of images and the role they play on student learning.

Peer-learning has long been understood as fundamental to visual art learning (Wilson, 1976). In fact, systems theories of learning have enjoyed periodic consideration over the past forty years in art education (Castro, 2012a; Kindler, 1999; Marshall, 2016). The field's latest engagement with systems theory is its attention to complexity science, theory, and thinking. The goals of complexity thinking seek to better understand the associations between levels of organization and its impact on learning (Davis & Sumara, 2006). For our study, we were specifically interested in how complexity thinking frames learning as a process of transformation to sustain "internal and external coherence" (Davis, 2018, p. 198) in a continually dynamic process of adaptation and transformation. Learning in these environments is an act of looking closely at images and reinterpreting to some degree the thematic or visual characteristics of images as a process of maintaining an internal and external coherence within the larger learning collective (Castro, 2012a). What this means is that students will adopt the stylistic and thematic tendencies of their peers. The difference in social media is that now students are able to view everyone's art, rather than those images made by peers sitting close to them in the classroom.

To understand how our participants learn with and through these practices on and offline, we attended to how they articulated their artistic development and document the evolution of their work in reference to the MonCoin curriculum, their peers, and environment. Encounters with the images produced by peers and the algorithms that delivered such images required a human and non-human approach to understanding learning online (Castro, 2015)—which was why ANT is well suited to attend to the role of the non-human and complexity thinking to the dynamics of complex decentralized learning networks. These two complementary frameworks enabled us to emphasize the impact of things, in our case—images, smartphones, digital networks, social media platforms, etc.—on student learning.

To account for movement, we drew from mobility studies (Cresswell, 2010), which attends to the flows of material (e.g., people, goods, images, etc.), and mLearning (Pachler, Bachmair, & Cook, 2010). Often mobility is assessed in terms of relationships between the relative movement between a set of actors and conditions. These relationships have been referred to as moorings/un-moorings (Urry, 2003) or (im)mobilities (Adey, 2010). What defines the qualities of these movement relationships can be physical or political. In our pilot research (Castro et al., 2016), we used Adey's (2010) theorization of (im)mobilities to understand better how young people's movement or lack thereof impacted their educational engagement. mLearning is not necessarily a fundamentally new way of learning; rather, it emphasizes incorporating the qualities of movement inside and outside of the classroom, all supported by mobile media (Kress & Pachler, 2007). The dynamics of movement through space amplified through mobile media form the foundations for our theorization, analysis, and the MonCoin curriculum.

The MonCoin Curriculum

The incorporation of the informal creative activities of teens and their smartphones into the art curriculum can generate high levels of student engagement (Black et al., 2015; Grauer et al., 2012; Lalonde & Castro, 2015). Making meaningful connections between the creative and cultural practices of students and curriculum content offers a solution to the never-ending game of "catch-up" that schools play when it comes to new technology. However, the adoption of new digital technology into schools and curricula has long had an uneven effect on student learning (Cuban, Kirkpatrick, & Peck, 2001). Part of the problem is the accelerated cycle of technological innovation and its impact on society. One solution is creating curricula that are co-constructed and negotiated between student's cultural practices and formal curricula. This in-between space, described as a third-space pedagogy by art education scholar Brent Wilson (2008), provides the opportunity for innovation and pedagogical possibility outside the realm of formal and informal education. The MonCoin curriculum is designed to incorporate the ubiquity of mobile media and social media practices in the lives of young people with the formal art curriculum.

The curriculum is structured on a series of missions that ask participants to start visually investigating ideas of self, moving to spaces and subjects less familiar. It is nested thematically by exploring ideas of expressing one's identity without showing themselves to exploring the areas around oneself. We named the prompts and questions as missions to create the sense of a game (Gee, 2003). The missions are delivered to the participants' devices at various times throughout the curriculum.

The missions are conceptually based on constraints that enable (Castro, 2007) a feature of complex systems. In complexity theory, the emergence of individual and collective knowledge is dependent on constraints that delineate boundaries and movement. In this sense, constraints can be the permeable cellular membrane of an organism or the atmospheric conditions that give rise to a hurricane (Mitchell, 2009). In the curriculum, constraints are conditions, prompts, questions, and missions that provoke physical and conceptual movement by primarily asking participants to examine prior knowledge in new ways. Qualities of successful constraints are the structure and clarity they provide, while also including enough ambiguity to encourage a diversity of responses. The curriculum theorist Bill Doll (1989) wrote about constraints in the mathematics curriculum as balancing being unfamiliar enough to challenge students, but not so much that students would not attempt the problem. In art, constraints reference prior knowledge while posing a reevaluation of the habitual ways of interpreting and enacting this knowledge. It is an understanding similar to constructivist and social constructivist theories of learning, especially concepts such as zones of proximal development (Vygotsky & Cole, 1978), which posit that learning best occurs by finding the right amount of support for a student to work toward independence. With constraints that enable, it is referencing what students know and gently nudging them to new understandings. For MonCoin, we primarily focused on conceptual development and taught skills as the need arose. In other words, we let the student's ideas drive the requirements for skill development. As I already pointed out from our pilot study, young people want to learn skills, and they want to explore big, meaningful ideas. We do not separate these dual aspects of making as we see them as two sides of a coin.

The work of Harrell Fletcher and Miranda July's Learning to Love You More (2007) project was the original inspiration for the kinds and quality of prompts that make up MonCoin's missions. Not a typical work of art in the sense of a painting or sculpture, Learning to Love You More is what is termed social practice art, which is a work of art that is concerned directly with the social relationships that are formed. Instead of a specific material considered the medium for a work of art, it is the quality of the social relationship that is created (Castro, 2012b). Learning to Love You More was a Web site that started in 2002. Fletcher and July posted assignments for people to respond to, which they then would send to the artists for possible posting. Assignments included "Make a child's outfit an adult size," "Draw a constellation from someone's freckles," and "Take a flash photo of under your bed." The artists would then curate and post the responses, sometimes using them as inspiration for future assignments. One assignment in particular—"Make a LYTLM assignment"—inspired our last two missions of posting a mission and responding to a mission. These missions allowed students to shape the trajectory of the curriculum by testing new ideas and assessing the response from their peers.

Missions

We structured the missions into four major themes: Self, My School, My Neighborhood, and Post/Respond to a Mission. The missions were delivered through the social media platform, and students were tagged (a process of marking their online profile), so they would receive notifications of the post. Each mission post was a photograph that related somewhat to the theme of the mission. Overlaid on the image was the title of the mission in bold lettering (Fig. 1.1). Accompanying each mission post was a detailed description that included an overview of constraint and reminders for appropriate behavior online. As part of the introduction to MonCoin, we would talk with students about their rights and responsibilities when posting content online and interacting—hence the constant reminder in each mission post to consider their responsibilities when posting and also traveling through their school and neighborhood.

It was also brought to our attention students' heavy reliance on Google Image search. Art teachers are now finding that some students will use found images online as their own, which is why we needed to remind students to use their own photos. Additionally, we would also cover the basics of photographic composition and free photo editing applications. Each mission description would also use hashtags to organize the posts making it easy for the art teachers to organize student responses based on the theme quickly. We found through our iterative process of testing and refining the curriculum that within the larger thematic missions, there needed to be smaller, more specific missions. We called these micro-missions (Fig. 1.1), which we would post to our closed social network on daily basis. We emphasized to participants that they did not need to respond to all of the micro-missions, though some students chose to take on the challenge and respond to each micro-mission.

Each major theme would last about a week, depending on the schedule of the school. Some of our participating teachers focused solely on the MonCoin curriculum and some used it as a supplementary activity where students would work on more traditional studio projects during class with some time devoted to the missions and requirements. Depending on the choice of the teacher to use the MonCoin curriculum in a focused manner or a complementary activity would impact how long each mission took.

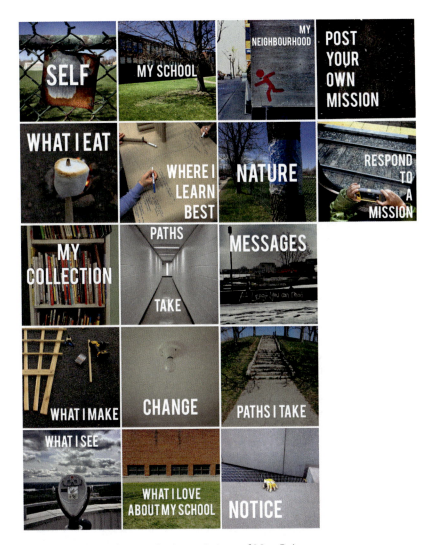

Fig. 1.1 The missions and micro-missions of MonCoin

Given the flexible nature of MonCoin, because it asks students to move through their spaces, it is relatively easy to adapt to a variety of teaching contexts. If an art teacher chose to focus solely on the MonCoin curriculum, in-class activities enriched students' understanding and practice of mobile photography and talking about each other's images.

Self.

In the first mission, we will explore the theme of identity. Show us something about who you are, but without revealing your identity—like showing your face.

Make sure you use the hashtags: #mission1_self. We will post more micro-missions related to this theme to inspire you each day. Remember only post contents (pictures and words) that are yours and that you would be comfortable sharing with your teachers and parents.

What I eat.
What you eat says a lot about you. Show us what you eat in a way that visually communicates why you love it.
This is the first micro-mission. It is related to the #mission1_self. The micro-missions are to help you explore the bigger theme. You do not have to respond to every micro-mission, only those that inspire you.

My collection.
Many of us collect things. Our collections are a reflection of who we are. Show us what you collect. Sharing a collection visually is all about showing many items in one image. Consider the composition techniques we shared at the beginning of the project: dramatic lighting, the rule of thirds, using the edges of the frame, frame within a frame, getting close. This is the second micro-mission related to #mission1_self.

What I make.
Many of us make things. What we make reflects who we are. Show us what you make. This is the third micro-mission related to #mission1_self.

What I see.
How we see the world and what we choose to look at define who we are. This micro-mission can be responded to in several different ways. One possibility is to visually communicate how you see the world—from what catches your eye to your philosophy of how the world works. *What I see* is very open-ended. This is the fourth micro-mission related to #mission1_self.

My school.

The second mission is about communicating what your school means to you. When walking through the school remember to response the other classes in session and the building. Remember only post contents (pictures and words) that are yours and that you would be comfortable sharing with your teachers and parents. Use the hashtag: #mission2_myschool.

Where I learn best.
Where do you learn best in school? There are places in every school where we feel smart, know something, and are confident to apply what we know. This is the fifth micro-mission and is related to the #mission2_myschool. The micro-missions are to help you explore the bigger theme. You do not have to respond to every micro-mission, only those that inspire you.

Paths I take.
What paths do you take through school?
This is the sixth micro-mission and is related to the #mission2_myschool

Change.
Is there something you would change about your school? What would it be? Why would you want to change it? Only show things that could realistically be changes with your positive contributions. This is the seventh micro-mission and is related to the #mission2_myschool

What I love about my school.
What makes your school special? What do you look forward to when you come to school? This is the eighth micro-mission and is related to the #mission2_myschool

My neighborhood.

The third mission involves visually exploring the neighborhood around the school and where you live. What does your neighborhood mean to you? Remember to respect the environment, people's privacy, and property. Do not post images that would identify yourself or others. Remember only post content

> (pictures and words) that are yours and that you would be comfortable sharing with your teachers and parents. Use the hashtag: #mission3_myneighborhood.
>
> Nature.
> The human-made environment is full of nature. Humans are not the only living thing in the city. Where does nature take over? Where is it subdued? Where is the natural world changing? Adapting? Thriving? What are your favorite aspects of the natural world in your neighborhood? What needs to be protected? This is the ninth micro-mission and is related to the #mission3_myneighborhood.
>
> Messages.
> In the urban environment, there are messages everywhere. There are loud messages and quiet ones. What are these messages telling you? This is the tenth micro-mission and is related to the #mission3_myneighborhood.
>
> Paths I take.
> What paths do you take through your neighborhood? This is the eleventh micro-mission and is related to the #mission3_myneighborhood.
>
> Notice.
> Look carefully and closely at your surroundings. Do you notice anything that you would not have noticed if you weren't looking carefully? For this micro-mission seek out and photograph the little or big things that go unnoticed. This is the thirteenth micro-mission and is related to the #mission3_myneighborhood.

The MonCoin curriculum leverages mobile media as a way to amplify peer-learning and educational engagement (Akbari, Castro, Lalonde, Moreno, & Pariser, 2016). The curriculum's design, especially the second half, evolved to directly ask students to respond to each other's images and ideas. We found that the creative potential in a group increases significantly when the source of ideas comes from the group, and this can only happen when there is open communication. Social media enables people to see ideas quickly in a learning environment that is not controlled by one individual. How mobile and social media changes the dynamic in the classroom is moving from a centralized network model to a decentralized one (Castro, 2013). A centralized network model of communication in education relies heavily on the teacher to communicate ideas. For example, in some classrooms, art teachers think nothing of controlling what gets posted on the walls of the classroom, including student artwork. A decentralized model opens up the possibilities for students to participate in what art is shared in the school—and especially in a social media learning environment. The role of the teacher changes, but the workload does not. Instead of directing and informing, the teacher is an active participant by making, observing, interacting, and intervening when appropriate. Interventions are not only relegated to correcting inappropriate behavior, such as posting offensive content, they are also useful when the ideation becomes homogenous. In decentralized networks, like the Internet, ideas and attention can quickly be monopolized (Watts, 2003). In online learning environments, stylistic trends or subject matter can become the norm (Castro, 2015). The art teacher can recognize when students gravitate toward one way of making and then introduce new ideas or skills to broaden their repertoire. This is not to say that converging on one way of making is necessarily detrimental, it may, in fact, mean a certain amount of mastery was achieved, which means that for the art teacher it is time to introduce new ways of knowing and making.

Post your own mission.

For this mission we want you to post a mission for your classmates and teacher to respond to. Good missions are specific, yet open-ended enough that you can't predict what people will post. Good missions get at what connects us as humans, but asks us about our own unique experience. Please ensure that your missions will not require the person who responds to them to harm themselves, others, or property. Remember only post missions that you would be comfortable sharing with your teachers and parents. Use the hashtag: #mission5_postmission and compose your own hashtag to keep track of who responds.

Respond to a mission.

Select and respond to one or more missions posted by your classmates. Make sure you tag the person who wrote the mission and use their hashtags. Also, use the hashtag #mission5_respondmission.

The MonCoin curriculum is not fixed. It is meant to evolve and adapt to the needs of teachers and students. The emphasis of the curriculum is to explore the everyday surroundings of students anew. Whether that is an emphasis on the school, the neighborhood, or another shared space, MonCoin is about using mobile media to create a collective experience—one that depends on the individual expression of students and the ability to share those experiences with the group. And this collective experience emphasizes the shared space of students, teachers, and community members.

THE MONCOIN RESEARCH

MonCoin is also a research study. We were interested in how a visual art curriculum, delivered through and utilizing mobile media, could increase the engagement of students. As described at the beginning of this introduction, we undertook our pilot study at a school that helped 16- to 18-year-olds stay in or get back into school and/or obtain their high school diploma. From our pilot, we expanded the project into three new schools: two primarily English speaking schools, one a private school and the other a comprehensive school; and one comprehensive French-language secondary school. Thousands of images were produced, and hours of interviews conducted. The teachers and students at each school shaped the design of the curriculum. They offered deep insight into how the use of mobile media inside and outside of the art classroom changes students' sense of identity, how they come to know, and how they learn.

Our methodological approach to MonCoin used design-based research (DBR) (Barab & Squire, 2004; Design-Based Research Collective, 2003; Wang & Hannafin, 2005). DBR is similar to action research in that it seeks to address a problem through iteration, analysis, and action. Yet the difference is DBR's dual focus on the design of educational interventions (e.g., curricula, technological support, etc.) and the development of theories of learning. The emphasis on education and learning stems from DBR's emergence from the Learning Sciences and clinical psychology. Researchers in the early 1990s wanted to take research out of the controlled laboratory and into the messiness of real-world classrooms (Brown, 1992).

The main qualities of DBR research are: interventionist, theory-driven, pragmatic, contextual, iterative, collaborative, and integrative (Barab & Squire, 2004). Intervention in the context of MonCoin was our involvement in providing a meaningful curriculum that actively involves the researcher's presence and positionality. MonCoin was driven and contributed to theories of learning, especially as they related to sociomaterialism, complexity, mobility, identity, and affect. The context of the classroom necessitated a pragmatic approach to our presence as researchers in the learning environment. Iteration was a key to the development of the MonCoin curriculum—at the end of each phase, participant feedback and responses were analyzed, and modifications were made in the next curricular iteration. The collaboration was a constant; extensive meetings with the participating educators throughout and especially at the end of each phase were a critical component to gain feedback to adapt the MonCoin curriculum better. Our close collaboration with the educators and students generated insights into the curriculum. DBR is dependent on the integrative assemblage of different research methods. In our case, we relied extensively on participant observation, pre- and post-interviews, and image-based analysis of posted content online.

DBR is not without its criticism. Given that the uptake of DBR has been broad and varied across educational disciplines, it has sometimes conflicting epistemological assumptions—meaning how knowledge is treated. Liam Rourke and Norm Friesen (2006) highlighted this contradiction when they argued that the positivist promises of mixed methods research cannot be conflated with the interpretivist position of the contextually sensitive emphasis of DBR. In MonCoin, we are firmly rooted in the interpretivist approach as it aligns with our theoretical assumptions of knowledge, which is an inter-objectivist position. Inter-objectivity, as defined by Brent Davis and Dennis Sumara (2006), holds that observations and descriptions of a phenomenon change the phenomenon.

The interpretations throughout this book and previous publications provide insights into a variety of pressing questions about teaching and learning with and through new technologies. Educational researchers Terry Anderson and Julie Shattuck (2012) in their analysis of the DBR literature reflected that most studies utilizing this methodology did not make claims of large-scale change or reform. Instead, the majority of DBR research is modestly situated in classroom environments and produces rich and deep descriptions, interpretations, and theorizations of learning. Anderson and Shattuck noted that even though large-scale change was not achieved in many DBR studies, small shifts in the attitudes and approaches of teachers and schools did. Herein lies the promise of DBR research—it is the multitude of small, in-depth projects that collectively can have an effect on the overall quality of education. Even though these changes are near impossible to measure due to the context-specific nature of DBR research, its impact cannot be ignored.

Organization of Book

With hundreds of hours of interviews and thousands of participant-produced images constituting our database, the MonCoin research team had no shortage of possible facets to explore regarding how young people use mobile phones inside and outside of the art classroom. In many ways, this edited book embodies the collective knowledge that MonCoin aimed to enact, made possible by the careful, insightful, and rigorous examination of our data by the project's researchers and collaborators. This book is organized into three themes. The first examines how young people's identities form and are performed through mobile and social media in an art curriculum like MonCoin. The second section considers the spatial dimensions of teaching and learning through mobile media. And the third section presents an additional set of curricular possibilities for using mobile media in the art classroom. The book concludes with a chapter that theorizes the materiality of learning in the MonCoin project.

In Chapter 2, Martin Lalonde, a former Research Assistant on the MonCoin project, takes an image-centric approach to how young people's identities emerge and evolve. Using affect theory, Lalonde traces the forces that move adolescents to use their smartphones to create, consume, and circulate images in acts of becoming. This means the constellation of images that young people live in, with, and through, is an essential part of who they are as individuals. He concludes with a call for schools to consider the role curriculum can play in creating a space for teens and adolescents to reflect and act on how socially mediated image making and consumption are an integral part of their development. David Pariser and Bettina Forget, Co-Investigator and Research Assistant, take a different approach to understand the identity formation and performance of our participants in Chapter 3. Using a contemporary interpretation of Goffman's (1959) theory of identity performance coupled with a method of mapping social relationships—sociograms—Pariser and Forget investigate the on and offline social engagement of students. While students have the potential to explore new ways of performing their identities online, thus creating new social relationships in the class, the more significant pedagogical value for the authors is the fine-grained knowledge teachers can learn about their students. In Chapter 4, Bettina Forget continues the examination of identity formation through mobile and social media by considering the smartphone apps that girls used to support their learning. Using interview and observation data, Forget analyzes how girls identify, select, and use mobile applications for education, art making, and social relationships. She advocates for teachers to cultivate careful and critical examination of the kinds of smartphone applications that end up on our student's phones.

Ehsan Akbari, a Research Assistant and Project Manager for MonCoin, conducts an in-depth analysis of the spatial missions in Chapter 5. Akbari introduces the theme of spatiality through an elaboration on cultivating awareness through mobile media photography. He couples theories of spatiality with complexity to discuss how participants' perceptions of their environments give rise to collective perceptions of shared spaces. In Chapter 6, Akbari looks at how missions that are designed to cultivate investigations of personal and civic environments can foster a deeper appreciation of the everyday spaces young people navigate. He does this by using spatial theory in conceptualizing the missions used in the MonCoin project. Akbari concludes with a set of recommendations for how art educators can design meaningful spatial missions for the needs of their students and context.

In Chapter 7, Anne Pilon, one of the MonCoin collaborating art teachers, presents a series of pedagogical activities using mobile media in the art classroom. Before working with the MonCoin project, Pilon was beginning to consider the possibilities for mobile media as her school recently instituted an iPad-per-student program. As a result of her participation in MonCoin, she designed a set of innovative projects using mobile media. In Pilon's reflection, she articulates the need to develop pedagogical activities that capture the salient qualities of new technology—not just replace what is already easily accomplished through traditional materials. Sabrina Bejba, another MonCoin collaborating art teacher, shares a set of photography projects using smartphone cameras in Chapter 8. As wet darkrooms are becoming less common due to high financial costs and traditional computer labs harder to maintain, art educators are increasingly using student's mobile media as a tool for fine art photography, animation, and filmmaking. Today's mobile media is powerful enough to shoot high-resolution images and video, including the ability to edit and distribute content easily. In Chapter 9, Lina Moreno provides us with a creative way of thinking about conversations in the art classroom using mobile media. Using constraints that enable, Moreno designed an in-class activity that reshapes how students can talk about each other's artwork. With simple tools like tape and markers to identify conceptual connections between the student's mobile devices, she pushes them to think about the relationships between images and each other.

G. H. Greer concludes this book with a meta-analysis of learning that was cultivated in the MonCoin project. Greer interviewed the research team and analyzed student interviews to theorize the materiality of learning, after joining the MonCoin project as a research assistant in the data analysis phase. The book concludes with Greer's chapter because it provides the reader with a deep understanding of how learning and teaching are a dynamic network of relationships between humans and non-humans.

Ultimately, learning in, with, and through new technology involves an ever-changing set of conditions. Artificial intelligence, machine learning, and powerful mobile computing technologies will increasingly shape the experiences of ourselves, each other, and the spaces we navigate. The reader of this book will notice that we do not delve too much into the specifics of technology as these will rapidly change. Rather, the curriculum of MonCoin is designed to be adapted to any platform or devices as long as images can be posted by students, and they can see the work of their peers. These two features define a significant portion of how young people spend their time interacting, and it is what undergirds our approach to the use of mobile and social media in MonCoin's curriculum. Technology will change, but the concepts in this book will hopefully outlive the life cycle of a smartphone. Young people will seek to connect with each other, and art teachers can amplify this inclination into creative activity to explore concepts of self, space, and material with or without new technology. Art teachers have the power to assemble complex competencies into cohesive explorations that are culturally relevant to today's teens and adolescents.

REFERENCES

Adey, P. (2010). *Mobility*. New York: Routledge.
Akbari, E., Castro, J. C., Lalonde, M., Moreno, L., & Pariser, D. (2016). "This allowed us to see what others were thinking": Curriculum for peer-initiated learning in art. *Art Education*, 69(5), 20–25.

Anderson, T., & Shattuck, J. (2012). Design-based research: A decade of progress in education research? *Educational Researcher, 41*(1), 16–25.

Barab, S. A., & Squire, K. (2004). Design-based research: Putting a stake in the ground. *Journal of the Learning Sciences, 13*(1), 1–14.

Bennett, W. L., Wells, C., & Rank, A. (2009). Young citizens and civic learning: Two paradigms of citizenship in the digital age. *Citizenship Studies, 13*(2), 105–120.

Black, J., Castro, J. C., & Lin, C. (2015). *New media usage in formal and informal educational settings*. New York, NY: Palgrave Macmillan.

Blandy, D., & Bolin, P. (2018). *Learning things: Material culture in art education*. New York, NY: Teachers College Press.

boyd, d. (2014). *It's complicated: The social lives of networked teens*. London: Yale University Press.

Brown, A. L. (1992). Design experiments: Theoretical and methodological challenges in creating complex interventions in classroom settings. *The Journal of the Learning Sciences, 2*, 141–178.

Castro, J. C. (2007). Enabling artistic inquiry. *Canadian Art Teacher, 6*, 6–16.

Castro, J. C. (2010). *An inquiry into knowing, learning, and teaching through new and social media*. Vancouver: The University of British Columbia. Retrieved from https://circle.ubc.ca/bitstream/handle/2429/14682/ubc_2010_spring_castro_juan.pdf?sequence=1.

Castro, J. C. (2012a). Learning and teaching art through social media. *Studies in Art Education, 52*(2), 153–170.

Castro, J. C. (2012b). Shaping a new social: Harrell Fletcher and The problem of possible redemption. In T. Quinn, J. Ploof, & L. Hochtritt (Eds.), *Art and social justice education: Culture as commons* (pp. 101–103). London: Routledge, Taylor & Francis Group.

Castro, J. C. (2013). Teaching art in a networked world. *Trends, The Journal of The Texas Art Education Association, 2013*, 87–92.

Castro, J. C. (2015). Visualizing the collective learner through decentralized networks. *International Journal of Education & the Arts, 16*(4). Retrieved from http://www.ijea.org/v16n4/.

Castro, J. C., Lalonde, M., & Pariser, D. (2016). Understanding the im/mobilities of engaging at-risk youth through art and mobile media. *Studies in Art Education, 57*(3), 238–251.

CEFRIO. (2017). *Mobilité au Québec en 2016: état des lieux*. Retrieved from http://www.cefrio.qc.ca/media/uploader/Fascicule_2016_mobilite_final.pdf.

Cresswell, T. (2010). Mobilities I: Catching up. *Progress in Human Geography, 35*(4), 550–558.

Cuban, L., Kirkpatrick, H., & Peck, C. (2001). High access and low use of technologies in high school classrooms: Explaining an apparent paradox. *American Educational Research Journal, 38*(4), 813–834. https://doi.org/10.3102/00028312038004813.

Davis, B. (2018). On the many metaphors of learning ... and their associated educational frames. *Journal of Curriculum Studies, 50*(2), 182–203.
Davis, B., & Sumara, D. (2006). *Complexity and education: Inquires into learning, teaching, and research.* Mahwah, NJ: Lawrence Erlbaum Associates.
Doll, W. E. (1989). Complexity in the classroom. *Educational Leadership, 7,* 65–70.
Design-Based Research Collective. (2003). Design-based research: An emerging paradigm for educational inquiry. *Educational Researcher, 32,* 5–8.
Duggan, M., & Rainie, L. (2012). Cell phone activities 2012. *Pew Internet and American Life Project.* Retrieved from: http://pewinternet.org/Reports/2012/Cell-Activities.aspx.
Fenwick, T., & Edwards, R. (2010). *Actor-network theory in education* (1st ed.). New York: Routledge.
Fenwick, T., Edwards, R., & Sawchuck, P. (2011). *Emerging approaches to educational research: Tracing the sociomaterial.* London: Routledge.
Fletcher, H., & July, M. (2007). *Learning to love you more.* London: Prestel.
Freedman, K., Heijnen, E., Kallio-Tavin, M., Kárpáti, A., & Papp, L. (2013). Visual culture learning communities: How and what students come to know in informal art groups. *Studies in Art Education, 53*(2), 103–115.
Gee, J. P. (2003). What video games have to teach us about learning and literacy. *Computers in Entertainment (CIE), 1*(1), 20.
Gee, J. P. (2009). *New digital media and learning as an emerging area and "worked examples" as one way forward.* Cambridge: MIT Press.
Goffman, I. (1959). *The presentation of self in everyday life.* New York: Anchor Books.
Goggin, G. (2006). *Cell phone culture: Mobile technology in everyday life.* New York: Routledge.
Goggin, G., & Hjorth, L. (Eds.). (2014). *The Routledge companion to mobile media.* New York: Taylor & Francis.
Grauer, K., Castro, J. C., & Lin, C. (2012). Encounters with difference: Community-based new media programs and practices. *Studies in Art Education, 52*(2), 139–152.
Ito, M., Horst, H., Bittanti, M., boyd, d.m., Herr-Stephenson, B., & Lange, P.G., Pascoe, C. J., ... Tripp, L. (2008). *Living and learning with new media: Summary of findings from the digital youth project.* Retrieved from http://digitalyouth.ischool.berkeley.edu/files/report/digitalyouth-WhitePaper.pdf.
Jenkins, H. (2006). *Convergence culture: Where old and new media collide.* New York: New York University Press.
Jenkins, H., Purushotma, R., Weigel, M., Clinton, K., & Robison, A. J. (2009). *Confronting the challenges of participatory culture: Media education for the 21st century.* Cambridge, MA: The MIT Press. Retrieved from http://books.google.com/books?.

Karpati, A., Freedman, K., Castro, J. C., Kallio-Tavin, M., & Heijnen, E. (2017). Collaboration in visual culture learning communities: Towards a synergy of individual and collective creative practice. *The International Journal of Art & Design Education, 36*(2), 164–175.

Kindler, A. M. (1999). "From endpoints to repertoires": A challenge to art education. *Studies in Art Education, 40*(4), 330–349.

Kress, G., & Pachler, N. (2007). Thinking about the 'm' in mobile learning. In *Didactics of microlearning: Concepts, discourses and examples* (pp. 139–154). Münster: Waxmann.

Lalonde, M., & Castro, J. C. (2015). Amplifying youth cultural practices by engaging and developing professional identity through social media. In J. Black, J. C. Castro, & C. Lin (Eds.), *Youth practices in digital arts and new media: Learning in formal and informal settings* (pp. 40–62). New York, NY: Palgrave Macmillan.

Lalonde, M., Castro, J. C., & Pariser, D. (2016). Identity tableaux: Multimodal contextual constructions of adolescent identity. *Visual Art Research, 42*(1), 38–55.

Latour, B. (2005). *Reassembling the social: An introduction to actor-network-theory.* Oxford, UK: Oxford University Press.

Lenhart, A., Smith, A., Anderson, M., Duggan, M., & Perrin, A. (2015). *Teens, technology and friendships.* Retrieved October 31, 2015, from http://www.pewinternet.org/2015/08/06/teens-technology-and-friendships/.

Marshall, J. (2016). A systems view: The role of art in education. *Art Education, 69*(3), 12–19.

Maturana, H., & Varela, F. (1992). *The tree of knowledge: The biological roots of human understanding.* Boston, MA: Shambhala.

Mitchell, M. (2009). *Complexity: A guided tour.* Oxford: Oxford University Press.

Pachler, N., Bachmair, B., & Cook, J. (2010). *Mobile learning: Structures, agency, practices.* New York: Springer.

Pariser, D., Castro, J. C., & Lalonde, M. (2016). Investigating at-risk youth visually examining their communities through mobilities, aesthetics and civic engagement. *International Journal of Education Through Art, 12*(2), 211–225.

Rourke, L., & Friesen, N. (2006). The learning sciences: The very idea. *Education Media International, 43*, 271–284.

Steeves, V. (2014). *Young Canadians in a wired world, phase III: Life online.* Ottawa: MediaSmarts.

Tavin, K., & Ballengee Morris, C. (Eds.). (2012). *Stand(ing) up, for a change: Voices of arts educators.* Reston, VA: National Art Education Association.

Turkle, S. (2011). *Alone together: Why we expect more from technology and less from each other.* New York: Basic Books.

Twenge, J. (2017, September). Have smartphones destroyed a generation? *The Atlantic*. Retrieved from https://www.theatlantic.com/magazine/archive/2017/09/has-the-smartphone-destroyed-a-generation/534198/.
Urry, J. (2003). *Global complexity*. Malden, MA: Polity.
Varela, F. J., Thompson, E., & Rosch, E. (1991). *The embodied mind: Cognitive science and human experience*. Cambridge, MA: MIT Press.
Vygotsky, L. S., & Cole, M. (1978). *Mind in society: The development of higher psychological processes*. Cambridge, MA: Harvard University Press.
Wang, F., & Hannafin, M. J. (2005). Design-based research and technology-enhanced learning environments. *Educational Technology Research and Development, 53*(4), 5–23.
Watts, D. J. (2003). *Six degrees: The science of a connected age*. New York, NY: W. W. Norton.
Wilson, B. (1976). Little Julian's impure drawings: Why children make art. *Studies in Art Education, 17*(2), 45–61.
Wilson, B. (2008). Contemporary art, the "best of art", and third-site pedagogy. *Art Education, 61*, 6–9.

CHAPTER 2

The Connected Image in Mobile and Social Media: The Visual Instances of Adolescents Becoming

Martin Lalonde

INTRODUCTION

Recent demographic research showed that young people in Quebec and the United States spend most of their time online through mobile social networks that are based on visual communication (Anderson & Jiang, 2018; Thoër et al., 2017). These online spaces have become indispensable places of socialization for the vast majority of young people. Whether to stay in touch with their surroundings to develop new relationships or simply to stay informed about what is happening in their environment (boyd, 2014; Lenhart, 2015), adolescents and young adults are striving to design and share an image of themselves on these platforms—an image that is both expressive of the internal mental and emotional states and representative of changes in the composition of the physical body. If it is unclear to understand whether these images are produced to meet the requirements of a social setting, what is clearly evident is the weight

M. Lalonde (✉)
Université du Québec à Montréal, Montreal, QC, Canada
e-mail: lalonde.martin@uqam.ca

and importance of these visual self-representation processes for the identity formation of many adolescents (Lachance, 2013).

Observing the visual and multimodal communications between young people on social media through affect theory (Gregg & Seigworth, 2010; Hogan, 2016) provides us a framework to understand image exchanges as mutual affections. Young people affect and are affected by the images they exchange. In social media environments, images can be understood as manifestations of their virtualities. They are produced in a process that is both conscious and unconscious. French psychiatrist and psychoanalyst Serge Tisseron (2001), a specialist in the impact of the digital image on socialization and identity construction processes, described this as a phenomenon of extimacy—that is, images are at the same time the documentation, the expression, and the reflection on oneself and one's relationship to the other. These processes of communication, developed in the informal educational setting of cultural practices according to French visual studies researcher André Gunthert (2015), have a significant impact on a young person's self-image, confidence, and sense of social competence. Canadian socioanthropologist specialized in youth visual practices Jocelyn Lachance (2013) has explained how social media and image now play a vital role in an adolescent's identity formation, one that can have significant positive and negative impacts on the social integration, identity development, and the empowerment of young people.

Schools and formal education writ large are slow to address this solidifying social phenomenon. First, there are the often-raised concerns of social transgressions online. What formal disciplinary school subjects can address such concerns? Then, there is the question of the integration and use of digital technologies in the learning environment. Whether it is the teacher's sense of technological competence in using new devices or software, or the means and resources available in a given educational context, the challenge is complex—from both theoretical and practical positions. Indeed, one can even ask the question of whether it is relevant to address these issues in a school setting, and if so, with what objectives?

In this chapter, I present a component of data and results from my doctoral research that examines the impact of image-making practices in mobile social media on youth identity development and their social integration in the context of a community of practice in a Montreal comprehensive secondary school. By collaborating with an art teacher and a group of 25 grade 11 students, I proposed to design educational activities that would consider the communication methods of mobile social networks prevalent in the digital culture of young people. This iteration of the MonCoin curriculum set the conditions for an analytical reflection on these modes of communication in mobile social media contexts to enable students to enrich their competence in the appreciation and personal visual production.

In particular, this chapter examines data from interviews with students and their teacher to formulate a hypothesis on the nature, function, and impact of the various modalities of visual communications between youth on social media. This hypothesis is based on a theory of affect as explored in the works of the French philosopher Gilles Deleuze and the Canadian philosopher Brian Massumi. To define the term affect, I mainly refer to the affect theory out of cultural studies. This particular approach, associated with poststructuralist thinking, employs concepts from psychoanalysis and, more specifically, from criticism of traditional psychoanalysis (Hogan, 2016). Speaking of affect from this point of view, therefore, implies to understand the term as referring to the fundamental motivations of being and its deep impulses while formulating a critique of the discourses, the practices, the structures, and the social institutions which relate to it. In the first section of this chapter, I will present some principles of affect theory by Deleuze's reflection on the writings of the sixteenth-century Dutch philosopher Baruch Spinoza. Following this, I will show how Massumi updates some elements of this theory through his work on the concepts of virtuality and actualization. The second part of this chapter will situate affect theory in an analysis of data from my doctoral research. In the third section of this chapter, I will demonstrate how the act of producing, sharing, and textually commenting images on mobile social media can be conceived as processes of mutual and auto affections among young teenage users. The fundamental desire to actualize the possibilities of the self is the driving force that pushes young people toward a process of viewing, producing, and sharing images that depict the potentialities of their being and the embodiment of all its possible trajectories.

The purpose of this chapter is to provide a theoretical contribution to the understanding of the visual communication of young people through social and mobile media to lay the groundwork for the design and implementation of formal visual arts curricula. This chapter is aimed specifically at researchers and teachers in the field of arts and communications who work with adolescents and who are interested in the issues of identity development, social integration, and school motivation.

A Theory of Affect

It is essential to clarify a definition of the term affect when discussing related theories. Taking us back to the Latin roots of the word affected, the comparison of French dictionaries' definitions helps us in highlighting the conceptual contours of the term. If one refers to a single definition describing an elementary state related to sensations (2013), another one proposes a psychological perspective where it relates to a primary impression of attraction or repulsion and a psychoanalytical perspective where it points to the satisfaction or repression of the emotions linked to the primary drives (2012). Although very brief, this definition is helpful because it allows us to differentiate the two new fields of study that relate to the term. Talking about the study of affect or English affect studies refers to two distinct areas of research (Hogan, 2016).

There are first the affective sciences, and then, there is the study of affect. These two fields are distinguished by the disciplines in which they are deployed, by their theoretical framework, by their methodology, and more particularly by their research objectives. On the one hand, we are interested in human emotional processes from psychology; on the other hand, we are interested in the motivations of the individual from a psychoanalytical and philosophical point of view. The first area is, therefore, empirical studies in the field of psychology and cognitive science, among others, while the second is in the field of cultural studies. The affective sciences, for example, refer to the work of the American psychologist Silvan Tomkins (1962/1995) and his theory of the nine fundamental affects of the human and present clinical studies in the psychology of human emotions. The theory of affect, on the other hand, emphasizes the difference between affect and emotion and is based on the classic philosophical writings of Spinoza (1677/1993) to develop a critical philosophy of contemporary social and political conditions. Deliberating about the concept of affect is therefore fundamentally different from deliberating about the emotional. This distinction represents a significant difference in posture between researchers who claim one field or the other. An encyclopedic article on this subject by the cognitive and affective science of literature scholar Patrick C. Hogan (2016) suggested that although fundamentally distinct, these two areas of research would benefit from developing in complementarity contributions to the complexity of affect. He pointed out that the affective sciences have methodological rigor and that their research is based on a solid empirical base, while the theory of affects challenges certain ideological assumptions on which research in the field of social sciences is based.

Spinoza's Theory of Affect

The theory of affect is based on Spinoza's Ethics (1677/1993) and proposes a framework that served as a precursor to the field of Freudian psychoanalysis (Hogan, 2016). By differentiating affect and emotion, several authors stress the unrepresentative nature of affect (Massumi, 2002; Shouse, 2005; Hogan, 2016). This principle would be analogous to the concept of the Freudian drive (Hogan, 2016) and does not necessarily represent the object pursued by the individual, instead treats the principle of the drive itself. The affect would thus be undefinable or irreducible to any definition because it evokes the physical sensation (Massumi, 2002) precisely. The body and its extensible parts feel the physical sensation. When the brain treats the force of the drive and translated through language, we are already moving away from its particular nature. Massumi (2002) elaborated in depth on this subject, stating that affect is unspeakable, especially when it is bodily. Not only does it belong to the domain of physical perception, but it is also continuous movement, which makes it impermeable in some way to a definitive representative framework. In reference to the quantum of affect (Affektbetrag) in Freud's theory of impulses, French philosopher specialized in aesthetic Baldine Saint-Girons (n.d.) describes affect in the same terms. She explains that it is the continually changing nature of the phenomenon, its mobility as well as its lack of support that make it a quantitative data that cannot be measured. It has significant impacts on the energy of a single body. If the phenomenon itself is unrepresentative, it is through the possibilities of energy deployment of the subject that we can perceive it, denote it. In this regard, the French philosopher Gilles Deleuze (1981) refers to the influential work on metaphysics and epistemology of early twentieth-century philosopher Henri Bergson (1934/2014) to explain how the concepts of passage and duration are distinguished precisely by their nature related to movement. Such a nature cannot be reduced to a representation. Such a definition would mark a stop or represent only a snapshot of a more complex process. What characterizes the notion of affect is, therefore, this continuous movement of becoming in the body.

Affected Body, Affecting Body

The body is never static—it is constituted of continuous movement, between rest and action, in terms of both its activities and its internal constitution (Deleuze, 1978). The body continually is in the process of composition, of becoming (Massumi, 2002). It responds to the affections it undergoes (Massumi, 2002). The concept of body is central to affect in the philosophy of Spinoza (1677/1993). Here, the mind is one with the body. There is the human body, but there are also the physical and ideal elements with which a body is in permanent contact. These elements are also kinds of bodies in that Spinoza evocation of corporality, that is, the physical dimension of ideas. Deleuze explains that ideas are autonomous in the sense that they express themselves in us. Elaborating on the concept of autonomous ideas, Deleuze (1978) stated that "it is less we who have ideas than the ideas that assert themselves." In the same way that noise would affect our hearing, a light source affects our sight, so do ideas affect us continually by influencing our power to act. Whether the elements are physical/external or they are in the realm of abstraction or interpretation, they are bodies that affect. Bodies affect each other and are determined by this ability to be affected by their power to be affected (Deleuze, 1978). For Spinoza (1677/1993), bodies seek to persist as beings; they seek to survive. This persistence is the expression of their conatus—Latin for our inclination as a living being to do our best to survive. It is a kind of innate tendency to stay alive. When bodies affect each other, when they are affected, it is their conatus that is affected, they desire to persist as a being that is either strengthened or weakened. The concept of affect is often confused with representative ideas (emotions) that cause or are caused by the constant movement of the body. Spinoza identifies three fundamental emotions: joy, sadness, and desire. Joy is positive affect; it increases the acting power of a body. Sadness is a negative affect that diminishes this power of action, and desire is a form of self-affection that concerns the conatus itself, that is, the consciousness of the body to want to persevere as an entity—to be and to be aware of the positive and negative affects that transform its becoming.

Deleuze (1978) explains that Spinoza presents the body as a whole, consisting of a large number of extensive parts. These parts are related to each other in a constituent relationship that represents the body as a whole. The relationship of the parts determines the body. These parts affect each other so that the body affects itself. A body is in a position to affect and fluctuate its conatus, the tendency to persist as a being. It is these constitutive relations, in regard to the relationships between the parts of the body, and in regard to the relations of the whole to other, external bodies, which determine its potential. Affect is, therefore, a continuous variation of the state of being (Deleuze, 1978). If this state of being determines the power to act, and the desire of this power to act, what is a body capable of? What is his potential? What are his possible trajectories? What affect can it, in turn, generate on other bodies?

Bodies do not exist in a decontextualized context where there is no consideration of the relational dimension. If bodies are in a state of continual becoming, if their components are in a continuous composition process as a whole in reaction to the tensions which mark the relations of the bodies, it is imperative to consider their relational nature. Spinoza uses the Latin term ocursus, or encounter, to illustrate this principle of how bodies are related. Encounters are the points of contact that energize the tensions of affect. Encounters that engage in positive affect strengthen the constituent rapport of a body, while encounters that cause a negative affect weaken and deconstruct it. It is the same for the physical body as for the mind. For example, too much heat could destroy the constituent rapport that creates the skin organism. In the same way but without direct physical consequences, negative external behavior toward a person could lead to the deconstruction of its psychological composition, therefore affecting his trust, self-esteem, or capacity to act for example.

The Three Types of Deleuze's Ideas

Deleuze speaks of three types of ideas in reference to Spinoza: affection idea, the notion idea, and the essence idea. The affection idea is when a subject realizes the effect of an affect. It will notice the result of a body on her or a part of her. In such a situation, the subject will continue in its trajectory or deviate from the representation of the affect in question without necessarily becoming aware of its cause. The second idea, the notion idea itself, is that in which the individual knows what is favorable or favorable to his constitutive relations. Here, he becomes aware of the cause of affect, he realizes which encounters are favorable or unfavorable to him, but he still does not know how to maintain his power to act. The third idea, the essence idea, refers to the knowledge of encounters that will favor its constituent relations but goes further by including the essence of being and external bodies. In essence, it is not only a question of what is favorable or unfavorable to him, but of the singular essence which is his and the singular essence which is that of God and the singular essence of things, or "exterior" (Deleuze, 1978). We return here to the starting point of this section where knowledge is not about a representative object, but about a "pure idea."

> ... si c'est vrai que, du point [de vue] des rapports qui régissent les parties étendues d'un corps ou d'une âme, les parties extensives, tous les corps ne conviennent pas les uns avec les autres; si vous arrivez à un monde de pures intensités, toutes sont censées convenir les unes avec les autres. (Deleuze, 1978)
>
> ...because, if it is true that all bodies do not agree with each other, if it is true that from the point of view of the relations which govern the extended parts of a body or a soul, the extensive parts, all the bodies are not suitable for each other; if you come to a world of pure intensities, all are supposed to agree with each other. (translation by the author)

According to Deleuze, it is, therefore, a question for the individual to reach a certain level of harmony between his essence, that of external things and that of ideas. He explains that Spinoza names this beatitude, a term which corresponds here to the auto affect, the auto affect where the individual is aware not only of his intensity threshold in his relationships with other bodies but is also able to influence his power to act and those of others in light of fundamental principles, of pure ideas.

VIRTUALITIES, POTENTIAL, AND ACTUALIZATION

Deleuze's idea of mapping humans affect to foresee their potential, their power to affect and be affected can be related to Massumi's (2002) more recent writings on becoming and affect. The latter insists on the unspeakable character of affect in the sense that it is above all an intensity. Intensities are perceived by the body, treated, and translated into an idea by the brain they become emotions, and emotions are already representations of a causal phenomenon. Elaborating on the concept of intensity, Massumi explains that the body is an envelope, a vessel, a system stored inside the shell of the epidermis. It is then most often through the skin that one would perceive affections. These sensations would flow between the parts of our body to eventually lead to the brain. Massumi, therefore, returns to the physical nature of perception. It is through the body that we perceive the intensities of the encounters we produce. These intensities would be duplicated and amplified in us by the fact that the brain creates representations, ideas, ideal inner bodies that would continue to affect us in a process Massumi terms resonance. In us resonate the images we form from our perceptions. He uses the term resonating vessel to illustrate his understanding of the relationship between the skin and the brain. Affects are doubled and amplified in a feedback loop that directly influences our power to act.

This reasoning leads us to an essential contribution of Massumi, the one where the body is both current and virtual. Intensities are for Massumi beginnings. Beginnings of actions and expressions. They happen so quickly that they exclude and cancel each other out. They are virtual germs of actions and expression. In this process, there is always one that matures and comes up. It would be, in fact, the multitude of tendencies that spring from the intensity of an encounter, a vast range of virtual possibilities from which a single beginning will emerge. From this point of view, the body is virtual and current. That is to say, it is made of these potentialities, of these tendencies which are not yet actions, but which are an experiential sum. The body is where the field of possibilities lies, the virtuality of the body, its potential, and its capability.

> The virtual is a paradox where opposites coexist, coalesce, and connect; where possibilities cannot be experienced, cannot be felt, and albeit be reduced and contained. An individual action or expression will emerge and be registered consciously. One "wills" it to emerge, to be qualified, to take on socio-linguistic meaning, to enter linear action-reaction circuits, to become a content of one's life by dint or by inhibition. (Massumi, 2002, p. 91)

When determining the possibilities of a body, it also defines the limits of its environment. It is the possible actions of a body that define the boundaries and circumstances of the field in which it is situated. When one of these possibilities is actualized, it marks at the same time its limitations. It is these two dimensions that constitute, according to Massumi, the two facets of what he means by emergence. There would, therefore, be a constant back-and-forth dynamic, a loop between the virtuality of the body and its actualization, perception, and cognition, these two poles feeding each other. Affect triggers movements that go through bodies, which resonates in and between them. It is through the actualization of bodies that potentialities emerge in and between bodies and systems. It is these virtualities that define the scope, therefore the limits of a body's spaces and possibilities.

Affect in Cultural Studies and Educational Research

Australian academics Melissa Gregg and Gregory Seigworth (2010) presented various open-ended social science research contributions and perspectives based on affect theory. They identified the need for research to focus on areas of tension in the constitutions of human, non-human, and machine actors; and on the blurring of affective boundaries in the relationship between human and machine. Seigworth and Gregg also advocated for the examination of the "regimes of expressivity" promoted by information communication technologies through questions, such as how intensities connect people in the context of image-based communication and how such spaces affect individuals and communities within mass movements on the Internet. They name this phenomenon as inter alia, that is "...to unfold regimes of expressivity that are tied much more to resonant worldings and diffusions of feeling/passions—often including atmospheres of sociality, crowd behaviors, contagions of feeling, matters of belonging ..." (Gregg & Seigworth, 2010, p. 8). The two authors underline how emotion—in the sense that it is a vector of affections—represents an important player in the actualization and potentials of groupings. In this regard, I will highlight how the social media used in my research is based on actor affection's dynamic—that is when individuals hit the "like" button on images and create a kind of emotional mark that determines and opens up possible social connections from an image and its role in the identity formation and dissemination online.

Pedagogy and Affect

Australia's Megan Watkins (2006, 2010), an educational researcher, has investigated the contributions of affect theory to curriculum research in the context of language instruction in an elementary school setting. She developed an approach she calls affect pedagogy (2006) that seeks to establish the value of reciprocity in student–teacher relationships. For her, technological advancements have cast a shadow over the role of the teacher by justifying student-centered pedagogical models or models of flipped pedagogy that evacuate the role of the teacher as a key actor in the process of teaching and learning. She also took the positions that went against critical pedagogy—where the teacher is positioned as the vector of oppressive power. Watkins saw the relevance of affect because it emphasizes the importance of the relationship between bodies in a learning space—a frame through which the body is perceived as an individual and a kind of society, as consciousness and unconsciousness, as a body and mind, as corporeal and cognitive. She questioned the impact of educational structures on students' willingness to learn. In other words, how does the school environment affect learners' desire to learn? How can reports initiated by the teacher increase or decrease the potential and the futures of students? How do students' existence and actions affect the potential of the teacher, her desire to persist in her being? Watkins conceives affect as the effects of teaching practices that seek to stimulate students' desire to persist as active actors in the learning process. In the school context, affect would be the embodied instantiations of the recognition between teachers and pupils (Yar as quoted by Watkins, 2010). The notion of recognition regularly returns in Watkins's work as a confirmation of the mutuality between teachers and pupils. Recognition acts, according to her, are considerations of the reciprocity of bodies and as a confirmation of individual value. Pedagogical gestures of recognition act as positive affections that accumulate, leaving traces in the learners' bodies. From this point of view, the desire to persist by the teacher and the student creates a dynamic of going back and forth, which generates an amplification of the essence between teacher and student.

The relationship between the teacher and the student is imbedded in a logic of reciprocity which, as she argues, reinforces their mutual desire to persevere and magnifies the essence of their role in this dynamic. Returning to affect, Watkins insisted on the principle where the affect is pre-conscious, where it precedes the emotional states that are generated in consciousness. These resonances would, therefore, be conditions that would allow the reinforcement or weakening of teachers and learner's capacities. In a way, this can be linked with the concept of affect maps of Deleuze where one could identify, for example, what is the potential of a student or a teacher, how can they affect and be affected, what are the thresholds of their intensities? Watkins (2010) insists on the fact that education has prioritized a psychological conception of consciousness to the detriment of a physical consciousness—that which perceives and accumulates perceptions before conscious awareness. Her assertion emphasized the role of the body as a physical organism at the center of learning and teaching.

THE AFFECT OF IDENTITY IMAGES IN SOCIAL NETWORKS

If we now look at the phenomenon of visual communication of adolescents on mobile social networks, we can easily observe the processes of affections that occur in these spaces. Indeed, thinking about platforms such as Facebook and Instagram, and especially about the modalities of communications they offer to their users, allows us to see that these are spaces in which users are affecting and affected by images. Not only can images be perceived as robust vectors of affection, but they can also be understood as forms of actualization of young people potentialities. In the next paragraphs, I will develop a theoretical hypothesis on the meaning, function, and effect of networked photography of young people on mobile media social networks based on affect theory. The purpose of this contribution is to provide a framework that allows us to understand better the issues, circumstances, and conditions of a learning environment mediated by social networks based primarily on the production and consumption of images.

RESEARCH DATA

The assumption presented in this section is based on data collected from one of the research sites. We worked with a group of more than twenty students from 16 to 17 years of a visual arts class located in a francophone public high school in the city of Montreal. These students, some of whom were enrolled in the enriched science program, had only one 75-minute art period per week, and the use of mobile technologies was prohibited in the school during class hours. Despite this situation, the majority of students had a smartphone and made extensive use of image-based social media on a personal level. Interview data showed us that addressing the dynamics and impacts of a common social media platform among youth at the time was a significant motivator for many participants. We conducted two 4-week research phases during the same school year at this particular research site. We proposed to the student participants to create an alternative Instagram account that they would reserve for their participation in the project. This second account would be part of a private Instagram group bringing together the student participants, their teacher, and the researchers. The only constraints that we formulated at the beginning of the project were the following: to avoid publishing images where we can recognize the identity of a person with his face; to draw inspiration from the visual themes proposed by the researcher; to avoid publishing content that encourages violence or drug use. While student participants were also free to publish photographic subjects of their choice, the context of the visual arts class justified the main goal we formulated of producing a personal aesthetic through the series of images they would publish.

I focus primarily on the analysis from semi-structured interviews with participating students. During these interviews, I asked questions about what motivated them to be present on mobile social media. I asked them about the role of the image, about their production methods, about the unofficial rules that govern the operation of their social relations online. These questions asked students to continually compare and differentiate what she or he was doing on the MonCoin social network and what she or he was doing on their social networks. The participants were urged to articulate their explanations and justify certain behaviors or attitudes that they took in one context versus the other using comparative analysis.

BODIES AFFECTING BODIES THROUGH IMAGES

In the first round of interviews, there was some evidence of the role of mobile and social media to serve as a forum for the expression of one's identity, governed by specific communication modalities. Most of the youth interviewed said they used these technologies and platforms for entertainment and to stay in touch with their friends. When questioned as to which types of images they produce, share, and consume, the vast majority of responses pointed to self-portraits (or selfies), social scenes, and pictures documenting everyday happenings. Even though many participants claimed to make casual images, a more in-depth questioning revealed that participants observed a rigorous set of codes of conduct and visual production within these online social spaces. There was some concern among participants of making gaps when they present themselves through their digital publications. If the action of publishing an image is wrought with doubt, it is because their identity, their reputation, and their social status are at risk. It is risky because participants expressed the virtualities of their bodies, and they realized, consciously or unconsciously, that their audience's feedback will affect their power to act as bodies.

A key finding present in almost all the interviews of participants is where they express their fear of being ridiculed online. They, therefore, sought to stand out to elicit reactions, interactions, and interest in their person, while at the same time remaining within a normative framework where they would not be identified as marginal. What they look for when they publish images of themselves are forms of validation and recognition of those around them. The returns they seek are positive affections, affections which could cause in them a variation toward the primordial feeling of joy—to use Spinoza's term (1677/1993). Moreover, what they fear are negative affections, those which will cause in them a feeling of sadness as a result of feeling ridiculed or excluded. From this point of view, young people demonstrated knowledge of Deleuze's affection idea (1978), where they pursue or flee, respectively the causes of movement on the state of their affect.

The representative and straightforward situations of daily social media interaction that produce feedback (or lack of) on images young people produce and share are in themselves affecting bodies that leave traces of positive or negative affects. Negative affects, those which create variations of sadness, reduce and weaken a body's power to act, its virtual potential, while positive affects will have the opposite effect. Positive feedback about images of themselves will increase their potential and their range of possibilities—it will support and strengthen exponentially their power to act.

This dynamic demonstrates how many young people approach image-based mobile social media from the affection ideas, the first form of an idea of Spinoza according to Deleuze. That is to say, they associate their representations of the effects of affections with the variations in their being without knowing the causes of these affections. As a result, they find themselves chasing positive affections and fleeing negative affections by ignoring what causes them. In social media, this mostly results in a situation where a young person directs his or her behavior online to obtain likes and favorable comments from followers and searching ways for his publications not to be ignored.

The interview database of participating students provides some insight into how, at the time of the research, Instagram was a space strictly normed by a series of unofficial rules. The participants' comments demonstrate how this is a space dedicated almost exclusively to photos of selfies and social scene type of images. Participants assert that, when they form the project to produce and share a picture, they do so thinking about their audience and how they could get endorsements from this audience. The words of the participant *Zonimorox* are representative of the general type of answer obtained to the question. They stated "What do you think when you publish an image on your personal Instagram? Why? I think of all my subscribers, my contact list. (…) I think of what they will think when they will see my picture."

Further, participant, *Youramazingstone*, explained how this search for "Likes" can negatively affect the self-esteem of young women by imposing a certain body aesthetic. It emphasizes the danger of indulging in the game of looking for likes, the danger of losing one's true personality in favor of a construction. She explained:

> It's also about self-esteem, all that (searching for likes in social media), if you do not really have a high regard for yourself, and you're going to register on Instagram, that may not be the way to go. Maybe you should build a good sense of yourself before, and after that, you'll be able to go to register, because you can see things that will completely make you question yourself.

The participating students who offered us their views on their personal use of social media also, for the most part, emphasized the risky and delicate nature of sharing content on these platforms. Comparing their application to the method that was suggested in the context of the project, many said they appreciated having a second account, specifically for the project, because they would never have risked going outside the scope of their established visual practice with their personal audience. They would avoid any misconduct for fear of being perceived as strange or for fear of losing the social capital resulting from comments and Likes.

Participant *Thebigdeal's* comments on this subject are unequivocal. Explaining that he would never risk such discrepancies (posting images related to the project's proposals) to his own Instagram for fear of seeing a decline in the likes and the rating of his friends: "No, because there are people who would have thought it's weird that I'm posting such pictures. Maybe they would have paid less attention to my posts after, and it would have had an impact on my Likes … "

However, it is also the fact that the project has allowed students to make a counterpoint to their common uses that seem to have allowed some of them to get rid of part of the influence of affection ideas. Although some of them initially balked at the thought of managing a second profile on this platform, the exercise allowed them to take a step back from their practice and observe how personal aesthetic research could be rewarding and potentially conceivable in the context of their practice. Participant *Deez_notz4* explains.

> If I publish a photo on Facebook or Instagram on my personal account, the goal is to have as much Likes as I can, it is to get the most possible recognition of other users. When I took a photo to publish for the project, my goal was more personal. If the others liked it, it was good, but I published it mainly because I found it interesting, because it met the criteria and because that represented me artistically, that was my style.

From this point of view, the project allowed some participants to realize the notion idea, the second type of idea by Spinoza (Deleuze, 1978), the one that identifies the causes behind the lived affections. By doing so, student participants were partially and gradually aware of what was causing variations in them in this context. They were beginning to identify how they could endorse practices that were favorable to them outside the established norms of such networks.

INSTANTIATION OF THE BODY
AND THE ACTUALIZATION OF VIRTUALITIES

These communicative dynamics—the visual exchanges in mobile social media spaces—bring us to see this context as a place where users update their virtualities through images, and that those images can be conceived as instantiations of their potentialities. As Massumi (2002) pointed out, it is the potentialities of a body that guide these actions, which are at the origin of its instantiations. Each encounter is a moment when bodies are affected and generate a multitude of possibilities of which only one is actualized in action or expression. Once again, digital images posted online are a form of these manifestations of an affect. When a user composes and publishes an image of her or himself, this image represents an update of a state—that which she or he is. Affected by this image, the receivers (members of an individual's social network) respond by displaying a reaction to that image. Whether it is the use of the like button function of the social media, the textual comments or the offline responses to this image, these reactions will, in turn, affect the author of the image and cause variations in his behavior and future creative productions and online posts.

What is unique in the context of connected photography on social media is that these updates are not just gestures or expressions; they are concrete in their visual dimension. The image persists by its permanence and continues to resonate in the body of their author. The image would be a body, both virtual and actualized that remains active in dynamic feedback with its author. We can relate this situation to French semiologist Laurence Allard's (2014) conception of the smartphone, which considers it as a device of conversation with oneself, as a mirror which reflects the virtualities that persist and affect us positively or negatively. Such an observation points to the impact and the power of a favorable self-image (an image of ourselves that positively affects us) in the context of digital social networks. For example, a user who creates pictures of her or himself that she or he likes can at the same time self-affect in a positive way and therefore, increase her or his potential and power to act, increasing his space of possibilities.

The spaces of visual communication, created by mobile and social media, foster images that are in themselves affecting bodies. These bodies affect the state and disposition of image producers and viewers. The intensities between these physical bodies (users and makers of images) and idealized bodies (images) are the factors underlying the variations of the power to act, therefore of the user's conatus. In other words, the process of visual exchanges has the potential to reinforce an image producer's sense of legitimacy or illegitimacy about their self-image that they project toward their social groups. An image producer who receives the positive appreciation of her or his images will be positively affected, and her or his potential would be increased while the image producer who goes unnoticed, or worse, the one who is ridiculed, would be reduced in her or his power to act.

Data drawn from observations in the physical and online exchanges showed that this concept is not as neatly defined. Many young people demonstrated a critical awareness of the effects of positive and negative feedback resulting from posting images of themselves online. Some participants spoke of the emptiness of such practices and the misleading aspect of identity development and empowerment. Several participants pointed out that by adopting such practices (where one seeks to obtain the appreciation of peers on one's network), one took the risk of losing sight of one's authentic personal motivations and that this search for validation often became an end in of itself. Participants shared how images they consumed affected their sense of power to act (the legitimacy and appearance of their physical bodies) and the expression of their potential (how they decided to actualize their potential, that is to say, to put it into an image). Thus, Deleuze's ideas (1978) are expressed in the words of participants. By the criticism it formulates, it demonstrates a retreat on the communication dynamics that govern these spaces and on what causes positive or negative affects for them. As Deleuze mentioned, the participants in this study were aware of the relationships that are favorable to them and can orient their everyday attitudes and actions accordingly.

The visual communication of adolescents through social media can be understood as a kind of update to their state—the sense of self and who they are and how they act in the world. Since affect is the continuous oscillation of their disposition that follows the ongoing encounters of their environment, the images they produce and share are actualizations of their potentialities, of their virtualities, they are instantiations of their continual becoming. Such a condition is fraught with consequences for their process of identity development and social integration. Taking into consideration the question of increasing and decreasing the power to act following the affect produced by ideal bodies (images), and considering that these affects can widen or reduce the range of possibilities an individual can become, it is essential to attend to the impact of these image-making practices in the becoming of adolescents.

Conclusion

Formal education programs do not yet have a space in the curriculum where young people can address the impact of social media on their development. The discipline of arts education represents a milieu from which it is relevant to analyze and maintain a critical discourse on the communication dynamics that animate such identity forming spaces. Participant's comments on the relevance of using social media platforms in the school setting provide relevant insight into the needs and motivations of adolescents to reflect on these practices in the classroom.

The position advanced in this chapter highlights an under-examined aspect of the impact of social media on the identity development and social integration of young people. With the ubiquity of digital technologies and the regular arrival of new features, new operating systems, and new architectures in social networking, the complexity of social interaction will continue to become an increasingly significant part of young people's lives. It is, therefore, necessary for the field of art education to develop approaches, methods, and pedagogical resources that will address these issues and allow different contexts to keep pace with changing cultural practices of young people. While some current demographic surveys find that many teachers feel unprepared when it comes to the use of new technologies or are afraid to invest the "youth" spaces of digital culture (Fiévez, 2017), there is still much research to be done to establish the theoretical and practical bases of teaching strategies that will consider the realities of new image-based communication modalities in teaching and learning.

In this chapter, I have argued that visual communication through mobile social media as a form of encounter with the potential and empowerment of adolescents. The results of this work will also lead us to present the impacts of such a framework of understanding on the approach and pedagogical strategies that were conceived and implemented in the context of this design-based research project.

References

Affect. (2012). *Le petit Larousse illustré 2013*. Paris: Larousse.
Affect. (2013). *Le petit Robert: dictionnaire alphabétique et analogique de la langue française*. Paris: Le Robert.
Allard, L. (2014). Express yourself 3.0! Le mobile comme technologie pour soi et quelques autres entre double agir communicationnel et continuum disjonctif soma technologique. In L. Allard, L. Creto, & R. Odin (Eds.), *Téléphone mobile et création* (p. 139–161). Paris: Armand Colin.
Anderson, M., & Jiang, J. (2018). *Teens, social media & technology 2018*. Pew Research Center. Retrieved from http://www.pewinternet.org/2018/05/31/teens-social-media-technology-2018/.
Bergson, H. (1934/2014). *La Pensée et le mouvant: essais et conférences*. Librairie Félix Alcan.
boyd, d. (2014). *It's complicated: The social lives of networked teens*. London: Yale University Press.
Deleuze, G. (1978, janvier). *Cours de Vincennes du 24 janvier 1978*. Université de Vincennes. Retrieved from https://www.webdeleuze.com/textes/11.
Deleuze, G. (1981, janvier). *Cours de Vincennes du 20 janvier 1981*. Université de Vincennes. Retrieved from https://www.webdeleuze.com/textes/35.

Fiévez, A. (2017). *L'intégration des TIC en contexte éducatif: modèles, réalités et enjeux*. Québec: Presses de l'Université du Québec.
Gregg, M., & Seigworth, G. J. (Eds.). (2010). *The Affect Theory Reader*. Durham and London: Duke University Press.
Gunthert, A. (2015). *L'image partagée: la photographie numérique*. Paris: Textuel.
Hogan, P. C. (2016). Affect studies and literary criticism. In *Oxford research encyclopedia of literature*. Retrieved from http://literature.oxfordre.com/view/10.1093/acrefore/9780190201098.001.0001/acrefore-9780190201098-e-105?rskey=8JWyCc&result=1.
Lachance, J. (2013). *Photos d'ados: à l'ère du numérique*. Québec: Presses de l'Université Laval.
Lenhart, A. (2015). *Teens, social media and technology overview 2015*. Pew Research Center. Retrieved from http://www.pewinternet.org/2015/04/09/teens-social-media-technology-2015.
Massumi, B. (2002). *Parables for the virtual: Movement, affect, sensation*. Durham, NC: Duke University Press.
Saint-Girons, B. (n.d.). Quantum d'affect. In *Encyclopædia Universalis*. Retrieved from http://www.universalis-edu.com/encyclopedie/quantum-d-affect/.
Shouse, E. (2005). Feeling, emotion, affect. *M/C Journal*, *8*(6). Retrieved from http://journal.media-culture.org.au/0512/03-shouse.php.
Spinoza, B. (1993). *L' Éthique* (A. Guérinot, Trad.). Paris: Les Éditions Ivrea. Retrieved from http://classiques.uqac.ca/classiques/spinoza/ethique/ethique_de_Spinoza.pdf.
Thoër, C., Millerand, F., Coutant, A., Bourget, C., Vachon, K., Lacombe, M.-È., & Centre francophone d'informatisation des organisations. (2017). *Visionnement connecté par les jeunes au Québec*. Retrieved from http://collections.banq.qc.ca/ark:/52327/bs3246439.
Tisseron, S. (2001). *L'intimité surexposée*. Paris: Ramsay.
Tomkins, S. S. (1962/1995). *Affect, imagery, consciousness*. New York: Springer.
Watkins, M. (2006). Pedagogic affect/effect: Embodying a desire to learn. *Pedagogies: An International Journal*, *1*(4), 269–282. Retrieved from https://doi.org/10.1080/15544800701341533.
Watkins, M. (2010). Desiring recognition, accumulating affect. In M. Gregg & G. J. Seigworth (Eds.), *The affect theory reader* (pp. 269–288). Durham, NC: Duke University Press.

CHAPTER 3

The Social Organization of Students in Class Versus in an Online Social Network: Freedom and Constraint in Two Different Settings

David Pariser and Bettina Forget

INTRODUCTION

Our primary focus in this chapter is to consider the social organization of our students in two of the linked worlds that they inhabit: a physical art classroom and the online world of the social network that is an extension of that art classroom. From what we have seen from our data, and that of other commentators (e.g., Bromwich, 2015) it is evident that some students function differently in the physical world of the classroom, versus that of an online social network. Thus, the same student may be a "loner" in the physical classroom—with few social contacts, while online this same student may be connected with many of their classmates. The reverse may be true as well—a gregarious student in the physical classroom may be something of an isolate in the social network (Akbari & Pariser, 2017). At first glance, these sorts of contrasting behaviors suggest the existence of an "inverse law" that

D. Pariser (✉) · B. Forget
Concordia University, Montreal, QC, Canada

© The Author(s) 2019
J. C. Castro (ed.), *Mobile Media In and Outside of the Art Classroom*,
https://doi.org/10.1007/978-3-030-25316-5_3

governs some students' social behavior in these two different contexts. Of course, "the inverse law" does not apply to all students' on and on off line situations. In looking at some of the data from the MonCoin research we also find students whose social profiles do not alter as a function of being on, or off line. That is, some students will have consistently low social connections on and off line, and others will have consistently rich and numerous social connections, on and off line.

In short, we do not claim that the effects of participating in both a physical and virtual classroom necessarily have the same impact on all students involved. As we note above, the effects are variable—a finding that we will illustrate at some length. What we do wish to emphasize is that by having access to a social network and activities of the sort offered in the MonCoin curriculum, some students will seize the opportunity to explore a central developmental issue for young adults, namely the exploration and construction of identities. Activity on line also gives some students a chance to explore new ways of interacting with their peers if they wish to do so. They can try out new "performances" of themselves (Goffman, 1959) and to curate online "exhibitions" that illustrate aspects of their identity (Hogan, 2010). For teachers, offering students this opportunity to explore their own identity via an exchange of visual images and comments may be the most useful benefit that the MonCoin curriculum can offer in the classroom. It may also provide a way of "normalizing" the use of mobile media and social networks in the classroom.

In what follows we will be presenting the varied data that we have gathered from a single iteration of the MonCoin curriculum in a Secondary 3 classroom in a Montreal urban high school. We will use this data to illustrate the ways in which students have responded diversely to arts-based activities and have used these activities as an occasion for social interaction among their peers and for exploring issues related to identity. We will also look in more detail at the ways in which the same individuals function differently, in the world of the physical classroom versus that of the social network. We will focus on students whose behavior clearly illustrates some of the ways in which they navigate the opportunities and challenges of the curriculum (Akbari, Castro, Lalonde, Moreno, & Pariser, 2016)—and the ways in which the students navigated the different worlds of on, and off line.

Theoretical Grounding

Writ large, the MonCoin project is grounded in several sociomaterial theoretical bases, however, for the purposes of the present discussion we will focus on research and approaches related to the sociology and psychology of on and off line learning, self-presentation, and interaction (Castro, Lalonde, & Pariser, 2016). In this respect, some key figures provide an important framework for our method and discussion.

The work of the social psychologist Goffman (1959) provides us a key theoretical framework. Goffman comes from the Symbolic Interactionists School (Mead, 1934) and remains a ubiquitous reference point for contemporary researchers who observe online behavior (Ganda, 2014; Oram, 2009). Goffman's fundamental interest was to examine the ways in which people present themselves to an audience. Goffman was convinced that the individual faces the basic challenge of presenting a controlled "performance" of themselves for the benefit of a given audience. In formal and professional settings, the rules for self-presentation are clear and boundaries are well known. Waiters, actors, politicians, doctors all have to work within the behavioral parameters established by the social expectations of the audience. But within those constraints, the individual still has the challenge of making their role/performance "authentic." Goffman's vision has been critiqued as a somewhat cynical vision of social interaction where everyone puts on an act calculated to conform to social expectations. In this respect, his notion of "backstage" and "public space" is particularly telling. Goffman notes that as with all theatrical performances, the audience is shown a selected sample of behavior—i.e., "on stage," while the "backstage" aspects of the performance are hidden from the audience so much so that it is considered a dramatic breach for the audience to witness what the actors are doing "backstage." Goffman illustrates this delicate balance in describing the backstage and front stage areas of a restaurant. What goes on "backstage" in the kitchen is not for the customer to see and in that space, actors can behave in ways that are at variance with the personae they adopt in the dining room—i.e., spitting in the soup, making rude remarks about the patrons, etc. This notion of the ways in which people present themselves in their onstage interactions raises the question—where in all this is there room for the "authentic" presentation of self? Yet, Goffman's model of contrived social interaction has had a powerful and long-standing hold on students of social interaction and his influence has been so pervasive that researchers who examine online interactions invariably cite Goffman as a resource for understanding what goes on in the "public space" of online social networks (see Boyd, 2014).

Although Goffman developed his theories for the presentation of self in a period well before the rise of the Internet, the basic question of performing one's identity remains a focal feature of the presentation of self regardless of the medium in which such a performance takes place. Bernie Hogan (2010) is a scholar who has adapted Goffman's theoretical model to accommodate the universe of online social media. His contribution to Goffman's performance model is to suggest that in addition to the real-time business of "performance" in front of an audience—individuals can in fact curate an "exhibition" of images, videos, and texts that present their own unique identities (see Lalonde, Castro, & Pariser, 2016). The audience for such displays of artifacts related to the self can "visit" the site at any time—so the individuals presenting themselves change their role from "actor" to "curator" (Davis, 2016). Thus, when the participants in the MonCoin curriculum responded to didactic prompts and posted images, we can view their choices not only as responses to the challenges offered by the "Micro Missions" but also as a way of developing a collection of images that demonstrated their sense of identity. Such demonstrations were carefully developed with an audience in mind and with the purpose of reinforcing the sort of self-image that the student wished to project. Thus, as we will show, "gamer boys" posted images of their equipment (Fig. 3.1). While other students were at pains to let their classmates into key aspects of their lives—see the varied and telling responses to the micro-mission that requested documentation of "My Collection." Collections were selectively documented, everything from astounding collections of sneakers to a drawer full of colorful head scarves. Clearly both individuals were engaged with two tasks simultaneously letting their classmates know something about themselves, while still adhering to a strong sense of their own unique identity whether it be sartorial or ethnic. In most cases, it was a balancing act.

Fig. 3.1 4×4 Matrix of posted images exploring identity

The Neo-Tribal and the Subcultural Nexus

In addition to the dimension of the public presentation of self whether in terms of performance (Goffman, 1959) or in terms of a collection of curated images (Hogan, 2010), there is also the matter of the types of social associations that students form voluntarily. And here the work of Robards and Bennett (2011) is relevant. These two Australian researchers have done work that examines the sorts of social associations that youths form in their on and off line presentations of self. Rather than looking at the ways in which student behavior and social associations are at variance with each other on and off line, the two researchers found that activity on and off line tended to reinforce each other. This observation is of special interest to us as it is our aim in this chapter to compare the social organization of a classroom with that of the classroom-based social network. Robards and Bennett (2011) stated "Rather than being used to meet new people, social network sites are instead being used to articulate existing and often off line networks of family, colleagues and more casual acquaintances…" (p. 307).

They make another observation as well, they note that earlier researchers (Hebdige, 1979) have seen youth online associations as examples of classic "subcultures," such as youthful groups united by a critique of society—as in the case of hippies or anarchists. Robards and Bennett suggested that contemporary youthful online associations can now be seen as the expression of a post-subcultural ethos—one such ethos being "neo-tribalism" (see Hesmondhalgh, 2005; Muggleton, 2000).

In their research, Robards and Bennett worked with and interviewed 32 young adults (11 males, 21 females) all aged 18–27 years old. The researchers reported that "the most salient result was to show how the virtual spaces offered by social networks…appear to accentuate existing trends towards reflexively derived, identity projects as defined by post-subcultural theorists" (Robards & Bennett, 2011, p. 304). They suggested that the sorts of associations typically formed by young adults online and in the physical world can best be characterized as "Neo-tribal." Neo-tribalism is one form of post-subcultural affiliation. The term is defined as "…without the rigidity of the forms of organization with which we are familiar (tribe) refers to a certain ambience, a state of mind, and is preferably to be expressed through lifestyles that favor appearance and form" (Maffesoli, 1996, p. 98). Unlike other manifestations of sub-cultural association, such as Hippies, Goths, and Hipsters, neo-tribal associations are characterized by a lack of political or class allegiance and critique and are instead groups whose members associate on the basis of a single shared interest. The classic example of neo-tribal association being groups of tourists who share an interest in travel and little else. Robards and Bennett indicated that a researcher in the area of sub-cultural groups online (Hodkinson, 2002) has identified the way in which the Internet has made it possible for traditional types of sub-cultural groups to thrive, while at the same time also providing a platform for multiple intersections of varying styles, tastes, lifestyles, and cultural practices, generating a sense of belonging more consistent with a neo-tribal model. Hodkinson stressed the former through his fieldwork with Goths, arguing that, "...just as in off line situations, individuals online tend to gravitate towards those with whom they share some familiarity" (p. 306). For our purposes here, it is significant that Robards and Bennett touched on the explorations of multiple identities as a key contributor to neo-tribal association. They cited Hodkins and Lincoln (2008) who noted, "...rather than forming fixed collective groupings young people today are more likely to... (negotiate) personal paths through a myriad of temporary and partial identities" (p. 9).

Robards and Bennett concluded their discussion with the following declaration, which helps to clarify the nature of their insight based on the empirical work that they have done with young adults on the Australian Gold Coast, when they stated, "as this article seeks to illustrate, when subject to empirical scrutiny, young people's use of the internet exhibits tendencies that align far more readily with post-subcultural/neo-tribal types of association than with subcultural models of explanation" (Robards & Bennett, 2011, p. 307).

Robards and Bennett's observations raise some interesting questions not only about the function of online social networks as reinforcers rather than diversions from "real world" social networks, but also about the function and maintenance of curated online "exhibits." As we noted, Hogan devotes a good deal of attention to the way that these exhibits function. It may well be that they serve the same dual function attributed by Robards and Bennett to social networks, in that they provide a space for fantasy and experimental role-playing while at the same time reinforcing real-world social ties. Then there is also the matter of the type of social cohesion played out within online social networks. As Robards and Bennett pointed out, the behavior observed in social networks aligns more closely with post-subcultural and neo-tribal sorts of affiliation, making a critique of the culture less of a common bond among the participants in the social network. What does create a strong bond among the individuals studied by Robards and Bennett are a wide range of intersecting interests rather than fealty to a shared ideology or political critique. In fact, we have found these sorts of crosscutting interests manifest in some of the posts and images offered by the students who participated in the MonCoin curriculum.

The Impact of Digital Media and Social Networks on Vulnerable Adolescents

As we are dealing in this research with high school students as our subjects, it must be noted that there is considerable debate about the impact of digital media, social networks, and smartphones on the mental well-being of adolescents (Terkel, 2011; Treem, Dailey, Pierce, & Biffl, 2016). This contributes to the reluctance of teachers and curriculum planners to integrate such technology into their classrooms. However, our use of this technology is central to the MonCoin curriculum, and we acknowledge the controversy. A recent article in the *Globe and Mail* (2018) is representative of the ongoing debate. Two key players in the world of high-tech mobilities—Jim Balsillie and Norman Doidge—examine the relationship between the corporations that design ever more addictive devices and the mental health effects of these machines. Balsillie is a corporate Co-CEO of the company that manufactured Blackberry smartphones. Doidge is a psychiatrist who feels that adolescents are particularly vulnerable in the face of a technology that exploits two paramount issues for young adults—developing a sense of identity, a sense of individuation, and the attendant need for peer approval. Doidge commented

> Social media is a 24/7 hall of mirrors, with everyone watching themselves and making comparisons all the time. How can anyone not become thin skinned living in a round-the-clock panopticon of peers all competing with each other for attention in an electronic coliseum? (p. 5)

Other researchers of youth and technology, such as Gardner and Davis (2013), have a more nuanced view of the impact of this technology and offer the view that, like all technology it can be used for good or ill.

METHOD, SOURCES OF DATA, AND INTERPRETATION—SOCIOGRAMS

In order to compare social activity and social grouping within and across the two environments we have chosen—the physical art classroom and the online social network—we have several sources of data that cover both settings. In the discussion that follows, we will be using material from student entry and exit interviews, teacher interviews, records of images that students posted in response to photographic assignments that are a part of the MonCoin curriculum. We will also refer to the frequency and focus of the comments made by students on each other's work. As one way of visualizing this complex material, we will employ a graphic convention called a "sociogram." Sociograms are tools that have been primarily used by social scientists as a way of illustrating the sorts of connections among social groups (e.g., Macdonald & Cohen, 1995). Sociograms show the high traffic and low traffic nodes associated with certain individuals. Thus, we may assume that a person with many connections is "socially central" and often, a person with few such connections is an "isolate." We have constructed two sociograms, one based on the seating chart of the classroom to illustrate the social structure of the physical classroom (Fig. 3.2) and the other, based on the interactions of students on their closed online social network (Fig. 3.3). In order to make these two illustrations we used several data sources—interviews with students and the teacher, and a seating chart, as a way of describing the social organization of the physical classroom.

For this chapter, we discuss a single classroom with 15 girls and 14 boys as a microcosm for study. We are fortunate that the art teacher (Ms. Lisbon) is a highly observant and empathetic art teacher with a strong relationship with her students. Ms. Lisbon provided us with rich information about the classroom friendships and connections that she observed among her art students. The classroom seating chart is also a good indication of the social bonds among the students—as Ms. Lisbon permitted students to sit in affinity groups in class. For a description of the social world of the physical art classroom, we will rely mainly on the teacher's comments and observations. In the course of her extended interview, Ms. Lisbon ranked all of the students in her class as high, medium/average, or low in terms of social connections. That is, she identified those students who in her estimation were highly social and therefore were at the center of large social networks, versus those at the other end of the scale who were not connected with a wide social web in her classroom. Ms. Lisbon's assessment of students' classroom social connections is one of the variables against which we can compare student activity and connectedness in the online social network. We asked, are those students judged by Ms. Lisbon as having a high social profile, equally active, and in evidence in the online social network?

For information about the organization of the students' online social world, we have an equally rich data source—namely images posted by students, the comments that they made and received, their "likes," and the comments that they made in their exit interviews. In our discussion

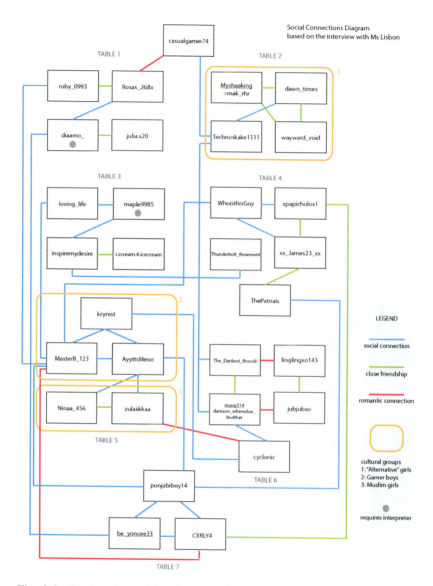

Fig. 3.2 Seating chart of the classroom showing affinity groupings

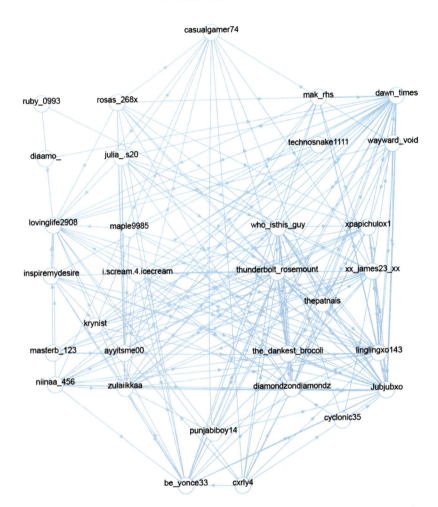

Fig. 3.3 Comprehensive sociogram showing major student connections in the online MonCoin class social network

of individual student cases, we will offer both qualitative and quantitative information that illustrates how these students function on and off line. We will look at the contents of student images, the frequency and volume of posts, and responses, and what students had to say about their intentions and reactions to posted images.

We were able to develop further data on these students as they participated in the online social network. We are able to produce some simple statistics that indicate the students' degrees of social connection (Table 3.1). We developed a simple count of the number of posts each student made, the number of "likes" that the student received for the images that they posted, the sorts of comments that their peers offered, and the average number of "likes" per image posted for each student. We refer to this as the "like-to-post" ratio. The meaning of the ratio of "likes" per image is debatable: does a high "like to post" ratio indicate images that student peers find very meritorious on the basis of the formal and thematic quality of the images? Or does a high ratio indicate that the

Table 3.1 Showing each student ranked according to 3 criteria: (1) The raw number of images they posted; (2) The number of "likes" their classmates gave them; (3) Each student's "like-to-post" ratios

student	like-to-image ratio	ranking	images posted	ranking	likes received	ranking
Be_yonce33	10.55	1	9	23	95	13
Lovinglife2908	10.45	2	22	6	230	2
diamondzondiamondz	10.14	3	7	28	71	20
ayyitsmee00	9.5	4	4	29	38	26
ruby_0993	8.88	5	9	24	80	15
jubjubxo	8.875	6	16	12	142	8
cxrly4	8.83	7	18	10	159	6
thepatnais	8.58	8	17	11	146	7
niinaa	8.36	9	11	19	92	14
The_dankest_brocoli	8.285	10	7	27	58	23
mak_rhs	8.06	11	23	5	186	5
diaamo_	7.9	12	10	20	79	16
i.scream.4icecream	7.79	13	43	1	335	1
maple9985	7.6	14	25	4	190	4
masterb_123	7.5	15	9	25	68	21
Julia-s.20	7.5	16	10	21	75	18
inspiremydesire	7.42	17	26	3	193	3
papichulox1	7.0	18	13	14	19	29
linglingxo	6.95	19	20	7	139	9
rosas_268x	6.545	20	11	18	72	19
wayward_void	6.36	21	19	8	121	10
dawn_times	6.15	22	19	9	117	11
krynist	5.5	23	10	22	55	24
xx_james_xx	5.2	24	15	13	78	17
who_isthis_guy	5.08	25	12	15	61	22
cyclonic35	3.58	26	12	16	43	25
zuulaiikkaa	3.27	27	11	17	[36]	27
casualgamer	3.13	28	8	26	25	28
Thunderbolt_rosemont	3.05	29	37	2	113	12

student is known to be "popular" and well integrated into a large social network off line. Of course, both interpretations may play a role in understanding a high "like-to-post" ratio.

General findings (Table 3.1) are these: The average no. of "likes" $=107/$per student; the average no. of images posted $=15.5/$ student; and the average ratio of images posted-to-likes $=7.09$. On the basis of the average ratio of posts to likes, we can portion the table for like ratios up into thirds—everyone from participants *thunderbolt* to *linglingxo*—is in the bottom third, *papichulo* to *ruby* are in the middle third, and *diamonzon diamondz* to *beyonce* are in the upper third.

An additional factor needs to be kept in mind when considering the like-to-post ratios—students who participated in the MonCoin social network were required to adopt pseudonyms as a way of masking their identities online. This procedure was adopted on the basis of findings from earlier research (Castro, 2014). Castro found that when students were able to mask their identities they seemed freer to experiment with various sorts of presentations of self—some female students in his research study went online under male pseudonyms and the images that they produced were markedly different from what they normally produced under their "real" names, to the extent their art teachers could not identify their work. However, there is an additional complication here. Although the students in Ms. Lisbon's class adopted pseudonyms, anonymity online was by no means perfect. In their exit interviews, two somewhat contradictory facts emerged. First, almost all of the students in Ms. Lisbon's class had varying degrees of knowledge of the aliases adopted by their classmates. Students admitted to knowing the real identities of anywhere from 5 to 20 of their classmates. They often said that identifying their classmates was quite easy and could be done on the basis of the "flavor" of the pseudonyms chosen, the sorts of images posted—and the sorts of themes explored—i.e., known "gamers" posted material associated with gaming, while others posted images that were easily linked by their peers to the persona they presented in the physical classroom. Second, the paradox is that although the pseudonyms were only partially successful as masks—offering freedom to explore new possibilities—a number of the students also stated that being anonymous, thanks to their pseudonym, was a real benefit. That is, the students felt liberated from the scrutiny of their peers (and negative judgments) even though they admitted that their online disguises were not perfect.

Discussion of Online Activity in the Social Network

Cases: Small Groups and Individuals

The Hubs

As in most classrooms, friends sit together at the same table, and so it is in Ms. Lisbon's art class. However, not all students are confined to a tight social circle. Ms. Lisbon identified *be_yonce33*, *cxrly4*, and *loving_life* as "travelers"—students who she can place at any table in the classroom and they will be comfortable. In our classroom sociogram, these students are social hubs: they have strong connections with students in their own social group, but also to students in other cliques and tables. These classroom connections are matched by the student's online interactions during the MonCoin project. For the discussion that follows concerning the rankings of students based on our three measures we refer to Table 3.1 and Fig. 3.4.

Be_yonce33 earned the highest like-to-post ratio score with 10.55. According to Ms. Lisbon, *be_yonce33* can "float to many tables," and "is a very high achiever, used to getting 100%, because [of] the detail and effort she puts into her work." *Be_yonce33* sits with her close friend *cxrly4*, another "extremely high achiever" according to Ms. Lisbon, another "floater," and also high scorer in our index. *Cxrly4* is interested in art, and Ms. Lisbon described her as "someone who is naturally active on social media on her own, and taking pictures as well." Indeed, *cxrly4* was active online: she was one of the top "likers" and commenters, and in the top quarter of posters with 18 images. *Cxrly4*'s many online connections were echoed by her connection to the rest of the class: nearly every student liked or commented on at least one of her images.

Loving_life has the second highest "like"-to-post ratio scores of the class. When it came to "likes" received, *loving_life* was the recipient of 230 "likes" from his fellow students. *Loving_life* is not new to Instagram; his own Instagram account has more than 4000 followers. Despite his Instagram-savviness, his images are unremarkable. His motifs are commonly found in many other students' photo streams and his images lack any creative flair. *Loving_life* posted a fairly high number of images (22), but he was rather stingy when it came to giving likes, scoring near the bottom of the class, the third lowest with only 8 likes given.

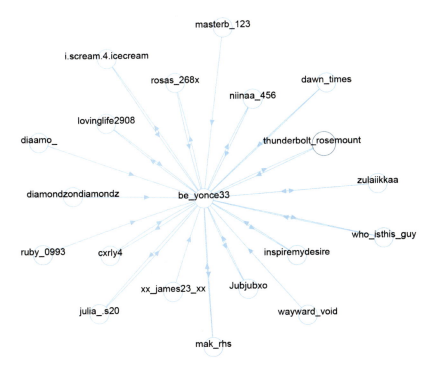

Fig. 3.4 Online sociogram for a student with many social connections in the classroom

We therefore conclude that *loving_life*'s high "like"-to-post ratio was not a result of image quality or reciprocity, but due to his social status in the class.

All three active social hubs in the class were also among the highest scorers; the online and offline sociogram was a close match. It is a similar picture with the students with a low social profile in class.

The Loners
Thunderbolt_rosemont is described by Ms. Lisbon as mildly autistic, and having a hard time with motor and social skills (Fig. 3.5). During group projects, *thunderbolt_rosemont* can get left out, as was the case during one of the MonCoin field excursions. Ms. Lisbon shared that

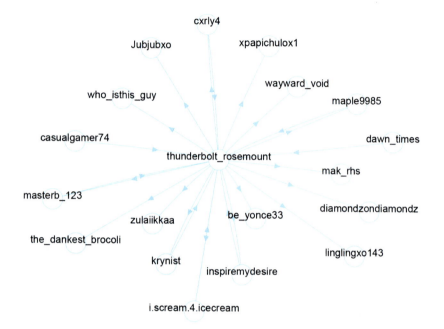

Fig. 3.5 Online sociogram for a student with few social connections in the classroom

It was hard for me, as a teacher, to see him not being included, because he was just so focused that they forgot him, almost. He was trying to interact, but as the project was moving on you could see he wasn't being included.

Thunderbolt_Rosemont's online and off line profiles were a close match. He was prolific, posting an impressive 37 images, the second highest after *i.scream.4.icecream*. However, he received the lowest like-to-post ratio score, a mere 3.05. It is worth noting that *thunderbolt_rosemont* did not give his fellow students much to work with: his images are unremarkable, often blurred, with a healthy disregard for formal features such as "rule of thirds." The MonCoin team emphasized the importance of formal features as a way of producing effective photographs—a goal that most of the students wanted to master. While *loving_life* received a relatively high like-to-post ratio by posting uninteresting images this may be attributed to his high social status off line in class.

Thunderbolt_rosemont's low like-to-post ratio may be due to both his low status in the classroom and to the lack of aesthetic value in the images that he posted.

Our second lowest post-to-like ratio scorer was *casualgamer*, who came in at 3.13. *Casualgamer* is described by Ms. Lisbon as someone who has a very small circle of friends outside of the class, and who doesn't connect with his fellow art-class students. "[He] doesn't like to divulge too much stuff about himself; hair in front of his face, hoodie off and on," observed Ms. Lisbon. *Casualgamer* received few likes, and no comments at all from his classmates. In turn, he also did not engage with other students, liking very few images and making no comments. Many of his images are missing hashtags, which are used to identify missions and to facilitate dialogue. As with the hubs, the loners' online and off line sociograms were a close match, the formal, aesthetic aspects of the images notwithstanding.

Motifs and Gender

While the motifs and quality of the posts may not influence popularity, they can indicate gender identity. Due to the nature of the missions, many motifs are ubiquitous: food was among the most popular, due to the mission "What I Eat," and there is a large proportion of photos from in and around the school, prompted by the missions "My School" and "My Neighbourhood." Images of nature, plants (especially dandelions) were also popular across the board, a response to the "Nature" mission. There were, however, motifs that were particular to each gender.

We found that only boys posted images of sports, gaming, and computers (Fig. 3.6). These images were mostly posted during the missions "Self" and "My School." Some photos are nearly exact copies of each other, such as closely cropped shots of basketballs and footballs, and photos of novelty keyboards with colored, backlit keys (Fig. 3.1).

A theme exclusive to girls was the art that they made. More than half of the girls in Ms. Lisbon's class photographed their sketchbooks, collages, origami sculptures, and paintings-in-progress, mostly in response to the "What I Make" mission (Fig. 3.6). These images did more than indicate a personal interest, they also revealed something about the person making the art. For example, *wayward_void* posted an image of her sketchbook with drawings of a bloodied face and a sketch of a person placing two fingers to the side of his head and gesturing to blow his brains out (Fig. 3.3). These drawings appeared to be deeply personal,

Fig. 3.6 4×4 Matrix of posted images exploring identity

and thanks to the teacher's intervention the student later amended the page by covering these drawings with Post-it Notes that featured more innocuous sketches of smiling faces. We saw none of the boys make these kinds of vulnerable, personal gestures in their photos. In fact, none of the boys posted any images of their artworks, not even *thepatnais*, who was described by Ms. Lisbon as a prolific and gifted artist.

Both girls and boys posted images of food in response to the mission "What I Eat," but the subject and aesthetics of the images revealed a gender divide. The girls produced the iconic food shots. Instagram is typically known for beautifully staged fresh fruit on French toast, a plate of carefully arranged sashimi, or a frothing strawberry smoothie. The girls' photos were crisp and well lit, with photographic filters applied to enhance the image (Fig. 3.6). In contrast, the boys' food was beige, blurred, and dead center. Examples included a plate of spaghetti, a cheese pizza, and a styrofoam container with an unknown meat on rice—all hurried documentary shots of food that had moments before being consumed (Fig. 3.6).

These images may be an indicator of the different relationship boys and girls have with food, but what can these gender-specific motifs tell us about the social connections in the class? While there are clear gender groupings in the motifs, the students' interactions with these images crossed gender lines. Both girls and boys liked and commented on the junk food images; both girls and boys liked and commented on the images of artworks. This suggested that the motifs were connected to the student's personal identity rather than to specific social groups on the sociogram. However, motifs can also be used to signal belonging to a specific interest group, such as the group we call the "Gamer Boys."

The Neo-Tribe: Gamer Boys

The Gamer Boys are identified through their pseudonyms. Following the adage "it takes one to know one," *punjabiboy* noted that many of the MonCoin pseudonyms are actually the usernames some students use for their online video gaming. Three of these boys sit together and are connected on the classroom sociogram: *krynist*, *MasterB_123*, and *AyyitsMe00*. They are, as Ms. Lisbon calls them, "the gaming table." Also associated with this group through online interactions are *punjabiboy*, *xx_james_xx*, and *casualgamer* (Fig. 3.7).

While the core group of Gamer Boys were easily identified on the classroom sociogram, this group's social connections extended beyond the students sitting at the same table. There were discrepancies between the online versus off line interactions of this group. While *xx_james_xx*, *casualgamer*, and *krynist* didn't connect on the classroom sociogram, they didn't like nor did they comment on each other's images. Two members of the group (*krynist* and *masterb_123*) even reached out to a student with a lower social score *thunderbolt_rosemont*, affording him a total of ten "likes."

Another discrepancy was the online and off line activity of the "hub" *masterb-123*, a highly social student on the classroom sociogram. He was

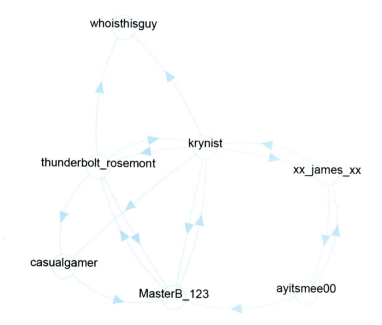

Fig. 3.7 Gamer Boys' sociogram

described by Ms. Lisbon as a traveler. She said "[he's a] big guy, one of our house leaders. He's a floater, he can go to multiple tables. Very social." However, *masterb_123* ran a fairly low profile online. His "like"-to-image ratios were middling at 7.5, and he posted nine images, which placed him in the bottom quarter of posters. Despite his popularity in class, *masterb_123*'s online profile was unremarkable.

Overall, the gamer group was not very active online. Their posting activity was low to middling (4–15 posts per student), and they typically gave each other few likes, usually one or two likes over the course of the MonCoin project. Their like-to-image ratios were also in the middle range, hovering around 5 (see Table 3.1).

Aside from the chosen pseudonyms and online interactions, this group of boys was also identifiable through the images they post. The motifs were gender normative, much as discussed above: gaming consoles, keyboards, sports equipment, junk food, and cars (Fig. 3.1). The images shared a candid aesthetic; they lacked creative touches such as filters or inventive angles, rather, they tended to be documentary shots more focused on content than on form. The function of the images was to identify the student as a gamer, as a member of the tribe. However, this strategy did not always lead to inclusion in the gamer club.

Whoisthisguy immediately identified himself as a gamer, the very first image he posted was of a game console with a matching headset (Fig. 3.1). Other motifs included luxury cars, sports equipment, and images of fast food. However, his "tribe" did not respond to him. While he received a few seemingly random likes from other gamers, the otherwise social *masterb_123* did not reply to any of his posts. *Whoisthisguy* was described by Ms. Lisbon as a loner, who connects with *xx_james_xx* and *xpapichulox1* in class, though they did not always reciprocate his advances. They certainly did not do so online: neither one liked any of *whoisthisguy*'s images. *Whoisthisguy* played it safe, he presented a typical "gamer boy" persona and did not stray from the "no frills" aesthetic shared by the group. However, much like in the case of *thunderbolt_rosemont*, social status superseded his online performance of identity.

Maffesoli (1996) described neo-tribes as a collection of individuals who share an interest, but not necessarily a political or class allegiance. Can the Gamer Boys and the Alternative Group be considered to be neo-tribes? The definition appeared to be a good fit for the Gamer Boys: the core group of *krynist*, *masterb_123*, and *ayyitsme00* are friends in class, but the other members of the group typically did not interact with each other off line. However, once they were online, the (partial) anonymity of the MonCoin project allowed them to bridge classroom cliques and to connect with each other through liking, commenting, and posting imagery that identified them as members of the gamer interest group.

In the case of the Alternative Group, the concept of the neo-tribe becomes less well defined. The three girls and the transgender boy student shared pronounced political convictions based on ideas of identity and gender. As Ms. Lisbon noted, "it's what defines them as a group." Their connections off line were echoed by their interactions online; they followed each other through liking and by posting artistic, and sometimes challenging imagery. While the Alternative Group itself may not have fit the definition of a neo-tribe, their online interactions with the duo *inspiremydesire* and *i.scream4.icecream* could have been seen as the creation of a loose, temporary tribe that was based on a mutual appreciation of artistic expression. We propose that the structure of the

MonCoin project facilitated this spontaneous formation of interest groups that transcended social classroom affiliations.

Reaching Out: Alternative Connections
A parallel to the Gamer Boys group is a foursome of three artsy, "alternative" girls who are fond of art and one transgender boy. Ms. Lisbon notes "That whole group is open about identity, sexuality, that's almost what defines their group, what really connects them." The group shared a table and included *mak_rhs, dawn_times, wayward_void*, and *technosnake1111* (Fig. 3.8).

In this tight-knit group, the three girls spent time with each other nearly exclusively, while the transgender student floated in and out. On our like-to-image social rating the "alternative" group is middling, ranging from 6.15 and 6.38 for *dawn_times* and *wayward_void* to 8.6 for *mak_rhs* (we have no data for *technosnake1111*, as he deleted his posts before we could capture them). The close off line bond was matched by the group's online activity—they supported each other by vigorously

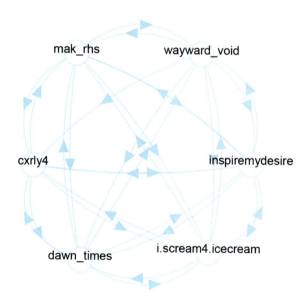

Fig. 3.8 Alternative Girls' sociogram

liking and commenting on each other's posts, such as *dawn_times* who liked 17 out of *mak_rhs*'s 23 photos. Similar to the Gamer Boys, this group also posted repeating images: the same peach was shown, abandoned and forlorn on the ground by both *technosnake1111* and ***dawntimes*** (Fig. 3.1), and all four members of this group took nearly identical shots of a wall in the art studio and a painted door. This artistically inclined "alternative" group-valued aesthetics. Its members made creative choices such as silhouetting figures against a brilliant sky, taking shots at unusual angles, playing with monochromatic images, and macro photography. The quality of their images garnered likes and comments from many students outside the "alternative" group's social circle, but we noticed an especially strong exchange of likes and comments between this group and another social node: the social hub duo of *inspiremydesire* and *i.scream4.icecream*.

Ms. Lisbon described *inspiremydesire* as "really active, she's one of the house leaders, extreme leadership skills, very mature." She is close friends with *i.scream4.icecream*, who sits beside her in class. In fact, according to Ms. Lisbon "inspiremydesire and i.scream4.icecream often get called sisters, they are mistaken for sisters because they're both tall and they're both blond, and they hang out a lot." *I.scream4.icecream* is an exchange student from Austria who is "extremely open to talking to people and social." She was the most active student online by far, both for liking images by other students and for receiving likes. She received a staggering 326 likes, more than 100 more likes than the next highest student. In turn, she liked nearly every other student's post and was the top poster, with 43 images.

In their classroom sociogram (Fig. 3.3), the "alternative" group and the two dynamic leaders do not connect at all. Online, it is a different story. The members of both groups reach out to each other by repeatedly liking and commenting on each other's images. There is even a repeated image, *i.scream4.icecream* also photographed the painted door (Fig. 3.1).

Perhaps it was the MonCoin project's mantle of anonymity that facilitated the connection of these two social groups, maybe it was the strong online activity that brought the students to each other's attention, or maybe the students appreciated each other's creative imagery. Whatever the reason, a connection was made online that was not present off line.

Comparing the Teacher's Assessment of Students' Social Connections In-Class with the Same Student's Network of Connections On Line

As we have mentioned, the teacher Ms. Lisbon offered an extensive and very useful discussion of the students in her art class. One indication that a student had access to a robust social network in the classroom was when Ms. Lisbon would refer to a student as a "traveler." This meant that the student was welcome to sit at a number of different tables, and in fact did move freely around the classroom. Let us take a look at a couple of the students identified by Ms. Lisbon as either minimally connected to social networks in the classroom, or as students who were "travelers" with easy access to multiple social networks in the classroom. So, for example *thunderbolt_rosemont* was, as we identified, a coded student diagnosed with mild social autism—and so, at the low end of the social connection spectrum. Similarly, *aka who is this_guy?*, *krynist*, and *dawn_times* were all identified by the teacher as occupying the low end of the classroom sociability continuum.

At the other end of the sociability scale, there are the students Ms. Lisbon identified as "travellers." These students have strong connections to a number of in-class social networks: *lovinglife2908*, *inspiremydesire*, *i.scream.for.icecream*, and *Be_yonce33/new*.

If we look closely at how the classroom "high social" and "low social" students performed online we will see that their in-class social status is often reflected in their online social connectivity. So, if we look at *thunderbolt_rosemont* we find the following: his status in class was identified as "low social" by the teacher. That is, he was not identified as a "traveler." He posted a very high number of images for the class ($n=37$), when the average number of posted images for his class was 15. For these 37 images, he gathered an above average number of "likes" ($n=113$), but his ratio of "likes" to images was the lowest in class ($r=3.05$), the average like-to-post ratio was 7.09.

What do we make of this? If the low ratio of "likes" to images was an indication of his social standing, then he appeared to be as low status on line as in the physical classroom. But what to make of his very large number of posts ($n=37$)? It would seem that this large number actually works against him—as other students with much smaller numbers of posts achieved much higher like-to-post ratios. Three factors need to be considered here: (1) the "cool kid" factor—suggested by fellow researcher Ehsan Akbari in a personal correspondence. That is, Akbari observed that some of the cooler kids in the class manifested their coolness by participating only sparingly in posting images on line. For example, *masterb_123* posted only 9 images. He was identified by Ms. Lisbon as one of the more socially important individuals in the class. He received a total of 68 "likes" from his classmates (the average number of "likes" for the class was $n=107$). His post-to-like ratio was mid-range as well ($n=7.5$), average for the class was $n=7$. So even though he had relatively few posts, there was something about his work that earned him a respectable showing in terms of "likes." As we have seen, this was not the case with *thunderbolt_rosemont* who posted many images but who collected relatively few "likes" and the lowest post-to-"like" ratio. It appeared that the classroom "loner" (as identified by Ms. Lisbon) did not do nearly as well (measured in "likes") as a "more socially important" member of the classroom. One possible explanation is that the classmates while working on line knew exactly who everyone was. This brings us to the thorny issue of the supposed anonymity of the participants.

(2) Anonymity on line: When the students were interviewed at the close of the project almost all of them admitted that they had a very good idea who at least 4–6 of their classmates were, regardless of the online pseudonyms they had adopted. Some students claimed to know who everyone was in spite of pseudonyms. Thus, it may be that *thunderbolt_rosemont's* classmates knew who he was on line and treated him with the same regard as he received in the physical classroom—that is as a student of low status. If we look at his rankings on Table 3.1 we see that in terms of the number of "likes" he sits slightly above average with a total of 113, but his like-to-post ratio is the lowest in the class ($n=3.05$). So, apparently his classmates were not too enthusiastic about the images he posted. Was this on the basis of the quality of the images or was it because they knew who had made them? Or a combination of both factors?

(3) Additionally, there is the fact that *thunderbolt_rosemont* photographic skills were not judged as especially accomplished, thus the fact that he posted a relatively large number of not highly polished images may also have resulted in a low ratio of likes to posted images. Whatever the case, it is clear from Table 3.1, that *thunderbolt_rosemont* ranks at the low end of the scale in the social network, as he does in class (if we accept Ms. Lisbon's assessment). In the case of *thunderbolt_rosemont*,

there is no real difference between his solid connections to social networks on line or off.

The same is true, but in the opposite direction for *i.scream.for.icecream*. According to Ms. Lisbon, *i.scream.for.icecream* is extremely well connected in the classroom having access to a large social network. It would seem that the same is true for her online. She posted the largest number of images ($n=43$) for her class and had gleaned the largest number of "likes" ($n=335$) in the whole class. Yet her like-to-post ratio was not spectacular ($n=7.79$), slightly above the average for the class ($n=7.09$). The highest like-to-post ratio in the class was *Beyonce33's* ($n=10.55$). This raised the question of which was a better measure of social connections on line: the raw number of "likes" or the ratio of likes to posts? In any event, it seemed that in the case of *i.scream.for.icecream* and *thunderbolt_rosemont*, there was no difference in their social standing in the physical classroom and in the online social network. In one case, they remained low status and minimally connected and in the other they remained high status and widely connected.

There are other individuals whose in-class status and online status were somewhat at variance with each other (unlike the two examples above): For example, *dawn_times* was identified by Ms. Lisbon as a quiet student in class. She is not a "traveler," with no obvious signs of entry into numerous in-class social networks. However, online she presents a more active profile: she posts 19 images, which is above the average number of image posts for her class ($n=15.5$). For these 19 images, she collected 117 "likes." These 117 "likes" are above the class average for the number of likes ($n=107.44$). As for the ratio of "likes" to images posted, *dawn_times'* performance ($N=6.15$) was below the class average of 7.09. The sheer number of her "likes" however suggested that her online connectedness was perhaps greater than her access to the physical classroom social networks.

Conclusion

There is no question that the opportunity to interact with their classmates online as well as in person, to respond to the images produced through participating in the MonCoin curriculum, have been positive experiences. Many of the students in this data set commented in their exit interviews that they had many kinds of learning experiences—ranging from learning about the way some of the other students lived—their pets, homes, and taste in food. The activity also gave students an opportunity to reflect on aspects of their lives that they had never thought about. For example, a well-spoken and articulate young man—of some standing in the classroom posted an image of his sneaker collection—a dazzling collection that he was proud of (Fig. 3.6). Yet, his comment in his exit interview was the sober realization that, actually he did not need that many shoes! He might have come to that realization without posting that image, but it seems likely that the knowledge that his classmates were looking at his extravagant lifestyle may have made him more self-conscious about his copious collection. Similarly, having access to the social network where one could post images semi- or completely anonymously gave a Muslim member of the class the chance to show uncharacteristic aspects of herself with a certain degree of privacy. Thus, in addition to posting a severely cropped self-portrait of herself in a hijab—she also posted a shot of her foot on a skateboard, and yet another of a drawer full of brightly colored head scarves, thereby signaling something about her relationship to religious custom while at the same time foregrounding the importance of personal expression.

As we have indicated, the relationship between how a student functions and socializes within the physical classroom, and how these same students function in a social network, is not simple. In some cases, the social dynamics that obtained in the classroom also obtained on line. However, in other cases, the pretense of anonymity, no matter how imperfect, allowed students to experiment with imagery and topical explorations with less fear of negative judgment from their peers. As we noted—the very same students who acknowledged that they had a pretty good idea which names their classmates had adopted were also quick to add that, in fact, being "anonymous" or disguised online was a positive experience, one that freed them to experiment with technical as well as substantive topics.

In the end, whether the students' online and off line personalities and experiences tend to match, may not be the most important issue, but rather that the opportunity to create an online persona offers students a chance to explore new ways of interacting with their peers and exploring aspects of their emerging identity, if they wish to do so. They can try out a new "performance"—or try curating a new "exhibit." For students, these opportunities will be of great value as they explore issues of identity and connect with other students in their class—on or off line. Enabled by the creative prompts and the (thin) guise of anonymity, students were ready to reveal personal information they may not otherwise have shared. They opened themselves up to new dialogues, even if they were confined to the online forum of Instagram posts and comments. In Goffman's terms, they are bringing the "backstage" into the "public space." The MonCoin project's digital "safe space" can allow students to go beyond the expectations and constraints imposed by a social neo-tribe. Through their online persona, a student can explore aesthetics and subject matters that are meaningful to them and make the art curriculum relevant to their own lives.

However, for teachers the MonCoin intervention offers a significant benefit as well. The careful use of closed social networks in class and the sociograms generated by on line interactions—such as the ones that were provided by the MonCoin project could be invaluable to a teacher who wants to perfect and personalize her teaching interventions. In effect, the approaches that were used for the purposes of our research could be easily transformed into tools for the teacher to use in order to get a better understanding of her classes and their social dynamics.

In the course of their demanding and busy days, classroom teachers do not have time to analyze and think about the unfolding social world that is their classroom. There is enough for a teacher to do to keep the class on track, handle lesson logistics, and make sure that content is covered. If provision could be made for the teacher to collect some of the same data that we did in the course of our study—then at her leisure, the teacher could develop a fine-grained understanding of the students in that class—far more detailed and nuanced than what a teacher can normally expect to achieve when placed at the center of the whirlwind that is a typical classroom. The technical tools that we used would provide the teacher with the luxury of a series of snapshots of her class as it functions as a social setting. The sociograms and the patterns of online interaction would help the teacher to identify the different players in her classroom—and this in turn would allow her to develop a more personalized teaching approach toward all of her students.

REFERENCES

Akbari, E., Castro, J. C., Lalonde, M., Moreno, L., & Pariser, D. (2016). "This allowed us to see what others were thinking": Curriculum for peer-initiated learning in art. *Art Education, 69*(5), 20–25.

Akbari, E., & Pariser, D. (2017, March 2). *Identity, mobilities, social media in art class.* New York: National Art Education Association Convention.

Boyd, D. (2014). *It's complicated: The social lives of networked teens*. New Haven: Yale University Press.

Bromwich, D. (2015, July 9). Trapped in the virtual classroom. *The New York Review of Books, 62*(12), 14–16.

Castro, J. C. (2014). Constructing, performing and perceiving identity(ies) in the place of on line art education. *Journal of Cultural Research in Art Education, 31*, 32–54.

Castro, J. C., Lalonde, M., & Pariser, D. (2016). Understanding the (im)mobilities of engaging at-risk youth through art and mobile media. *Studies in Art Education, 57*(3), 238–251.

Davis, J. (2016). Curation: A theoretical treatment. *Information, Communication & Society, 20*(5), 770–783. https://doi.org/10.1080/1369118x.2016.1203972.

Doidge, N., & Balsillie J. (2018, February 17). Smartphones: Have we alone made ourselves addicted? *Globe and Mail*, 1–6.

Ganda, M. (2014). *Social media and self: Influences on the formation of identity and understanding of self though social networking sites* (Doctoral dissertation). Portland State University, Portland, OR.

Gardner, H., & Davis, K. (2013). *The app generation: How today's youth navigate identity, intimacy and imagination in a digital world*. New Haven: Yale University Press.

Goffman, E. (1959). *The presentation of self in everyday life*. New York: Anchor Books.

Hebdige, D. (1979). *Subculture: The meaning of style*. London: Routledge.

Hesmondhalgh, D. (2005). Subcultures, scenes or tribes? None of the above. *Journal of Youth Studies, 8*(1), 21–40 (published online January 23, 2007).

Hodkinson, P. (2002). *Goth: Identity, Style and Subculture*. Oxford: Berg.

Hogan, B. (2010). The presentation of self in the age of social media: Distinguishing performances and exhibitions online. *Bulletin of Science, Technology & Society, 30*(6), 377–386.

Lalonde, M., Castro, J. C., & Pariser, D. (2016). Identity tableaux: Multimodal contextual constructions of adolescent identity. *Visual Art Research, 42*(1), 38–55.

MacDonald, C. D., & Cohen, R. (1995). Children's awareness of which peers like them and which peers dislike them. *Social Development, 4*(2), 182–193.

Mead, G. H. (1934). *Mind self and society*. Chicago: University of Chicago Press.

Maffesoli, M. (1996). *The time of the tribes: The decline of individualism in mass society* (D. Smith, Trans.). London: Sage.

Muggleton, D. (2000). *Inside subculture: The postmodern meaning of style*. Oxford: Berg.

Oram, A. (2009, October 26). *What sociologist Erving Goffman could tell us about social networking and internet identity*. Retrieved from: http://radar.oreilly.com/2009/10/what-sociologist-erving-goffma.html.

Robards, B., & Bennett, A. (2011). My tribe: Post-subcultural manifestations of belonging on social network sites. *Sociology, 45*(2), 303–317.

Terkel, S. (2011). *Alone together: Why we expect more from technology and less from each other.* Philadelphia: Basic Books.

Treem, J. W., Dailey, S. L., Pierce, C. S., & Biffl, D. (2016). What we are talking about when we talk about social media: A framework for study. *Sociology Compass, 10*(9), 768–784.

CHAPTER 4

Girls and Their Smartphones: Emergent Learning Through Apps That Enable

Bettina Forget

INTRODUCTION

The smartphone is a young woman's constant companion: It is a conduit to her peer group, her photo camera, her news feed, and her game center. It is a private space where she expresses her individuality by downloading apps which reflect her needs and likes. Could a girl's mobile device be integrated into an educational framework that promotes a more active engagement with creativity and digital technology? Which mobile apps are most conducive to creating a learning environment that connects to girls' learning styles? This chapter investigates how ninth-grade girls from two Anglophone secondary schools in Montreal used their smartphones both at school and at home. The girls I interviewed used a wide variety of mobile applications, from apps for chatting with friends, to art-portfolio apps, and apps that connect a smartphone to a microscope. I examine the range of the girls' favorite mobile applications and assess the apps' social, functional, and creative aspects.

I look at smartphone apps through the lens of complexity thinking and a student-based, constructivist teaching approach. A central component of this theoretical stance is the idea of constraints that enable (Castro, 2007),

B. Forget (✉)
Concordia University, Montreal, QC, Canada

an educational framework where creative prompts allow students to "enter into spaces of uncertainty and be able to reorganize previous understandings into new patterns of knowing about themselves in the world" (p. 8). I draw a parallel between constraints that enable—in the form of MonCoin missions (see Chapter 1)—and apps that enable learning (Gardner & Davis, 2013) through a critical examination of mobile app functionality, highlighting apps that foster open-ended play, collaboration, discovery-based learning, and that connect with the students' own interests. The qualities of enabling apps dovetail with the ways girls learn best. Given that girls are highly relational, and that peer learning and collaborative learning play a major role in their learning style (Cooper & Heaverlo, 2013; Jacobs, Kuriloff, Andrus, & Cox, 2014), I explore how the social media apps on the girls' phones relate to the functionality of apps for learning. I propose that engagement with mobile devices and apps can create an access ramp to digital technology and the STEM field (Science, Technology, Engineering, and Math), an arena where women and girls are currently underrepresented. For educators who aim to integrate mobile technology into their classroom, wading through myriads of apps is a daunting, if not impossible task. New apps and new versions of mobile devices are continually being deployed in the digital marketplace, and by the time you read this chapter new apps and new interfaces may well have superseded those I am describing. Accordingly, this chapter is not intended to be a "buying guide" for the top ten best apps for teaching girls. Rather, it is my aim to create awareness about the creative potential that apps may offer while being mindful of their capacity to exploit my psychological vulnerabilities and limit learning. The MonCoin project offers insights into how girls relate to their smartphones, and this chapter discusses both the pitfalls and the creative successes from using mobile media in the visual art classroom.

IDENTITY AND GENDER STEREOTYPES

Philosopher and neuroethics scholar Alicia Juarrero (2002) likened identity to a complex dynamic system that is delineated by a boundary, which she described as a permeable, active site of phase change. Here existential decisions are made about which outside influences to integrate into the system, and which to reject. In the balancing act between inclusion and exclusion of stimuli, the self is being continually constructed in a feedback loop with its cultural environment. Psychologists Daphna Oyserman, Kristen Elmore, and George Smith (2012) concurred, observing that "Self and identity theories converge in grounding self and identity in social context" (p. 76). The authors posited that self and identity are social products, and that endorsement from within an individual's social hierarchy is a particularly important factor, as it reinforces one's sense of value. As a result, people respond to their cultural and social environments by structuring their self-concepts to harmonize with others' expectations of them. Not only is identity meshed with the expectations of my social context, it is also in constant flux. Oyserman et al. (2012) observed that "identities are not the fixed markers people assume them to be but are instead dynamically constructed in the moment" (p. 70). In the temporal flow of experience, there is a recursive and ongoing reconstruction of myself as I respond to different environments and social contexts in which I find myself.

The external, societal pressures are especially pronounced for women and girls. Patricia Yancey Martin is a sociologist and scholar who specializes in gender studies. She sees gender as a social institution that is established and sustained through recursive performative acts. Yancey Martin (2003) proposed that women and men routinely practice gender "in embodied interactions that are emergent and fluid, grounded in practical knowledge and skills, and informed by liminal awareness and reflexivity" (p. 342). Gendering practices are based on tacit knowledge that is acquired over time and deployed through repetition. They are recursive scripts that both inscribe past performances and prescribe future performances. These practices are learned and enacted in childhood, it is, for example, how one learns how to "act like a girl" (p. 351). Gendering practices recursively construct gender stereotypes, which define how women and girls see themselves as individuals, understand their place in society, and shape ideas about their strengths and weaknesses.

Connecting Girls with STEM

Gender stereotypes influence how women and girls engage with certain fields of knowledge. While recent studies show that girls are enrolling in greater numbers in higher education (*The Economist*, 2015) and that they outperform boys throughout their academic career and across every social category, such as race, ethnicity, and socioeconomic status (Jabobs et al., 2014), gender differences persist when it comes to specific academic subjects. According to an analysis by *The Economist* (2015), girls do especially well in reading, where they outperform boys to such an extent that it is equivalent to an extra year of schooling, whereas boys are still ahead in math, where they are ahead an equivalent of three months' schooling. The gender divide is pronounced in the STEM field overall, which is seen by girls as lacking femininity. The perceived mismatch between girls' self-concepts and the stereotypes associated with science as "boys' subjects" cause girls and women to abstain from STEM disciplines (Kessels, 2014, p. 281). A poll conducted in 2009 by the American Society for Quality of Children between the ages of 8 and 17 showed that only 5% of the girls expressed an interest in an engineering career, compared with 24% of the boys. However, girls tend to do as well as boys in math and science during adolescence (Leaper, Timea, & Spears Brown, 2012, p. 269). It is therefore not the girls' abilities that are holding them back, but their ideas about gender norms. Can this misconception be mitigated in an educational context?

Computer scientist and educator Margaret Grimus (2013) suggested that the introduction of mobile devices could create an access ramp for girls into the domain of digital technology and the STEM field. During a study she conducted that researched the conditions and perceptions of K-12 students using mobile phones in regard to informational learning, she discovered that girls may feel at ease using mobile devices for communicating with their peers, but they feel less comfortable than boys at exploring their mobile devices beyond using the apps. This, posited Grimus (2013), may be due to gender socialization: "boys are often taught to explore and be more creative with technology; they tend to use mobile devices as a gadget" (p. 3). The author further noted that "boys are more active in free exploration and learning new applications—games in particular" (p. 8). In contrast, girls perceive themselves as less skilled when it comes to technology. Grimus (2013) stated, "[i] f this perception continues, it can limit young girls. It can impact the types of jobs and courses that girls take; hence it could lead to a different type of digital divide...much has to be done to teach girls about the technical and more advanced multimedia features of their mobile devices" (p. 3).

Girls' App Use and Learning Styles

If educators want to embark on the idea of connecting girls with STEM subjects, or better engage with girls generally through the use of mobile technology, what do I know about how girls prefer to learn, and how do these preferences connect with how they use their smartphones? A study by educational researchers Shannon Andrus, Peter Kuriloff, and Charlotte Jacobs (2015) investigating girls preferred learning styles discovered that "relationships are central to girls' learning" (p. 17). While girls form relationships with both their teachers and their fellow students, the girls surveyed in this study stated that they found connecting to other girls especially rewarding, both intellectually and emotionally. The girls especially enjoyed learning situations that included discussions, working in teams, and participating in collaborative projects. Girls' preference for learning experiences that are based on relationships and collaboration is echoed in studies by museum education researchers Toni Dancstep (née Dancu) and Lisa Sindorf (2010, 2016), who examined how girls interact with didactic exhibits in science museums. The studies found that girls learned best when exhibits "encourage collaboration by allowing for shared goals in the exhibit experience" (Dancstep & Sindorf, 2016, p. 15) and that girls enjoy exhibits that offer playful and open-ended learning situations. The second-most emphasized aspect of learning for girls described by Andrus et al. (2015) was that curricula should be relevant to girls' lives and to their world. The authors noted that "girls respond to lessons that encourage them to study on their own ideas, lives, and families but also lessons that teach them about the current and historical lives of women and girls around the world" (p. 17).

In their article "Reaching Girls," Jabobs et al. (2014) examined a survey that collected responses from both teachers and female students from grades 7 through 12. The authors identified lesson characteristics and activity components that were particularly effective and engaging for girls. Most notably, they found that lessons should clear, collaborative, and relevant to students' lives, as mentioned above. Particular class activities that were brought up repeatedly by students and teachers were "class discussions, hands-on projects, multimodal lessons, creativity and creative arts, and out-of-class experiences" (p. 69). It is interesting to note that the above-mentioned class activities and lesson characteristics find parallels in the use of mobile technology. Think only of how social media apps foster relationship building, how image and video editing apps can promote creativity and creative arts, and the potential of taking learning outside the classroom by using mobile technology, much like the MonCoin "missions."

TEENS, MOBILE TECHNOLOGY, AND INDIVIDUALITY

Educators contemplating the integration of smartphones into their curricula will find that a staggering number of teenagers already own a mobile device, and that they are populated by a wide array of apps. Popular social media apps and utilities such as email and web browsing are complemented by idiosyncratic choices that evolve from the student's hobbies, such as photo and music editing apps, fitness apps, and game apps. Think of the apps you have chosen to add on your own mobile device and how they connect to your interests. Could someone who looks through your collection of apps guess what kind of person you are? Developmental psychologist Howard Gardner and media technologies researcher Katie Davis (2013) equated the collection of apps on someone's device with a fingerprint, "only instead of a unique pattern of ridges, it's the combination of interests, habits, and social connections that identify that person. The app identity, then, is multifaceted" (p. 60). Educational scholars Michael Stevenson, John Hedberg, Kate Highfield, and Mingming Diao (2015) remarked that many apps are "atomized," a term that refers to the deconstruction of desktop software into smaller, single-purpose functions, allowing for more targeted use and individualization. Since many apps are free or come at a low cost, experimenting with a variety of app functions comes at a low risk for the teens and so encourages a more varied spread of literacies. The authors noted that as a result, young people today are more than passive consumers of knowledge, but are able to create, co-author, invent, publish, and share content that both reflects and creates their world.

I propose that the smartphone can be thought of as a concrete, pocket-sized "space of emergence," an idiosyncratic place where students can construct their individuality by compiling their unique app collections. These collections are in a dynamic flux, as apps and data are added and deleted in response to the constantly unfolding self. If, as educational theorists Deborah Osberg and Gert Biesta (2008) proposed, student-based education should foster individuality, then the smartphone can offer a means to connect curricula to a learner's specific sphere of interest. However, while mobile devices and apps offer great potential to educators, I should also take a moment to highlight areas of concern to be better equipped to anticipate eventual pitfalls.

Addictive Apps

Apps and mobile devices are engaging today's youth, and that is not by accident. The captivating aspects of smartphones lie in their tactile interface and intuitive software design. As Rosin (2013) remarked, my ability to activate and manipulate apps on a smartphone directly with my finger instead of a mouse is a parallel to what the psychologist Jerome Bruner (1964) termed enactive representation, the developmental stage in a child's learning when objects in the world are classified by making gestures. The gesture of swiping on a touch screen can turn a mobile device into a "rattle on steroids" (p. 60) for toddlers, as the children's hands become a natural extension of their thoughts.

This rattle on steroids is not only addictive to toddlers. The smartphone with its tactile interface and its array of seductive apps can become a tether that keeps me bound to the device, whatever my age. This is a point of concern for Tristan Harris, former Design Ethicist at Google, who today writes about how technology exploits my psychological vulnerabilities and how it is hijacking my agency. In his article "How Technology Hijacks People's Minds" (2016) Harris revealed a series of strategies app designers employ to monopolize my time and attention. For example, Harris pointed out that an app's menu options present an illusion of choice, when in reality each function that is offered to the user is tightly controlled by the app developer. The author suggested that when an app offers a menu of choices, I should critically examine the programmer's intent by posing questions such as "Why am I being given these options and not others? What types of options have been excluded and why?" Typically, the intent is to keep me continually engaged with my phones. In fact, Harris called my smartphones a "slot machine in our pockets" (par. 21). Each time I pull out my phones, I bet on the chance that someone responded to one of my posts or emails; it is the "variable reward" characteristic that is the hallmark of most addictive activities. Harris noted that apps and Web sites hijack people's minds is by inducing a 1% chance that I could be missing someone's message. This tension, which Harris termed Fear of Missing Something Important (FOMSI), creates the strongest pull, because social approval is one of the prime motivators for being on social media to begin with. Harris noted that teenagers are a specifically vulnerable demographic when it comes to social approval, both for receiving it and for feeling the need to reciprocate it. Reciprocity, the tit-for-tat game of following someone or liking someone back is another way app developers keep me hooked. Harris termed email, texting and messaging apps "social reciprocity factories" (par. 37).

While I are waiting for my virtual pats on the back, I experience tension. Professor of psychology Jean M. Twenge (2017) called the state of anxiously awaiting a reply from one's peer group, "a psychic tax." She noted that for teenagers, and teenage girls in particular, the feeling of missing out and loneliness has seen a sharp upswing in recent years. According to her survey, 48% more girls said they often felt left out in 2015 than in 2010, while only 27% of boys felt sidelined. Since girls spend most of their time on their devices on social media sites, they are more likely to see their peers engaging in social activities without them, exacerbating the problem. The gender disparity in FOMSI may be due to gender differences in the use of smartphones. According to a study by information science researchers Ionut Andone et al. (2016), women spend more time communicating on social apps than men, and they use their smartphones for longer periods, with the highest mean phone usage for teenagers between 12 and 17 years old. In fact, a 2017 study by Ofcom found that girls aged 12–15 estimate that they spend an average of 21.5 hours a week using their smartphones, compared with 15 hours for boys. When girls are online, they spend most of their time on social media sites such as Snapchat and Instagram (Pew, 2018). Grimus (2013) summed up the gender difference in the use of smartphones as "boys like digital games and girls like talking" (p. 2).

Given how apps can negatively affect girls, how can educators balance the smartphone's potential for creating a space of emergence with its danger of becoming a social reciprocity factory? In the wild array of ever-changing apps, how can educators select apps that could be the most beneficial for students in an educational setting?

Apps Can "Drill and Kill" or Be a "Guide on the Side"

Gardner and Davis (2013) offered an excellent approach of examining apps in terms of their educational potential by dividing apps into two groups: apps that enable and apps that make me dependent. "App—enabling" functionalities encourage users to create their own content, they are open-ended, and offer unexpected possibilities. In contrast, "app-dependent" functionalities offer a small array of pre-packaged choices, they are restrictive, and funnel users toward a predetermined goal. Gardner and Davis observed that apps can make you lazy, discourage the development of new skills, limit you to mimicry or tiny trivial tweaks or tweets—or they can open up whole new worlds for imagining, creating, producing, remixing, even forging new identities and enabling rich forms of intimacy (p. 33).

The authors connected these two app categories with two distinct teaching philosophies: Behaviorism and Constructivism. Behaviorism favors efficient learning environments with well-structured curricula and quantifiable tests which target goal-oriented outcomes. Gardner and Davis (2013) remarked that this teaching philosophy is sometimes unkindly referred to as the "drill and kill" method (p. 28). On the other hand, Constructivist teaching offers the "guide on the side" approach, where educators offer rich, complex problems and then get out of the way, much like the "missions" structure of the MonCoin project. The authors see a parallel between "app-enabling" functionalities and constructivist teaching, and "app-dependent" functionalities and the behaviorist teaching approach. Behaviorist educators tend to employ apps with the aim to streamline the curriculum, to more efficiently meet teaching goals, and to more effectively assess learning. Gardner and Davis (2013) argued that the vast majority of educational apps on offer tend to be geared toward the behaviorist teaching methods, and lamented that these apps are simply digital textbooks and preprogrammed educational conversations. A study by educational researchers Beth Bos and Kathryn Lee (2013) confirmed this assessment, noting that most mathematical apps, for example, are nothing more than "simple flashcards, numeric procedures of mobile textbooks... and do not support sense-making... active learning, or integrated visual models" (p. 3655).

Gardner and Davis advocated for the Constructivist approach of teaching and the use of "app-enabling" functionalities. Apps that enable offer opportunities to explore many possible courses of action, offer open-ended play, and encourage original content creation. For example, creative arts apps allow students to create, to manipulate, to deconstruct, and to reconstruct content. However, Gardner and Davis cautioned that some of these apps rely on prepackaged creative components such as audio loops, filters, and text quotes, which means that the outcomes more closely resemble the app developer's vision than that of the user's. As the authors put it, "What may be creative on the surface may actually be re-creative" (p. 145). Instead, enabling apps should provide a scaffold to create content but not the content itself, and allow for playful exploration that does not prescribe a specific outcome.

Constructivist educators typically use mobile technology and apps to provide open-ended tasks and free exploration. In the case of MonCoin, the combination of the mission prompts and the functionalities of the Instagram app provided a creative framework that allowed students to respond with unique, personal, and sometimes unpredictable images. The project's grounding in constraints that enable echoes Gardner's idea of enabling apps. The Instagram app offered the research team a platform that allowed students to take, manipulate, and share their images. While the app comes preloaded with an array of standard filters, each filter can be individualized, and images can also be edited directly without the aid of a filter. There was no prescribed imagery, no pre-made content, no boxes to tick. Instagram's social media component served as an opportunity to elicit peer-to-peer learning as students responded to each other's images through likes and comments. The research team was aware of the social pressures these online interactions may introduce to this online community of teenagers and asked students to create their accounts using a pseudonym, which afforded a measure of anonymity. The MonCoin team employed an interplay of enabling constraints, an enabling app, and a critical stance toward app functionality to build a project that created a space for students to discover themselves and connect to their peers.

MonCoin and Girls

The MonCoin project was grounded in complexity thinking and a student-based, constructivist teaching approach that foregrounds the learner's individuality and uniqueness. This teaching philosophy creates a pluralist "space of emergence" while also considering the recursive co-construction of identity and gender norms in response to an individual's social context. For girls, gender norms create stereotypes that discourage them from a deep engagement with digital technology and STEM subjects. However, mobile devices could create an access ramp for girls into the STEM field. Girls' preferences for relational and collaborative learning and open-ended play dovetail with the characteristics of enabling apps, which provide opportunities for peer learning and open-ended, playful exploration. The girls who participated in the MonCoin project were enthusiastic users of mobile technology, the vast majority owned a smartphone and had already established an online presence. My interviews with the girls provided salient insights into their use of apps, which apps they favored, and how mobile technology connected to their personal lives.

METHOD AND DATA COLLECTION

The data that forms the basis for this chapter was sourced from entry and exit interviews with female students from three 9th-grade classes that participated in the MonCoin project. One class attended a private girl's school, and the other two classes attended a coed public school, both schools are located in Montreal, Canada. During the 15–30 minute interviews, I asked the students a series of questions regarding their use of mobile media, their interest, and questions specific to the MonCoin photography missions. For the purpose of this chapter, I focused on the questions pertaining to the students' favorite apps, particularly social media apps, and how these apps were used. I also tracked how much time the girls said they spent online, the reason for their online activity, and their interests and motivations. I collated the answers in data tables and tagged specific narratives that related to mobile app use. The data from these three particular classrooms is by no means meant to be representative of all female students in North America, but the findings do correlate with the observations made by the previously mentioned scholars regarding girls' interests in communication, relational learning, and playful content creation.

Step 1: Organizing Apps by Type

To organize the plethora of apps for my data analysis, I created five categories of apps: social media apps, art apps, school apps, games, and "other" apps (see Fig. 4.1). Social media apps are defined as apps that permit communication via text, audio, or video as well as sharing of images, video, and audio content to a group of followers. Art apps are defined as apps which allow the creation and modification of images and videos. The school apps category concerns only the students from the private girl's school. Their iPads come preloaded with educational apps. Games are apps which allow users to play puzzles, quizzes, action adventures, or create virtual objects. The category of "other" apps includes utilities, brand-related apps, and entertainment apps such as video streaming services.

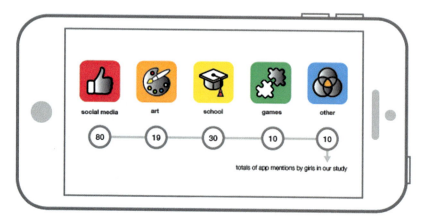

Fig. 4.1 Apps by type

Step 2: Identifying the Most Popular Apps
To identify the most popular apps, I listed all apps mentioned by the girls during the interviews and counted how many girls used each app. In total, I counted 17 different social media apps, 11 art apps, 7 school apps, 8 game apps, and 8 apps in the "other" category. For a short description of the top ten most popular apps mentioned in this section, please refer to Table 4.1.

It came as no surprise that social media apps were both the most numerous and the most popular of all apps among the students of my study. This finding correlates with the surveys conducted by the 2018 Pew Research Institute mentioned earlier. Instagram, Snapchat, and Facebook made up the top three most used apps, respectively, though students noted that they rarely used Facebook anymore. A distant fourth were Twitter, Tumblr, and Pinterest. Loosely associated with the group of social media apps are the communication apps iMessage and FaceTime, which allow streaming and chatting between one or more friends.

Among the art apps, the image editing apps Snapseed and Fuse were the most popular among the students. Snapseed is an image editing app that allows users to add filters, perform some basic photo-retouching, and add text to images. Fuse, also an image editing app, allows users to superimpose two images. Equally popular was VSCO, an art-portfolio app that sits at the crossroads between an art app and a social media app.

Table 4.1 Overview of the top ten most popular apps mentioned by the girls in my study

App	Type	Description
Instagram	Social media	Share still images and short, looping videos either by taking them directly with the mobile device or by selection from the user's media library. The app offers an array of filters, image captioning, hashtagging, and location tagging before posting. Users can follow other Instagrammers and can "like" and comment on their images
Snapchat	Social media	Communicate with a friend through text and image messaging. Posts auto-delete after a specific time. Snapchat allows users to annotate images by doodling and adding graphics
Facebook	Social media	Share text, images, web links, and video to a group of accepted "friends." Users can like, comment on, and share friend's posts. Facebook also offers users the opportunity to create interest groups, event pages, and pages for commercial businesses
Twitter	Social media	Share short texts (up to 280 characters), images and gifs. Users can follow Twitter accounts and like, reply to, and share posts
Tumblr	Social media	Blogging platform that allows users to post short texts and images. Users can follow other user's blogs
Snapseed	Art	An image editing app developed by Google. Users can add filters, do some basic photo-retouching, and add text to images
Fuse	Art	An image editing app that allows users to superimpose two images
VSCO	Art	A subscription-based photo-sharing app. Share still images by taking them directly with the mobile device or by selection from the user's media library. The app offers an array of filters, image captioning, and location tagging before posting. Users can publish their images to VSCO journals or to their own profile, where they can add hashtags and captions
Stop	Game	A word-game app, where players challenge friends to find words starting with a randomly selected letter that correspond to five randomly selected categories
Netflix	Other	A subscription-based video-streaming app that offers a selection of movies and TV shows

The app offers an array of filters, image captioning, and location tagging before posting. Users can publish their images to VSCO journals or create portfolios on their own profile.

The most popular game was Stop, a word-based game app where players challenge friends to find words starting with a randomly selected letter that correspond to five randomly selected categories. During the time of my interviews at the private girl's school, this game was taking the class by storm. Among the "other" apps, Netflix was the most mentioned, a guilty pleasure of students admitting that the iPad got in the way of their studying.

In Focus: Snapchat, the Most Popular App

Snapchat was a favorite with the girls for several reasons. The students appreciated how Snapchat facilitated casual communication. The girls used Snapchat to send each other quick messages, sometimes embellished with stickers and filters. "Snapchat is just quick little updates of what I'm doing, you know, if I saw something funny, stuff like that," remarked *technosnake1111*. The students valued the social aspect of the app, such as the ease with which friends and locations can be tagged in a post. "Snapchat also does this really cool thing where, like, it tracks down where you are, so, like, it knows… so like, let's you put the location and has, like, cool stickers sometimes." Many girls enjoyed the small creative touches Snapchat offers through its selection of stickers and filters. *Princess Consuella Banana Hammock* even used Snapchat for some spontaneous doodling on top of a photograph of a friend. She shared, "I drew, like … my friend was in the picture, and I drew her, like, on a little swing… I'm really bad at, like, drawing on the iPad. Or, drawing in general. But I'm just drawing on, yeah, it was funny."

This casual, creative play makes Snapchat conversations fun and compelling for the girls. A Snapchat conversation is exactly that: a conversation. During the interviews, the girls often compared Snapchat with Instagram, noting that on Instagram the focus is on the person who is posting images, whereas on Snapchat the communication engages both parties. As *Maria* explained, "Instagram it's more like, yourself as, like, the center of attention type of thing, where on Snapchat it can also be your friends that are the center of attention" (Maria, Personal Communication, May 9, 2016). *Rainy_.dayz* agreed, "A Snapchat is more, like, I'm not wearing a bunch of makeup and I'm not, like, high class and, like, wearing nice clothing. Snapchat is just, like, I'm having fun with my friends and then Instagram is more, like, I got done up." Gardner and Davis (2013) observed that Snapchat is intended to be a platform for a "series of mini-performances for an audience of one." This means that there is no need to project a polished profile to the world at large, there is less pressure to be perfectly presented. Rather, a Snapchat is intended to be an intimate, personal conversation. The conversation is also ephemeral. Snapchat creates a space for unguarded, no-makeup conversations by employing a simple feature: All messages are auto-deleted after both parties open them. This means that if a Snapchatter posts an unflattering picture or says something regrettable, it leaves no permanent digital footprint that can later come to haunt her. Or, at least that is how Snapchat is designed to work in theory. It is worth noting that this function can be circumvented by simply taking a screenshot with the mobile device, leading some girls to send messages that they did not intend to be kept, or worse, shared. *Princess Consuella Banana Hammock* engaged in some reciprocal psychological warfare on Snapchat "Um, I screenshot my best friend's sister on Snapchat, because she has really ugly pictures. And I do it back. And I have a folder of her, so it's like a really bad blackmail thing, but it's mutual."

Balancing the short-lived nature of the messages is the "Snapstreak" feature, which encourages uninterrupted, long-term conversations. Next to each Snapchat message, a number and a fire emoji indicate how many days in a row friends have chatted with, or "snapped" each other. Users make sure to keep the conversation going to maintain a high Snapstreak number. This gives the relationship a quantitative value, since a higher Snapstreak number implies a deeper social connection. The Snapstreak introduces an element of social pressure; it is a "social reciprocity factory" as mentioned earlier by Harris, a feature that is especially addictive for teenagers.

The popularity of Snapchat can be traced to a perfect mix of app-enabling and app-dependent functions: The easy relationship building in a low-pressure environment, the creative playfulness, and the ability to create original content are coupled with the hook of social reciprocity, making Snapchat (for now) the number one most popular app for girls.

Step 3: Grouping Apps by Function
Besides examining the apps by category, I also explored what the apps are designed to do, organizing them by functionality. The groupings are

Fig. 4.2 Apps by function

communication; content creation; reposting and sharing; research for information; research for inspiration; organization; active entertainment such as games; and passive entertainment such as watching movies (see Fig. 4.2).

This list of app functions is organized so that they scale from the most active to the least active function. For example, a girl communicating with her friends on Snapchat is an active behavior, whereas sitting on the sofa and watching videos on Netflix would count as a passive behavior. I considered creating original content to be more active than reposting existing content. I also distinguish between research that is active information gathering, such as tracking, reading, understanding, and applying information as part of a homework assignment, and research that is geared toward inspiration, such as browsing a Pinterest board and looking at images created by others. Finally, I differentiate between active entertainment such as games, where players strategize, participate, and even sometimes build virtual content, and passive entertainment such as watching TV on YouTube.

The idea of examining apps in terms of active and passive behaviors was inspired by Gardner and Davis' (2013) definition of app-enabling and app-dependent characteristics. I see active functionalities such as communication and content creation as supporting enabling characteristics, and passive functionalities such as consuming entertainment and inspiration browsing as supporting app-dependent characteristics.

Deconstructing apps according to their functions provides both educators and students with a tool to critically examine the apps they are already using or planning to add to their smartphone. In class, students could be asked to classify their favorite apps according to type and function, evaluate whether the apps elicit active or passive behaviors, examine the menu options, and identify any social reciprocity "hooks." A deeper awareness of how apps are constructed may encourage students to select more creative, enabling apps, and focus more on the active functions those apps provide. At the same time, students will be mindful of the passive and addictive functionalities of popular apps, especially social media apps. However, as I have seen in the above examination of the Snapchat app, most apps are a combination of both enabling and addictive components. The questions then is, what is the apps' proportion of active versus passive functionality? What would be the optimal balance to ensure that girls are engaged but not addicted to an app?

In the section below, I examine each app function and highlight examples of how girls discovered creative potential in apps that helped them in their learning.

APPS AND LEARNING: HOW GIRLS FIND CREATIVE USES FOR APPS

Communication

Since the most popular apps are social media apps, it stands to reason one of the most popular app functions is communication. The most cited reason to use the Internet for the students in my study was communication. This includes direct communication with peers, as well as sharing one's own content or reposting others' content. On social media apps that mostly means texting: twelve of the 17 social media apps include a functionality that can be used for messaging, for eight of the apps it is their primary function. This correlates well with the study by Grimus (2013) mentioned earlier, who noted that girls prefer to communicate with their peers using text messages and messages on social networking sites.

The girls I interviewed also enjoyed chatting via video apps. A group of students at the private girls' school found an interesting way to use the video chat app FaceTime. After school, the girls would get together online to help each other study for upcoming tests. They went through the material together, explained test questions, and demonstrated the answers. "One person does it, and the other person watches," *magenta.a* explained. "It's a fun way of studying. Like, we do a two-on-two. It can be like a study group, except we're not- we're, like- we're not together, together. It's over the Internet." In this example, the girls found a way to learn collaboratively using a ubiquitous utility app that comes pre-installed with the iPhone OS. Rather than learning alone in their rooms, they leveraged the app's functionality and their existing social connections to turn learning into an enjoyable, social, and rewarding activity.

Content Creation

By far the most popular function of apps is content creation. This is not only due to the student's interest in art apps, but also because apps of many other categories also contain a content creation component. As noted above, some social media apps are multifunctional: Snapchat provides the option to draw onto images or enhance them with stickers, filters, and animations. Instagram allows users to take images through the app, and users can then edit their images using a selection of filters and editing tools before posting. Facebook offers the Facebook Live option, where users can create live videos that stream on their Facebook wall and which can later be archived. Games can also allow players create original content, for example Sim games like Minecraft allow players to create and share virtual objects.

When girls create content, they may both seek out specialized, single-function creative apps or use apps that contain content creation functionalities. *Goldberg005* is a student who enjoys art, especially drawing comics, an art form she practices so much that she jokingly complained, "I have tendinitis now." Over a holiday break she discovered the app Stopmotion, an app which allows users to create animations from a series of drawings.

> I did, like, a drawing of somebody, like, running and I did the... I took a picture each like different motion and actually it looked pretty cool. I like cartoon stuff so I wanted to try doing one of my own.

While in this instance, *Goldberg005* experimented with a new art form on her own, she also worked collaboratively with her friends to create videos. For these video projects, her motivation was both focused on creative exploration and the playful interaction with her friends.

I have a lot of videos, like, my friend who goes to another high school... we have all videos, no pictures of us, just videos. There's one we took a bottle, put a lot of sand in it just from sec 1 and we threw it up a slide for... I don't know... it was fun back then. A friend of mine, she smashed an apple, she did it in slow motion and it was really cool and it went like a giant explosion.

This creative activity is without a specific aim, it is open-ended, collaborative, and videos are shared with friends. Playfulness, social interaction, and collectivity are enabling characteristics that are also the hallmarks of the way girls prefer to learn, as mentioned earlier in my review of the studies by Dancstep and Sindorf (2016) and Andrus et al. (2015). Note, also, that both learning situations took place outside of the classroom, hinting at the potential of apps to extend the curriculum beyond the confines of the school.

Research

Online research can be a leisurely browse through an Instagram feed in search of inspiration, or it can be a deep dive into online forums and instructional videos. *Notfluffysheep666* frequently engaged in in-depth online research, particularly on the platform YouTube, and her needs were specific. She is interested in computer science, electronics, and robotics, and she mostly searched for solutions to specific problems she encountered in her projects. *Notfluffysheep666* was taking charge of her learning by independently seeking out information such as "programming and videos on how to, like, code for a certain function." Rather than relying on books, she took advantage of the vast community of YouTube users who share instructional videos and demos. The platform is more than a repository of information, but also features a social media component that offers interactions such as commenting and liking videos. Viewers can ask the poster of a video questions and so engage in a dialogue, developing and informal community of teachers and learners.

Organization

Mobile devices come with an array of native apps that are designed to organize and facilitate your life. These include utilities such as calendars, agendas, address books, and the handy app that turns your phone into a flashlight. Utility apps can also inadvertently facilitate creative production. Following her interest in science and engineering, *notfluffysheep666* is a member of a robotics club, where she discovered an app that connects her iPad camera to a microscope. Apps such as these are typically developed by the microscope manufacturer and are designed to facilitate the capturing of live images and videos directly from the microscope. *Notfluffysheep666* used the app strictly as part of her science club, but the microscope app has the potential to be used beyond its function as a simple interface. What may an art teacher make of this seemingly simple functionality? The microscope app could be used to create images that could be artistically edited and shared, the app could facilitate collaborative work, and may even be integrated in the production of videos. This utility app offers an opportunity to expose more girls to STEM subjects by fusing compelling imagery and creative play with scientific research. How many other modest utility apps may serve as a bridge between disciplines and curricula?

Entertainment

On the far end of the functionality scale is the passive pastime of watching movies and TV on apps such as YouTube and Netflix. Most girls mentioned that, to some extent, they spend too much time on this guilty pleasure. A particularly avid TV addict, *Princess Consuella Banana Hammock*, joked that she is on the Internet "25 hours a day" watching TV shows on Netflix. "I watch, like, videos of Once Upon a Time, Grey's Anatomy edits …Sidewinders 2, and I'm just like, 'Oh my God, no.' I just like, ruin myself." She was aware of her own TV addiction and was also concerned about the effect of entertainment apps on her peers. She cautioned that allowing the use of mobile devices in schools could lead to students failing their classes because they get absorbed by passive entertainment.

> Like, this person, she got a really bad mark on a math test, because she was on her iPad the whole time. And she wasn't listening like … some people have no self-control. And some people have a bit, and some people don't care. There's a difference between people who want to actually succeed in school and people who use the iPad to play during class.

During my interviews, many students expressed similar sentiments. While they are aware how easy it is to get hooked on watching TV online or playing online games and they are spending too much time doing so, they may not understand how the apps are keeping them dependent. Here a critical examination of the enabling, active and addictive, passive functions of apps may provide the girls with tools to mitigate their entertainment addiction, or shift to apps that incorporate more app-enabling functionalities.

In Focus: Multifunctional YouTube Versus Unifunctional Netflix

YouTube may encourage passive, addictive behaviors such as watching endless hours of mindless entertainment, but as I have seen earlier, the same app can also be used for active research, such as *notfluffysheep666*'s dive into instructional videos for her computer coding project. On the surface, YouTube is a simple video-sharing platform, but its open-endedness and the sheer volume of users have transformed it into a multifunctional space that allows users to engage in multiple modes. This stands in contrast to Netflix, the most popular app for entertainment among the girls in my study. Netflix is a unifunctional, narrowly designed app built specifically for passive consumption. Netflix users may not upload their own content, nor comment or interact with the content that is provided, there is no dialogue, no community building, and no participation. In contrast, YouTube is open to communication on many levels. Besides the social media functionality of liking and commenting on other users' videos, some users also create video-responses to existing videos, creating a continuous stream of participation.

YouTube also fosters content creation. Many of the girls I interviewed stated that they create videos with the specific aim of sharing them on YouTube. For example, while *Princess Consuella Banana Hammock* admitted to spending too much time watching videos, she was also actively adding to YouTube's video library. She is an avid horseback rider, and she and her friends videotape each other during riding classes. *Princess Consuella Banana Hammock* isn't afraid to take a fall for her craft:

> I fell on Saturday, and it was a really bad fall. I really wanted to get it, like, videotaped, I had a video of me falling, and it was really funny. So I want to see it. But, if it really hurts, I don't want to see it.

Through watching endless hours of TV shows, *Princess Consuella Banana Hammock* appears to have developed an understanding of a video's entertainment value and how to engage her viewers.

YouTube is a multifunctional app that provides content for passive entertainment as well as active research, supports several modes of communication, and invites content creation. This broad structure creates the conditions for emergent knowledge production, in contrast to the restricted unifunctionality of the Netflix app. Educators who are discussing app functionalities and the addictive characteristics of entertainment apps may want to steer their students toward apps with a wider spectrum of functionalities, which offer more potential for active engagement.

SUMMARY

In the fast-changing digital landscape, teachers and students are learning about digital technology at the same time. As Stevenson et al. (2015) pointed out, "educators are struggling to keep pace with the speed of technological development and demand" (p. 369). Educators interested in the integration of mobile technology into the curriculum are faced with innumerable apps that offer educational value, but may not be more than mobile textbooks, as noted earlier by Bos and Lee (2013). Meanwhile, a digital divide is opening up, as girls disengage with science and technology due to restricting gender roles. How can teachers choose apps that foster creativity and engage with girls' learning styles, while avoiding those apps that funnel students into preconceived, prepackaged learning outcomes?

As I highlighted above, girls prefer to learn collaboratively, they are relational, they like to connect their learning to their own lives, and they favor open-ended play and creativity. These characteristics are echoed in the app-enabling functionalities described by Gardner and Davis (2013). Apps that enable learning create the conditions for emergent knowledge production; much like a petri dish they provide a fertile ground for new ideas, experimentation, and play. Evaluating an app's enabling and addicting functionalities can provide a road map for choosing apps that promote active engagement with creativity and are most conducive to creating a learning environment that connects to girls' learning styles.

In my survey of teenage girls from two Montreal secondary schools, I determined their most popular apps and collected stories about how and when they use their smartphone apps. I then organized the apps by type and by function to determine their learning-enabling potential. I scaled app functionalities form the most active to the most passive and connected them with enabling and addicting characteristics. This helped me to understand what made apps popular, and also helped me discover their creative potential. I found that girls were drawn to apps that offer intuitive and enjoyable modes of communication, apps functionalities that relate to their interests, and apps that foster-peer learning.

By deconstructing the most popular apps' functionalities, I noticed that the most popular apps are multifunctional. They offer a wide range of app-enabling functionalities but also tend to incorporate a measure of addictive, "hooks." Both students and educators should critically examine mobile apps for their enabling and addictive characteristics. By critically examining mobile apps with their students, and by choosing multifunctional apps that offer a broad range of actions, teachers can engage with girls and potentially lead them to explore digital technology in new and exciting ways.

References

American Society for Quality. (2009). *Engineering image problem could fuel shortage*. Milwaukee, WI: Author. Retrieved May 1, 2016 from http://www.qualitymag.com/articles/86139-asq-engineering-image-problem-couldfuel-shortage.

Andone, I., Blaszkiewicz, K., Eibes, M., Trendafilov, B., Markowetz, A., & Montag, C. (2016, September 12–16). *How age and gender affect smartphone usage*. Ubi/Comp/ISWC '16 Adjunct, Heidelberg, Germany.

Andrus, S. H., Kuriloff, P. J., & Jacobs, C. E. (2015). Teaching middle school girls more effectively. *Independent School, 73*, 16–18.

Anonymous. (2015). The weaker sex; gender, education and work. *The Economist, 414*(8928), 61–62.

Bos, B., & Lee, K. (2013). *Mathematics apps and mobile learning*. In Society for Information Technology & Teacher Education International Conference (Vol. 2013, pp. 3654–3660). Retrieved from http://www.editlib.org/p/48675.

Bruner, J. S. (1964). The course of cognitive growth. *American Psychologist, 19*(1), 1–15.

Castro, J. C. (2007). Enabling artistic inquiry. *Canadian Art Teacher, 6*(1), 6–16.

Cooper, R., & Heaverlo, C. (2013). Problem solving and creativity and design: What influence do they have on girls' interest in STEM subject areas? *American Journal of Engineering Education, 4*(1), 27–38.

Dancstep (née Dancu), T., & Sindorf, L. (2016). *Exhibit designs for girls' engagement: A guide to the EDGE design attributes*. San Francisco: Exploratorium.

Dancu, T. (2010). *Designing exhibits for gender equity* (PhD dissertation). Systems Science: Psychology, Portland State University, Portland, OR, USA.

Gardner, H., & Davis, K. (2013). *The app generation: How today's youth navigate identity, intimacy, and imagination in a digital world*. New Haven and London: Yale University Press.

Grimus, M. (2013). *Mobile phones and gender: Chances and challenges in education around the world*. Graz University of Technology. Retrieved from http://www.education-and-gender.eu/edge/pdf/MOBILE_PHONES_AND_GENDER_13.pdf.

Harris, T. (2016). How technology hijacks people's minds—From a magician and Google's design ethicist. Retrieved May 20, 2018 from http://www.tristanharris.com/essays.

Jabobs, C. E., Kuriloff, P. J., Andrus, S. H., & Cox, A. B. (2014). Reaching girls. *Phi Delta Kappan, 96*(1), 68–75.

Juarrero, A. (2002). Complex dynamical systems and the problem of identity. *Emergence, 4*, 94–104.

Kessels, U. (2014). Bridging the gap by enhancing the fit: How stereotypes about STEM clash with stereotypes about girls. *International Journal of Gender, Science and Technology, 7*(2), 280–296.

Leaper, C., Timea, F., & Spears Brown, C. (2012). Adolescent girls' experiences and gender-related beliefs in relation to their motivation in Math/Science and English. *Journal of Youth and Adolescence, 41*, 268–282. https://doi.org/10.1007/s10964-011-9693-z.

Ofcom. (2017, November 29). *Children and parents: Media use and attitudes report*. Office of Communications, UK. Retrieved from https://www.ofcom.org.uk/data/assets/pdf_file/0020/108182/children-parents-media-use-attitudes-2017.pdf.

Osberg, D., & Biesta, G. (2008). The emergent curriculum: Navigating a complex course between unguided learning and planned enculturation. *Curriculum Studies, 40*(3), 313–328.

Oyserman, D., Elmore, K., & Smith, G. (2012). Self, self-concept, and identity. In M. R. Leary & J. P. Tangney (Eds.), *Handbook of self and identity*. New York and London: Guilford Press.

Pew Research Center. (2018). *Teens, social media & technology 2018*. Washington, DC: Pew Research Center.

Rosin, H. (2013, April). The touch-screen generation. *The Atlantic*, pp. 56–65.

Stevenson, M., Hedberg, J., Highfield, K., & Diao, M. (2015). Visualizing solutions: Apps as cognitive stepping—Stones in the learning process. *The Electronic Journal of e-Learning, 13*(2), 366–379. Retrieved from www.ejel.org.

Twenge, J. M. (2017, September). Have smartphones destroyed a generation? *The Atlantic.*

Yancey Martin, P. (2003). "Said and done" versus "saying and doing" gendering practices, practicing gender at work. *Gender & Society, 1*(3), 342–377.

CHAPTER 5

Spatiality of Engagement

Ehsan Akbari

INTRODUCTION

This chapter examines how MonCoin students engaged with metaphorical, online, and physical spaces while they learned through mobile and social media. I posit that one of the keys to the success of the MonCoin project in engaging youth was in creating opportunities for students to actively engage with their immediate physical space in their online network through photography. Often, the use of online technology in education implies a binary opposition between physical space and online space, even in learning contexts where the two are integrated. In the MonCoin project, however, when students take pictures of their immediate surroundings in response to specific missions, learning in physical and online spaces not only coexisted and complemented each other, but also enriched and co-constituted each other. Furthermore, I consider the metaphorical space of photography as one that triangulates the binary between face-to-face and online learning that creates bridges between the two, which motivates students to participate.

In this chapter, I focus on the notion of spatiality in the MonCoin curriculum. First, I present a literature review on how educational approaches to online learning, blended learning, and place-based learning address the spatiality and temporality of learning and engagement.

E. Akbari (✉)
Concordia University, Montreal, QC, Canada

The discussion of the role of space and time in education is anchored in a theory of spatiality that views space as multiple, co-constitutive, and dynamic. In this view, spatiality is an emergent property of interactions among human and non-human actors in space and time. I use these theoretical insights to analyze the MonCoin curriculum by drawing on interview data with students and participating teachers at Hill Academy and Elm Secondary (pseudonyms). I discuss how spatiality in each context affected the curriculum design, and the specific in-classroom activities of going for walks to do photography in the school and neighborhood. Based on this analysis, I posit that spatiality in the MonCoin curriculum was co-constituted through interactions online and in the physical spaces of the classroom, school, and students' everyday surroundings, and photography mediated between the physical and online spaces to provide a space for metaphorical and visual expression.

BACKGROUND AND LITERATURE—ONLINE AND PHYSICAL SPACES IN EDUCATION

When the MonCoin curriculum was first implemented, one of the key objectives of the research team was to motivate educational engagement among students in an education program for youth who were at risk, or had dropped out of school (Castro, Lalonde, & Pariser, 2016). We presumed that having an online curriculum that allowed students to participate anytime and from anywhere would help them to be engaged in their education even if they did not attend school. A surprising finding from this pilot phase was that the more students engaged in the online space they accessed through their mobile devices, the more they wanted to meet and be together in the physical space. This resulted in a number of after school meetings and field trips where we gathered together to take pictures.

These findings influenced how we approached later iterations at Hill Academy and Elm Secondary. We were aware of the role physical and online interactions play in motivating engagement. In these iterations, especially at Elm Secondary, we also aimed to take advantage of the potential for this curriculum to motivate youth to engage with their surroundings and their school environment. Engagement with everyday civic and educational spaces is a central topic of this and the next chapter. Our understanding of the spatiality of engagement is informed by literature on online learning, blended learning, and place-based education.

These approaches provide insights on how mobile technologies, which enable learners to connect anytime and anywhere, can be used to enrich students' engagement in their everyday civic and educational spaces.

Online Learning—Expanding Learning Space and Time

One of the most useful aspects of online and mobile technologies is their ability to connect learners and teachers who are not in the same place at the same time. The attempt to expand education's reach beyond the classroom time and space stems from a long tradition of distance learning by correspondence, radio, and television (Güzer & Caner, 2014; Moore & Kearsely, 2011). These technologies along with more recent web-based platforms have been used to make education available beyond legal, financial, or geographical constraints expanding access to learning as a fundamental right (Geith & Vignare, 2008). Distance learning, thus, has benefited students who live in rural areas and remote communities and who would not have access otherwise (Barbour, 2007). The Canadian province of Newfoundland and Labrador, for instance, has incorporated distance learning strategies since 1988 to provide access to education for rural populations in the province. Initially these strategies utilized telecommunication technologies such as the phone, telegraph lines, fax, and later web-based platforms, which according to Barbour (2007) rendered distance transparent and eliminated geographical and demographic barriers to access quality education.

Online education can be delivered both synchronously and asynchronously. In the former, learners and teachers are connected in real time through chat, video conference call, or other means. In the latter, learners and teachers access the course on their own time to post blogs, read e-mails, or access course readings. Barbour and Hill (2011) found it was during times students were connected synchronously that they were most productive and engaged with the course material. This suggests that social connectivity is as important to one's engagement online as it is offline. The literature on online learning addresses this by emphasizing the importance of building a sense of community within online social networks to maintain its cohesiveness and engage students effectively (Ubon & Kimble, 2004; Rovai, 2002). This has also been a key aspect of the MonCoin curriculum, for which we created closed social network to maintain group cohesion. One of our key objectives was to enable social interactions that inspire peer-to-peer learning, where students learn as a collective from what others posted and how others responded to their posts (Akbari, Castro, Lalonde, Moreno, & Pariser, 2016; Castro, 2012).

Another important aspect of online learning for MonCoin is expansion of the space and time of learning. In recent years, mobile devices such as tablets and smartphones have amplified our ability to connect from anywhere and at anytime. This means a student can connect to a school project while they are at school, home, in their neighborhood, in the morning, in the afternoon, or at night. Students also connected to our online network synchronously, during class time and photo-walks, for example, and asynchronously. Example of asynchronous connectivity includes a student stopping to photograph a path they take every day and posting it on their walk home from school, or a student lying in bed and scrolling through our project's Instagram feed to like and comment on their peer's photographs. In this way, online connectivity through mobile devices allowed us to expand both the spaces and times in which learning occurred. We valued the affordances of synchronous and asynchronous online connectivity. However, we were also fully aware of the importance of face-to-face interactions in motivating students to engage with their education. MonCoin was never purely an online curriculum; rather, one that combines elements of online and physical interactions to engage students and enrich their learning in art.

Blended Learning Environments—The Best of Both Worlds

While online learning has often been understood as an alternative to face-to-face education to provide access to distant learners and to expand the space and time of learning, *blended learning* embraces the possibility of merging the most effective aspect of online-based platforms with face-to-face education. As defined by Dziuban, Hartman, and Moskal (2004), blended learning is "a pedagogical approach that combines the effectiveness and socialization opportunities of the classroom with the technologically enhanced active learning possibilities of the online environment" (p. 3). The term "blended learning" was first used in a paper about blending play and work in early childhood education settings (Cooney, Grupton, & O'Laughlin, 2000). Since the early 2000s, this term is used to describe educational interventions that integrate online and physical interactions to enable learning in instructor-led classes (Güzer & Caner, 2014). Scholars argued that the blending of online and physical spaces should involve an in-depth integration where the curriculum and teaching methods are designed to take advantage of the best elements of face-to-face and online learning to build off each other (Garrison & Vaughan, 2008; Osguthorpe & Graham, 2003; Vaughan, 2014). However, the balance between face-to-face elements and online activities varies depending on the purpose and outcomes to be achieved and is guided by pedagogical design principles (Partridge, Ponting, & McCay, 2011). Models can vary from involving predominantly face-to-face or online interactions, and everything in between, but the central question throughout the literature is how one should organize physical and online environments to support learning effectively (Güzer & Caner, 2014).

One common answer is to draw on constructivist and collaborative learning and teaching models that are contextual, and encourage active learning and social interactions in physical and online spaces (Brown, 2005; Güzer & Caner, 2014). As Osguthorpe and Graham (2003) pointed out, this requires one to go beyond merely showing a page from a Web site on a screen to maximizing the potential of various kinds of face-to-face interactions, including group work and informal discussions, as well asynchronous and synchronous online interactions.

Oblinger (2006) argued that "space—whether physical or virtual—can have an impact on learning" (p. 1.1); and thus, space is an important consideration when designing blended learning environments. Oblinger's (2006) book of collected essays explored various ways educators conceptualized "learning spaces" in order to facilitate active, social, and experiential learning. Learning spaces can occur online or offline, and in formal educational contexts as well as informal settings. Brown (2005) offered the examples of "discussion pockets," which are small, curved spaces in the corridors and hallways outside lecture halls on college campuses with a table and bench to accommodate meetings among four or five people, as an informal physical learning space. This space can allow students and teachers to engage in spontaneous conversations after lectures as a part of their active learning.

Technological online tools can also be utilized to create formal and informal learning spaces online. Online, groups of learners can connect synchronously through live chat or messaging, for example, or connect asynchronously, via e-mail or Instagram posts. Such spaces can be spontaneous or deliberate, and participants can engage in multiple spaces and at the same or different times. In this sense, designing blended learning environments requires one to consider not only how space facilitates and enables learning, but also how interactions and learning occur in time. A practical implication of this for the MonCoin project was that we had to consider the time of the day we sent out a mission. For example, we only sent out missions at the end of the school day so as not to disturb students in classes outside of art.

The literature on blended learning provides important insights for the MonCoin project. Firstly, it highlights the importance of integrating face-to-face and online interactions in ways that support learning. This is often done by drawing on models of teaching that promote active learning and social interactions. Secondly, the conceptualization of blended learning environments and learning spaces take seriously the role that space and time—physical and online; formal and informal; synchronous and asynchronous—can play in facilitating active learning. However, there is a tendency to focus more on how spaces serve active learning, and less attention is paid to how one learns from and about specific spaces through interactions in space. There is also little attention paid to how online space can transform and co-create physical spaces.

In the MonCoin project, we considered space, and by extension time, not as preexisting structures that can be put to the service of teaching and learning. Rather, space is a teacher and learner as well. One of the key goals we had in the project was to enable encounters within the physical and online everyday spaces in students' lives that would enrich their perception and engagement with those specific spaces. It was important for us to design interactions in physical and online spaces that facilitated students' engagement with their school and surroundings. We drew inspiration from place-based pedagogy, which provided an educational model for attending to one's everyday spaces.

Place-Based Education—Attending to Place

Place-based education (PBE) refers to pedagogy that connects learning to students' local environments and communities. Sobel (2004) described PBE as "the process of using the local community and environment as a starting point to teach concepts in language arts, mathematics, social studies, science and other subjects across the curriculum" (p. 6). He offered various examples of project across the United States that involve connecting schools to local governments, community organizations, and other citizens. PBE seeks to help the local communities through school projects, and, in turn, deepen and enrich students' connections to their local environments. Scholars have argued that *critical pedagogy of place* can make a valuable contribution to PBE by adding a critical social-political lens that advocates for transforming systems of oppression within local spaces (Ball & Lai, 2006; Gruenewald, 2003; McInerney, Smyth, & Down, 2011). Gruenewald (2003) argued that this approach can strengthen students' connections to their communities and "help communities of learners conserve and transform their living environments" (p. 11).

In art education, Mark Graham (2007) presented some particular ways that critical pedagogy of place can be applied in art classrooms. For example, educators can teach about the natural history of a place by getting students to go outside to explore nature or through mapmaking. Cultural journalism can also deepen connections to place by allowing students to explore "the cultural life of their community through local histories, stories, traditions, and the artifacts and performances of local cultural production" (p. 380). Finally, learners can play an activist and transformative role in their local communities by creating art that reflects on and addresses environmental, social, and political issues that are pertinent to the local community.

Land-based pedagogy also builds on PBE by integrating the "spiritual, emotional and intellectual aspects of land," which are at the heart of indigenous ways of knowing (Styres, Haig-Brown, & Blimkie, 2013, p. 37). Tuck, McKenzie, and McCoy (2014) emphasized the importance of land-based pedagogy for the project of decolonization, which must involve reconnecting Indigenous peoples to the materiality of the land, as well as the social relations, knowledges, and languages that emerge from the land.

PBE, critical pedagogy of place, and land-based pedagogy take seriously the role local places play in facilitating learning and individuals' connection to their environment and communities. These approaches, to varying degrees, also acknowledge the transformative role learners can have on these places as active and engaged citizens. In these approaches, space does not merely serve learning. Learners can also transform space. Space affects learners, and learners also shape and construct the space in which learning occurs. This view of space and learning is consistent with the socio-materialist framework discussed in throughout this book, which posits that humans and non-humans—including space and time—affect are affected by social processes.

The educational theories discussed here provide some insights on how asynchronous connectivity of mobile technologies can be used in ways that enrich learning in art classrooms. Blended learning provides a framework for using technology in ways that take advantage of the best aspects of face-to-face and online interactions to enrich learning. There is also consideration of the influence of space and time on learning. PBE and related theories offer a perspective that anchors learning in local ecological and social places, and also acknowledge the capacity of learners to transform these places. These ideas are critical for our understanding of spatiality, a central tenet of which is that online and physical spaces are co-constituted through interactions among learners and teachers, human and non-human. I elaborate on this notion in the next section.

THEORY OF SPATIALITY

Spatiality is the notion that our ontological and epistemological assumptions about space are fundamental to our ability to understand culture, society, politics, learning, and indeed most aspects of our everyday lives. The "spatial turn" refers to the intellectual movement since the 1990s, which has placed an emphasis on space, place, and mapping in various disciplines in the humanities including geography, history, cultural studies, and education. The various approaches to spatiality share in common the fundamental assumption that space is not a static container, but rather "a dynamic multiplicity that is constantly being produced by simultaneous practices-so-far" (Fenwick, Edwards, & Sawchuck, 2011, p. 29). In this conceptualization, space is the product of a multiplicity of human and non-human interactions, and time and space are inseparable from each other. The concepts of *relational space* and *space-time* are fundamental to our theorization of spatiality.

Relational space is rooted in the metaphysical notion that space is composed of relationships between objects, rather than a container in which objects exist. Relational space is the product of interactions and cannot exist with them. For Massey (2005), this notion had profound social and political implications. She pointed out, for example, that the Euclidian concept of three-dimensional space—that can be mapped on X, Y, and Z coordinates—played a role in validating the colonial conquests of the Americas by implicitly equating "the land and sea," and conceiving of "other places, peoples, cultures simply as phenomena 'on' this surface" (p. 4). In her seminal work, *For Space*, Massey (2005) offered a theorization of relational space, in which space is understood as "the product of interrelations; as constituted through interactions," space is "multifaceted" and "co-constitutive," and space is dynamic and "always under construction" (p. 9). Individual identities and social entities, "the relations 'between' them, and the spatiality which is part of them, are all co-constitutive" (p. 10). In this conceptualization, the individual and collective interactions, and the spatial arrangements among them, create, or "co-constitute" space.

Massey (2005) also maintained that in order to think about space as multiplicitous, open-ended, and dynamic, we must also attend to time. For her, space and time "are integral to one another" and "must be thought together" (p. 47, 18). Time introduces the element of change, movement, and dynamism, while "space unfolds as interactions" in the social dimension (p. 57). Massey argued that "it is on both of them, necessarily together, that rests the liveliness of the world" (p. 56). Fenwick et al. (2011) discussed the educational pertinence of this theorization of relational space-time, which shifts the focus of educational research from "individuals to individual interactions to the ordering of the human and non-human in space-time" (p. 129). This notion is particularly relevant for educational approaches that incorporate online learning, which allows for different kinds of spatial and temporal arrangements and interactions.

The concept of relational space-time has some practical implications for the MonCoin curriculum. In MonCoin, spatiality is co-constituted through online and face-to-face interactions among students, teachers, researchers, school policy, the curriculum, the school's architecture, chairs and tables in the classrooms, students' mobile devices, and so on. Our curriculum aimed to promote positive interactions among human and non-human actors within these multiple spaces—online and in the classroom, school, and students' everyday surroundings.

Spatiality and temporality were important components of the design, implementation, and analysis of the MonCoin curriculum. Firstly, the asynchronous connectivity of mobile devices allowed us to extend learning beyond the bounds of the classroom space and time. Our curriculum enabled participants to connect to closed peer network anytime and anywhere; thus, allowing the group to keep a sense of coherence even when they were not physically present at school. Secondly, we understood the importance of enriching online connectivity through interactions within the students' physical surroundings. Classroom time was devoted to giving instructions on effective photographic composition and editing, giving participants time to edit and upload of images, as well as going on school and neighborhood walks to do photography together. Providing participants with opportunities to meet and work within physical proximity influenced students' engagement online, and engagement online also influenced interactions within physical spaces.

In this sense, the online spaces of MonCoin and physical spaces in which learning occurred were co-constitutive. Our online closed network, the physical environments and interactions among teachers and learners, in space, built on and influenced each other. In our analysis, we view photography as another kind of space that mediated between the physical and online spaces. Photography provided a kind of space for visual metaphors, styles, and expression to find form, and influence how students engaged with each other in their online and physical spaces. In the MonCoin curriculum, the metaphorical space of photography, the online space of our closed network, and the physical spaces in students' lives—such as their classroom, school, homes, neighborhoods, and commute—all co-constituted, affected, and shaped each other.

Spatiality of Designing and Adapting the Curriculum

When designing a curriculum using design-based research (DBR), it is vital to be responsive and adaptive to the spatiality of the specific context in which research is conducted. This spatiality emerges from interactions among factors such as the school's history, demographics, policies toward the use of mobile devices, and each teacher's educational goals and priorities. These factors greatly influenced how we designed classroom activities and structured the missions to guide student learning and engagement. Our curricular design was grounded in the idea that learning spaces are fundamentally social, relational and co-constituted through interactions. The existing dynamics among students and teachers as well as actors such as the schools' policies and teachers' approach to monitoring and controlling student activities online and within the school environment had a significant impact on how we approached the MonCoin curriculum at each partner school. By collaborating closely with the teachers at each site, we were able to identify some of these key factors to adapt our curriculum to the particular educational context.

In the remainder of this chapter, I discuss iterations of the MonCoin curriculum that occurred at two different high schools—Hill Academy and Elm Secondary. The first site is a private school, which requires all students to purchase an iPad and teachers are required to use the iPads and the education content management application "Haiku" to share information with students. Therefore, there was an incentive for the teacher to collaborate with us to explore ways of effectively using iPads in her classroom. Mandating students to use iPads at school also necessitates the development of school rules and policies. The school administration was grappling with the problem of how to monitor and control student activities to ensure safety. The teacher at Hill Academy raised concern about this issue when she stated,

> We (teachers and administrators) struggle so much with damaging kinds of remarks that they (students) make to each other anonymously that I think maybe the school administration is finding it hard to see the positive ways that they can interact too.

The aim of our research was to promote positive online interactions among the students in the art classroom, while monitoring to ensure damaging remarks and images were not posted. In our first phase, we decided to use the content management system (CMS) that was used by the school, called "Haiku," which gives teachers the ability to post and share classroom content. The discussion feature also allowed students to share images and respond to each other's words. Teachers and members of our research team monitored the content posted by students. "Haiku" allowed the teacher to control what was being posted and delete inappropriate content. Our research team also needed to take into consideration the school's policy around where and when the iPads could be used. One restriction was that students could not use their iPads in the school's hallways. During the first phase of the research at Hill Academy, these policies influenced how we approached the school walk.

After the first iteration, the teacher expressed some frustration at the structural limitations of the "Haiku" platforms and the prohibition of using devices in the hallways. Also, the art teacher concluded the iPads were best utilized for their mobility to expand learning outside of the classroom and school spaces. She stated,

> What really works well for me on the project was really fixing the notion of using the iPad outside of the classroom. I was using the iPad for reporting but not making art. So, for me that was a very important thing that I learned I could do. The iPad should not be restricted to being used within the classroom but should be the opposite, should be used only outside of the classroom, because it's a mobile device. The classroom is where you want to engage the students and creative things with your hands or in your writing.

For the second phase of research at Hill Academy, we decided to use Instagram instead of "Haiku" and focus more on utilizing the iPads as a tool to do creative work outside of the class. Therefore, we did not do a school or neighborhood walk during the second phase at Hill Academy. Instead we focused on the theme of "My Surroundings" to encourage students to use their devices to explore the world outside of their school. At Hill Academy, key factors in the design and development of our curriculum included balancing control and asynchronicity, and the schools' restrictions around where and when iPads were permitted within the spaces of the school.

Elm Secondary is an Anglophone public high school in Montreal that offers programs in drama, music, and art. At the time of the research, the student population had been gradually shrinking and the numbers of empty classroom growing, but student numbers have stabilized since. The mandated policy around mobile devices was not strict at that time, and students could use mobile devices in some classes with the permission of their teacher. There were no bans of using mobile devices in the hallways. The issues and concerns raised by the art teacher mostly related to technical issues and accessibility. When asked about potential challenges that she foresees, she stated

> ...issues can include anything from the wifi not working to they didn't charge their phone that day to even they don't have a phone. So, that's an issue, it's accessibility, because I have, in every class, I'll have at least one or two, maybe three students who don't have access to a phone, and I really think it's important to make them feel included, and that's always one of my first priorities is, how can I make that student feel, like not stand out, because it might be an issue of their parents not wanting to, or even funds, and that happens in our schools.

To address some of these issues of accessibility, we provided extra iPod mobile devices with downloaded software, and a WiFi hot spot Internet connection in case the school WiFi did not work. The hot spot could also travel with us during the neighborhood and school walks. Another important factor was the teacher's approach and attitude toward the space of the school and its surroundings. For the teacher, a big incentive in using the MonCoin curriculum in her class was to engage her students to their surroundings. In response to why she wanted to do this project she stated,

Actually, I think it's in order to motivate the students to get them engaged in school, in order to get them to recognize their surroundings, to know that they have resources, to know that education is important and that it can be fun, and really open up their opportunities. I think a lot of students maybe go through their day without a bit of brightness and I think I can bring that with the art class for them.

For this teacher, connecting students to their school environment was a priority; and thus, the school became a major theme in both phases of the research at Elm Secondary. We also incorporated school and neighborhood walks in both phases. These walks provided students with opportunities to explore, photograph, share and preserve their perspectives of their schools and their neighborhood. The walks will be discussed in the following sections. A discussion of the factors such as school policies and teacher attitudes provides necessary background information for understanding how we approached the theme of spatiality in our research from phase to phase, and from context to context.

School and Neighborhood Walk

> We walked as a group and took pictures, but it helped us expand our mind, like anything we saw, like it could be the street, it could be the sewers, it could be like Dunkin Donuts, it was closed but it represented something to us, so I was wondering if we keep exploring, there will probably be things that we have never seen.
>
> —*Johnbook*

An integral part of the MonCoin curriculum was a series of walks around the school and neighborhood during which the students were invited to take pictures in response to specific missions. The number of walks, their duration, and the intentionality behind them changed in each iteration of the project in response to the context. These walks were key not only to integrating learning in online and physical spaces, but also to foster the student's connection to their surroundings and the use of photography as a space that mediates between the physical and online worlds expanding the possibilities of both.

In the quote above, participant *Johnbook* described the experience of going on a neighborhood walk during class time. For him, walking as a group and taking pictures of the neighborhood around the school piqued his interest in exploring his surroundings through photography. In this instance, the act of being together in physical space and exploring one's surroundings were a significant part of the learning process of the project, and the walks had an effect on the kinds of images that were posted on our online network. Furthermore, the kinds of images that were being posted online had some influence in how some participants explored and represented their surroundings.

In the following sections, we describe three walks to illustrate how photography mediated between physical and online spaces, and how these spaces reinforced and enriched each other. First, we describe a school walk at Hill Academy in which we asked participants to photograph comfortable and uncomfortable spaces in their school. Next, we describe the school walks and neighborhood at Elm Secondary, respectively.

COMFORTABLE, UNCOMFORTABLE—EXPLORING THE HALLWAYS OF THE SCHOOL

Our first school walk took place during the first iteration at Hill Academy and was guided by a mission called "Comfortable/Uncomfortable." The students were encouraged to walk around the school and take pictures of places where they felt comfortable and uncomfortable using photography to highlight their perception of such spaces. The class time immediately before the walk was devoted to exploring the use of different elements of composition in photography to convey a variety of moods and atmospheres through a presentation that introduced visual art vocabulary such as lighting, framing, contrast, angles, etc. Thus, one of the main objectives of the school walk was to explore, in a hands-on manner, the compositional elements that had been introduced in class.

It is important to note that the policy for using the iPads in this school did not allow students to use their devices in the hallways and in between classes. Since they were not usually allowed to walk around taking pictures, this mission was an extraordinary experience for some students. However, it complicated the logistics and required the use of hallway passes with specific hours to justify the students walking around the school and using their iPads. Some students felt a sense of freedom in being able to walk around the school's hallways during class time and use their iPads to take pictures. *Princess Consuella Banana Hammock* described this sense of freedom of walking anywhere and getting "dirty looks," from other students who she presumed were thinking, "why are you taking pictures in school?" In this case, the school walk was a rebellious act in defiance of the school's policy of not allowing iPads in hallways.

In other cases, the walk opened a space to reflect on their relationship to their school and to how they interacted within it. Participant *Barbara* said, "the third mission: where I'm comfortable and where I'm uncomfortable in the school [...] made me look a bit deeper into what I liked and what I didn't like." For this participant, applying the technical skill she had just learned while walking around the school to photograph the space in this manner opened the possibility of becoming more aware of how she experienced her immediate school surroundings.

Some students also discussed learning from the multiple perspectives of their peers by viewing their images online. For Tara, for example, the main learning outcomes of the school walk were learning about "how people perceive things differently and how, color, lighting and angle affects photos a lot." By sharing images of the same familiar space, the multiple perspectives of how each student interpreted this space became visualizable in their photographs.

In the case of the "comfortable/uncomfortable" mission, the sharing of images online also led to a clear and observable emergence of a visual style. That is, several participants used the same set of visual approaches with lighting, color, and camera angles to convey the notions of "comfortable" and "uncomfortable." *Chamilla* describes the emergence of this particular visual style online,

> My friend posted an "uncomfortable" picture about the hallway and she made it really dark, so I wanted to kind of reproduce that. Well, she put it on the floor. I didn't, but we kind of had similar, with the type of lighting we used. So, I had seen her picture before I took mine, and her "uncomfortable" picture was really dark and her "comfortable" picture was really light so it kind of gave me the idea to make my pictures dark and light as well.

This approach of using sharp camera angles, dark lighting, and a black-white color scheme to convey discomfort, on the one hand, and bright, colorful imagery to convey comfort, on the other, was a visual strategy deployed by a number of the participants. A clear and distinct visual style and trend emerged in response to this mission (see Fig. 5.1a). This may have been influenced by examples our research team presented to the class, but this trend was amplified on our peer network. Our approach to the school walk changed somewhat after phase 1 at Hill Academy. First, we did not do walks again at Hill Academy in phase 2, but we continued to do school walks in both phases of research at Elm Secondary. However, our approach to the school missions changed as we felt that giving students a mission that was a binary—comfortable/uncomfortable—led to a conventionalized visual style. We were interested in providing more open-ended missions and activities in subsequent phases.

School Walks at Elm Secondary

I had difficulty in was snapping pictures in my school because normally I feel like my school is very dull and maybe sometimes the walls, there's not a lot of color but then once certain projects were posted, I realized, with the editing on my phone and with close-ups, just viewing the school in a different way really helped, and I actually learned to take good pictures of my school.

—*inspiremydesire*

At Elm Secondary, one of the main objectives of the participating teacher was to use photography to foster a sense of connection to place and sense of belonging to the school environment. Thus, we were able to build on the experience we had at Hill Academy and emphasize this connection to place through walks in the school, as well as in the neighborhood. We structured these walks to give opportunities for students to engage with the physical space around them through the online spaces of the MonCoin curriculum. We wondered how we could articulate those two spaces in ways that made the most of the mobile and asynchronous characteristic of social media, and face-to-face interactions while being in the same space at the same time.

For the school walks at Elm Secondary, we invited students to respond to the missions "My School," and the related micro-missions "Where I Learn Best," "Change my School," and "What I Love About my School." One clear theme that came through in student interviews is that this mission was among the least popular among participants. *Sophieshadowhunter* summarized the sentiment of some of her peers with her response to the question, "what was your least favorite mission?" She stated, "School. I don't like school! I can deal with school, it's part

Fig. 5.1 These images were taken during the school and neighborhood walks. They are organized top to bottom, left to right, from **a** to **f**. **a** Samnantha La Rose—comfortable/uncomfortable. **b** xpapichulox1—My School. **c** illogic_13—Nature. **d** Ehsan Akbari—Neighborhood walk documentation. **e** Artistic_101–MyNeighborhood. **f** liliespinosa2000—MyNeighborhood

of everyday life, but I don't want to go around and take pictures of my school." Others echoed this view that their school was too dull or too ordinary to warrant taking pictures.

However, there were also examples of participants who reported learning from this mission, particularly from going on walks during class to take pictures. Participant *Cxrly4* for example talked about being able to "explore the different parts of the school; I actually found places that I didn't even know we had in the school, when we went around, so it was interesting to see that, and to explore more than usual." *Iscreamforicecream* also discussed how going through school to take pictures helped her look at the school differently. These participants identified the "My School" as a favorite mission due in part to the exploration of the school they did during the walks.

Moreover, there are examples of participants who reported not liking the mission, but learning something useful because of the school walks. Participant *pxeppermint*, for example, at first responded that "My School" was his least favorite mission because the school was not "photography-worthy." When asked if the walk changed his feeling toward taking pictures in the school, *pxeppermint* responded,

> Yeah, it helped, I know for sure because when we walked through school, I ended up posting a picture, I posted two, but I know, one of them I posted outside, but one of them was like a lock on the gate and it was cool because I never really noticed that before, so I said I was changed about "My School" with the lock, like to unlock it.

For *pxeppermint*, the walk was helpful in generating ideas, and also noticing different aspects of the school. Others discussed the peer learning during one of those walks. *Cxrly4*, for example, talked about how she decided to help her peers during the school walk. She said, "because I could see some of their focusing the lens, and angle, and more stability, it definitely helped, because I could see how their pictures improved as well." In such cases, taking photographs together in the physical space of the school enabled peer learning because students could see each other take a shot and provide feedback or observe new skills. This learning is further reinforced online as students are able to see the images their peers posted, and the improvements that were made in their photography. As such, physical and online peer-to-peer interactions informed and reinforced each other in the learning process.

From the examples above, we infer that although some students at Elm Secondary expressed resistance to a mission that required them to photograph their school, the perspective of some students changed due in large part to the school walks, which allowed them to explore their physical space together. There is also some evidence that students taught and learned from each other during these walks, and being together and moving through the space of their school had a positive impact on their learning. (see Fig. 5.1b)

Neighborhood Walks

At Elm Secondary, we did one neighborhood walk during each iteration. These walks occurred about a week after the school walks. For the walks, participants responded to the mission "My Neighborhood," which included micro-missions such as "Nature," "Messages," "Paths I take," "Art," and "Notice." Having the micro-missions allowed students to have more choices and more concrete points of entry to begin taking pictures during their walk. *Rainy_dayz* referred to this in their interview saying,

> I liked (the micro-missions) because …let's say the mission was My Neighborhood is a bit confusing, "what am I supposed to post? Am I supposed to do the street name?" and the micro-missions gave 'hints' of what to photograph, and how make personal connections to the mission.

This is one of several examples of participants who expressed similar views about the importance of the micro-missions for motivating engagement, particularly for the neighborhood mission. While diversity of entry points in the form of a micro-mission was a key motivator for the neighborhood mission, another motivator was the neighborhood walks. These walks provided the class with an opportunity to be together while moving through the neighborhood surrounding their school and taking pictures. Some participants reported learning by being in close proximity with peers and taking pictures. *Tropicalrain*, for example, talked about learning how to take pictures from different angles "will change the whole picture." *Illogic* discussed how the micro-mission "nature" got her to engage with her surroundings in a different way during the walk. She described how she took a photo:

During the walk, before we went back down towards the school and walked to the Dairy Queen, there was this row of trees on both sides and one half had leaves, the other half didn't so I lay on the ground and just got a few leaves on the foreground to focus but while the background was still in focus.

In this example, the participant is thinking carefully about the angle and the focus while photographing her surroundings. She is also changing her perceptive of her surroundings by changing the position of her body. Others that see her taking this picture can later see the photograph online. In this way, peers can learn from each other by observing the body language of doing photography in physical spaces, and view the photographic outcomes of these gestures online (Fig. 5.1c, d).

Also, being together in the same space motivated some to pose for each other's pictures. In one instance, four male students posed with their back to the camera, while a few students photographed this scene. In other cases, several images of the same space and subject were posted, offering a multiplicity of perspectives. One example of this is the running track, which appeared in three different images posted by different participants (see Fig. 5.1e, f). Each image conveyed a different mood and sense of textures.

It can be surmised that the neighborhood walk was received positively as a learning experience by several of the participants. A couple of them suggested doing more walks in the future, to other places. *Johnbook* was particularly enthusiastic,

> If we walk together as a group and, I'm not saying go far far, but at least walk somewhere where we know that somewhere is really artistic, like it could be graffiti, it could be an abandoned building, it could be a museum, it could be anything, like if we explored more, that would probably open up our minds more and plus it would expand it to give us ideas, like 'oh, I like this! This looks nice! I'll take a picture of it!" because usually about half of our pictures are from school or at home.

In spite of this enthusiasm, it is important to note that not all participants were equally engaged during the neighborhood walk. One common reason was that there were, in their opinion, no great photographs to be taken in the surroundings of their neighborhood. *Cxrly4* summed up this feeling by describing the frustration she felt during the walk.

I feel like, especially in class, when we had to go around this neighborhood, it was kind of difficult sometimes because, especially with the type of photography you're into, not always the surroundings are helpful, depending on what you like taking pictures of, so that was very challenging and it wasn't the best, but… Yeah, when we went around, it was interesting, but the surroundings weren't particularly perfect for the types of pictures that some people like to take.

The idea of a photograph-worthy environment was an attitude we had faced during the school walks as well. However, we emphasized that having an eye for a compelling image is as important as having an ideal environment. The images of the school and neighborhood posted by participants illustrated that very compelling images were created largely because of the creativity, vision, skills, and effort of the photographer, rather than being in a photogenic space. In fact, one important potential benefit of engaging in a photo walk is the development of the awareness to recognize and represent the extraordinary in the ordinary and mundane. This ability to notice one's environment with a photographer's eye was identified by some students as one of the main learning outcomes of the MonCoin project. In response to the question, "How do you know if you learned something?" *rainy_dayz* responded,

When you notice something different with yourself, like instead of just walking past someone and being like 'aw, that's cool,' you're like 'huh! I have to take a photo of that!', and then after you're like 'no, the lighting is bad,' so you turn on the flash, or like 'aw, ok wait, I have to go grab a chair, I need to get a higher angle,' so it's like, when you are starting to put in motivation, I guess that's when you know you're learning stuff.

In this case, we can observe how the activity of walking and taking photographs during class time had an effect on the participants outside of class time. By giving students opportunities to do photography within close physical proximity, we were able to encourage certain habits and perceptions among students. For some, these habits carried into their daily lives. This was reinforced online with the constant flow of images from their peers, and missions and micro-missions posted by the research team. As such, doing photography together in physical spaces, and sharing photographs of these spaces online were consequential in the learning process, and influenced student engagement.

Conclusion—Implications for Practice

At the end of the school and neighborhood walks, we would return to the classroom and take 10–15 minutes at the end of the class for students to upload their pictures and comment on their peers images online. During these moments, students were physically in the same space of the classroom, but they were in different spaces in their mobile device's screen. In such instances, the relation between physical and online is more than a duality. These spaces are layered and they reinforced one another. In the case of MonCoin, photography was an important intermediary between these spaces. We have found that the combination of taking pictures in physical spaces with peers, and viewing photographs online positively affected students' perceptions and interactions in their everyday physical and online spaces.

Space and time are key factors in designing and implementing curricula that incorporate the asynchronous connectivity of mobile devices in classroom settings. In our research, school policies about mobile devices, demographics, the physical architecture, and location of the school were integral to how we designed and implemented the project at each school. We aimed to anchor our curriculum within the physical space of the context in which the project took place, and also take advantage of the asynchronous connectivity of mobile devices to expand the space and time of learning. This asynchronous connectivity allowed us to create prompts (missions) that encouraged students to explore their school, neighborhood, and everyday surroundings through photography.

We also found it essential to use classroom space and time to reinforce engagement online. School and Neighborhood walks were particularly effective in encouraging peer learning and noticing one's environment. By doing photography together in the same space at the same time, students observed their peers move and engage with space in different ways to do photography. Online, students were exposed to multiple perspectives of these familiar spaces by viewing their peer's photos from the walks. Students learned about photography from their peers online as well as by making images together in physical spaces. This act of photographing one's surroundings also had an impact on how students perceived and engaged with their school and everyday surroundings. These classroom activities provide some examples of how physical and online learning spaces can be combined to enrich learning and interaction in spaces.

Acknowledgements I would like to thank Lina Moreno for her contributions to the literature review and for helping me develop some key concepts in this chapter. Our conversations about the spatiality of engagement in the MonCoin curriculum have been pivotal for forming the central thesis of this chapter.

REFERENCES

Akbari, E., Castro, J. C., Lalonde, M., Moreno, L., & Pariser, D. (2016). "This allowed us to see what others were thinking": Curriculum for peer-initiated learning in art. *Art Education, 69*(5), 20–25.
Ball, L. B., & Lai, A. (2006). Place-based pedagogy for the arts and humanities. *Pedagogy, 6*(2), 261–287.
Barbour, M. K. (2007). Portrait of rural virtual schooling. *Canadian Journal of Educational Administration and Policy, 59*, 1–21.
Barbour, M., & Hill, J. (2011). What are they doing and how are they doing it? Rural student experiences in virtual schooling. *International Journal of E-Learning and Distance Education, 25*(1). Retrieved from http://www.ijede.ca/index.php/jde/article/view/725/1248.
Brown, M. (2005). Chapter 12: Learning spaces. In D. G. Oblinger & J. L. Oblinger (Eds.), *Educating the net generation.* Boulder, CO: EDUCAUSE. Retrieved from https://www.educause.edu/research-and-publications/books/educating-net-generation/learning-spaces.
Castro, J. C. (2012). Learning and teaching art through social media. *Studies in Art Education, 52*(2), 153–170.
Castro, J. C., Lalonde, M., & Pariser, D. (2016). Understanding the (im)mobilities of engaging at-risk youth through art and mobile media. *Studies in Art Education, 57*(3), 238–251.
Cooney, M. H., Gupton, P., & O'Laughlin, M. (2000). Blurring the lines of play and work to create blended classroom learning experiences. *Early Childhood Education Journal, 27*(3), 165–171.
Dziuban, C. D., Hartman, J. L., & Moskal, P. D. (2004). Blended learning. *Educause Center for Analysis and Research—Research Bulletins, 7*, 1–12.
Fenwick, T., Edwards, R., & Sawchuk, P. (2011). *Emerging approaches to educational research: Tracing the socio-material.* London, UK: Routledge.
Garrison, D. R., & Vaughan, N. (2008). *Blended learning in higher education: Framework, principles, and guidelines.* San Francisco, CA: Jossey-Bass.
Geith, C., & Vignare, K. (2008). Access to education with online learning and open educational resources: Can they close the gap? *Journal of Asynchronous Learning Networks, 12*(1), 105–126.
Graham, M. A. (2007). Art, ecology and art education: Locating art education in a critical place-based pedagogy. *Studies in Art Education, 48*(4), 375–391.

Gruenewald, D. A. (2003). The best of both worlds: A critical pedagogy of place. *Educational Researcher, 32*(4), 3–12.

Güzer, B., & Caner, H. (2014). The past, present and future of blended learning: An in-depth analysis of literature. *Procedia—Social and Behavioral Sciences, 116*, 4596–4603. https://doi.org/10.1016/j.sbspro.2014.01.992.

Massey, D. (2005). *For space*. London, U.K.: Sage.

McInerney, P., Smyth, J., & Down, B. (2011). "Coming to a place near you?" The politics and possibilities of a critical pedagogy of place-based education. *Asia-Pacific Journal of Teacher Education, 39*(1), 3–16.

Milne, A. J. M. (n.d.). Chapter 11: Designing blended learning space to the student experience. In D. G. Oblinger (Ed.), *Learning Spaces*. Boulder, CO: EDUCAUSE. Retrieved from https://www.educause.edu/ir/library/pdf/PUB7102k.pdf.

Moore, M. G., & Kearsley, G. (2011). *Distance education: A systems view of online learning* (3rd ed.). Belmont, CA: Wadsworth Publishing.

Oblinger, D. G. (Ed.). (2006). *Learning spaces*. Boulder, CO: EDUCAUSE. Retrieved from https://www.educause.edu/research-and-publications/books/learning-spaces.

Osguthorpe, R. E., & Graham, C. R. (2003). Blended learning environments: Definitions and directions. *The Quarterly Review of Distance Education, 4*(3), 227–233.

Partridge, H., Ponting, D., & McCay, M. (2011). *Good practice report: Blended learning*. Sydney, NSW: Australian Learning & Teaching Council.

Rovai, A. P. (2002). Building sense of community at a distance. *The International Review of Research in Open and Distributed Learning, 3*(1), 1–16.

Sobel, D. (2004). Place-based education: Connecting classroom and community. *Nature and Listening, 4*(1), 1–7.

Styres, S., Haig-Brown, C., & Blimkie, M. (2013). Towards a pedagogy ofand: The urban context. *Canadian Journal of Education, 36*(2), 34–67.

Tuck, E., McKenzie, M., & McCoy, K. (2014). Land education: Indigenous, post-colonial, and decolonizing perspectives on place and environmental education research. *Journal Environmental Education Research, 20*(1), 1–23.

Ubon, N. A., & Kimble, C. (2004, July). Exploring social presence in asynchronous text-based online learning communities (OLCS). In *Proceedings of the 5th International Conference on Information Communication Technologies in Education* (pp. 292–297).

Vaughan, N. (2014). Student engagement and blended learning: Making the assessment connection. *Education Sciences, 4*(4), 247–264. https://doi.org/10.3390/educsci4040247.

CHAPTER 6

Spatial Missions: My Surroundings, My Neighbourhood, My School

Ehsan Akbari

Ever since the project began, I actually started to realize the beauty of my city a little more than I normally did. I would bike around the city of Montreal with my friends and snap beautiful photos throughout the day. At the end of the day I would go through the photos and see what interesting photos I was able to capture just of my phone
—inspiremydesire

INTRODUCTION

This chapter explores the theme of spatiality in relation to the missions "My Surroundings," "My Neighbourhood," "My School," and the related micro-missions "Nature," "Notice," "Change," "Paths I Take," "What I Love About My School," and "Where I Learn Best." The aim of this chapter is to offer insights for researchers and educators for designing effective *spatial missions*, which aim to encourage youth to attend to their everyday surroundings. We begin with a theory of spatial awareness, which posits that most of our perceptions and interactions within familiar spaces are guided by automatic and pre-conscious mental

E. Akbari (✉)
Concordia University, Montreal, QC, Canada

© The Author(s) 2019
J. C. Castro (ed.), *Mobile Media In and Outside of the Art Classroom*, https://doi.org/10.1007/978-3-030-25316-5_6

processes. Spatial missions are described as prompts that intervene in such automatic processes by guiding students' attention to particular aspects of their environment. This theorization is followed by a series of specific examples of missions and micro-missions from the MonCoin curriculum at Hill Academy and Elm Secondary. Here, we provide a detailed qualitative description of how each mission and micro-mission influenced students' perceptions and interactions with their everyday civic and educational spaces in order to derive some general principles for designing spatial missions. These principles will be presented in the conclusion.

Spatial Awareness: Observe, Pay Attention, Be Aware of Your Surroundings

Let's begin with a simple thought exercise to highlight some of the ways that people generally perceive and are influenced by their perceptions of their surroundings.

- Imagine a path that you take every day. This could be your daily commute to work, school, the store, jogging route, etc. What do you see along the way? Take a few seconds to imagine and make a list.
- Now imagine yourself in a new place you have always wanted to visit. This could be a noisy urban centre like London, Tokyo, or Beirut, or in calmer places like the mountains of Machu Picchu or Northern Scotland. You are walking along a path you have never walked on. What do you see along the way? Take a few seconds to imagine and make a list.
- Now compare these two scenarios. Is it easier to recall things that you see in either situation? Is there a difference in the kinds of things you imagined seeing? Is there a difference in *how you see* when you imagined yourself moving through these spaces?

One can infer some answers to these questions based on general principles about how a person perceives their environment in such circumstances. In the first situation, you have a clear and specific idea of what to expect on your path. Recalling a few of the key items that you see should be easy as you see these things almost every day. While moving on this path, you're not paying attention to a lot of details, as you already know clearly the pertinent information to get to your destination.

Whether driving, biking, walking, or taking a train, you don't need to close pay close attention to details unless you encounter something surprising or out of the ordinary. In the second situation, you are more likely to paying attention to details, looking around, and taking in what you are seeing in your surroundings. This is partly out of curiosity and interest in the new place and may be out of necessity for survival if you do not have a trusted guide. You have to pay attention to be able to navigate this space because you have yet to build a detailed mental map of all the pertinent information you need to know to navigate. You are seeing with more attention.

In the first scenario, moving through and perceiving space is mostly an automatic mental function requiring little sustained attention. Performing such routine activities is the domain of what psychologist and behavioural economist Daniel Kahneman called *System 1*. Kahneman (2013) used this term to describe mental activities that operate "automatically and quickly, with little or no effort and no sense of voluntary control" (p. 20). System 1 activities include detecting distances between objects, completing the phrase "bread and…," making a "disgust face" when shown a horrible picture, and driving on a familiar empty road (p. 21). The commonality among these activities is that they are performed automatically and without conscious effort. Subjective experience of agency and choice is the domain of *System 2*, which "allocates attention to the effortful mental activities that demand it" (p. 21). Shifting from System 1 to System 2 requires one to pay attention and apply mental effort.

Remarkably, System 1 is capable of performing a vast number of operations including navigating through a familiar path and perceiving our everyday surroundings with very little awareness. In fact, a great deal of what we perceive in familiar spaces does not register our conscious awareness. Tor Norretranders (1999) also described this dynamic between the conscious players he called the *I* versus the *me*, which is the person in general who processes information and performs actions without requiring intervention from the conscious *I*. Norretranders drew on research in Artificial Intelligence and Information Theory to demonstrate the difference between these two players in terms of numbers. He posited the rates of our conscious awareness to be between 16 to 40 bits a second compared to the millions of bits of sensory information that are taken in every second (pp. 138–139). The total bandwidth of the eyes is 10,000,000 bits/sec compared to 40 bits/sec for conscious awareness;

this number is 100,000 to 30 bits/sec for the ears (p. 143). This indicates that a great deal of our perception and mental activities happens without our conscious awareness, since the bandwidth of conscious perception is so narrow.

While we may not be fully aware of the majority of the sensory data we pick from our environment, this data affects our perceptions and behaviours, nonetheless. This fact was demonstrated in a study by Bateson, Nettle, and Roberts (2006), in which they measured the effects of subliminal visual cues in the environment on cooperative and pro-social behaviour. They conducted the study in an office break area where there had long been an "honesty box" placed next to the tea and coffee machine allowing office members to pay for their beverage. Their experiment involved placing near this box an image of a pair of watching eyes some days and the control image of flowers on other days. They compared on which days department members contributed more and found a significant increase in the amount contributed on days in which the peering eyes were present in the environment. Whether research participants were aware of the eyes or not, their behaviour was influenced by subtle visual cues. Bateson et al. (2006) posited that the images "exerted an automatic and unconscious effect on the participants' perception that they were being watched," which led them to contribute more (p. 413). This study shows that while we may not be giving focused attention to every sight and sound in our environment, we are still affected by subtle cues.

For Kahneman (2013), the susceptibility to be influenced unconsciously in this way is a key feature of his System 1, which is easily influenced by the *priming effect*. The priming effect occurs when an individual is exposed to stimulus that automatically and without conscious effort creates a series of associations within the mind. For example, "if you have recently seen or heard the word EAT, you are temporarily more likely to complete the word fragment SO_P as SOUP than as SOAP. The opposite would happen, of course, if you had just seen WASH" (p. 52). In these and other instances of the priming effect, exposure to a particular cue influences how one perceives and behaves. This process happens automatically and without conscious awareness.

These insights on how we perceive and are influenced by our environments are relevant for designing the missions and micro-missions discussed in this chapter. The goal of these spatial missions is to intervene in the automatic functions of systems 1 and guide students' attention towards various aspects of their everyday surroundings. These missions combine image and text to influence what students notice and how they see their surroundings. For example, the students' attention is directed to the murals, graffiti, and myriad hidden messages on the street of the city when they see the micro-missions "art" and "message" on their mobile device. After seeing the micro-mission "Paths I Take," a student might slow down or stop on her walk home to take a few pictures. An enthusiastic student will bend down or lie on the ground to capture the perfect angle. By using such spatial missions as part of a mobile photography curriculum, educators are priming students to observe, pay attention to, and be aware of various aspects of everyday surroundings.

Spatial Missions to Attend to Everyday Surrounding

Spatial missions are visual prompts that encourage students to observe, photograph and share various aspects of their everyday surroundings. Many of the principles discussed in Chapter 2 about designing missions, such as the need for redundancy and variety, apply to here as well. Spatial missions use these general principles for the specific purpose of interrupting the students' habitual patterns of being in and perceiving everyday spaces. They do this by asking students to seek, photograph, and share images of specific aspects of their surroundings that are identified by the educator who designs the missions. In this context, the educator's main role is to identify the aspects of the environment that are important to attend to in a particular location.

To consider how educators can design effective spatial missions that encourage students to meaningfully engage with their everyday surroundings, we draw on the experiences and feedback of the students who participated in second iteration the MonCoin project at Hill Academy and two different iterations of the MonCoin project at Elm Secondary. At Hill Academy, we used the "My Surroundings" mission as the general theme and included micro-missions that asked students to attend to both the civic and educational spaces. At Elm Secondary, the spatial missions were divided into two themes missions: "My Neighbourhood" and "My School." As noted in the previous chapter, our rationale for doing this was to address the specific and local needs and restriction of each collaborating teacher. At Hill Academy, photographing in the hallways of the school was discouraged by the schools' administration, while, at Elm

Secondary, a key incentive of the teacher to do this project was to get students to notice and take pride in their school.

In the following sections, we describe the main missions "My Surroundings," or "My Neighbourhood," and "My School"—and a selection of their related micro-missions. The specific micro-missions were chosen to provide diverse examples of and insights into how students experienced their everyday surroundings through mobile photography. Through a systematic analysis of student interviews and visual responses to the missions, we address the following questions: How do these missions influence students' perception and interaction with their everyday surroundings? What can we learn from the students about the limitations and affordances of each mission and micro-mission? And, what are some general principles that we can infer from this?

Methods of Research

To examine the above questions, we draw on datasets from iteration 2 at Hill Academy and iteration 1 and 2 at Elm Secondary. Specifically, we focused on transcripts of students' final interviews, students' visual responses, and numeric information about each mission and micro-mission. 20 transcripts were analysed and coded using the qualitative data analysis software MAXQDA. We did lexical searches of the keywords: "Neighborhood," "Surroundings," "My School," "Nature," "Notice," "Change," "Paths I Take," "Where I Learn Best," and "What I Love About My School." We also looked specifically at student responses in which they mentioned a specific photograph and a comment they gave or received on a photograph. Also, the interview questions of "what was your favorite and least favorite missions" and "what did you learn MonCoin?" provided insights into students' views of the mission and their learning.

We also analysed the students' visual responses to each spatial mission using compositional and content analysis techniques suggested by Rose (2016). We looked at images posted in response to each mission and assigned each image at least one technical and one conceptual code. Technical codes addressed photographic skills and strategies such as "Low Angel," "Dramatic Lighting," and "Close-up." Conceptual codes addressed the subject matter of the photograph and included codes such as "Nature," "Sunset," "Social Justice," and "Food." We also matched up what students said about the images with what they posted in order to learn more details about the images.

Furthermore, numeric information provides an overview of how enthusiastically students responded to the different missions and how they felt about them. We incorporated in our analysis the number of responses for each of the missions and micro-missions, and the number of times a particular mission was identified as a favourite and least favourite mission. However, as it will be made clear in this chapter, popularity of mission was not always a simple and clear means of gauging engagement. When considering what students said about the missions and the photos they posted, it is clear that the relation between numbers of responses to a mission and students' perception and learning from the mission is complex.

Transcripts, images, and numbers are the bases for developing a qualitative and descriptive account of how the spatial missions influenced students' perceptions, interactions, and learning in their everyday spaces. In the following sections, we describe the missions "My Surroundings," "My Neighbourhood," "My School," and their micro-missions in depth by drawing on specific examples of students' experiences with these spatial missions.

My Surroundings, My Neighbourhood

Description of Mission: "The second mission involves visually communicating what the neighborhood around the school and where you live means to you. #mission2_myneighbourhood"
Total Posts: 195 Neighbourhood; 97 Surroundings; 292
Student Comments: 4 Favourite Mission; 3 Least Favourite Mission

The missions "My Surroundings" and "My Neighborhood" aim to engage students with their everyday civic spaces. These missions were deployed on the second week of the project, after the "Self" mission and micro-missions. The total number of student responses was highest for the mission "Self" with 441 responses, followed by "My Neighborhood" and "My Surroundings" missions with 292 total responses. By the numbers, these were the second most popular missions, and students expressed mixed views about the missions in the interviews. Four identified these as their favourite mission, while three had unfavourable comments about them. Some were inspired by the mission and its micro-mission to explore their city and represent their neighbourhoods, while others expressed disinterest in taking pictures of surroundings they felt were unworthy of photography. The views students expressed about the missions provide insights into some of the benefits and limitation of these spatial missions (Fig. 6.1).

The case of *inspiremydesire* highlights some of the benefits and learning that can occur from doing photography in response to the spatial missions. For *inspiremydesire*, the Neighbourhood mission and its micro-missions deepened her engagement in the project and encouraged her to view photography with a smartphone as a powerful creative tool. Generally, *inspiremydesire* was a highly motivated art student and was very active online during the project. At the beginning of her interview, she pleasantly surprised the research team member interviewing her by reading a prepared statement to thank us for the project. In the prepared statement, *inspiremydesire* expressed the learning outcomes of the project in general, and how the neighbourhood mission and micro-mission influenced her engagement with her city:

> Before the project began, I saw my phone as a device just to call, message, or text. I never thought I would use my phone as a camera for photography. Throughout the project I began to learn what great photos I can capture and edit by just using my phone. This project has actually widened my view of photography. I always thought the only possible way to be a photographer and to take photos was with a professional camera but this project has made me realize that you can take great photos no matter what type of device you use. Not only did this project improve my knowledge of photography skills, it also made me a better photographer. Ever since the project began, I actually started to realize the beauty of my city a little more than I normally did. I would bike around the city of Montreal with my friends and snap beautiful photos throughout the day. At the end of the day I would go through the photos and see what interesting photos I was able to capture just of my phone.

The project had the outcome of encouraging *inspiremydesire* to see her phone as a creative tool. More pertinent to this chapter is her statement about seeing the city of Montreal in a new way, and the role the spatial missions had in facilitating this transformation. *Inspiremydesire* attributed some of her learning to the diversity of micro-mission, which incentivized her to explore her city and attend to different things she notices in her environment. She identified the missions "nature," "unique," "the messages on the wall," and "art" as prompts to look for while moving

6 SPATIAL MISSIONS: MY SURROUNDINGS ... 135

Fig. 6.1 - Inspiremydesire's responses to spatial missions (from top left to bottom right): #Micromission_Nature, #Micromission_Unique, #Micromission_notice, #Micromision_pathsItake, #Mission_myneighbourhood, #micromission_notice

through the city. By looking for photographic responses to the textual and visual prompts of the missions, she was able to look at her surroundings with more scrupulous eyes. After a day of biking, looking and taking pictures, she would end up with "a lot of pictures of art, paintings and stuff on the wall, and a lot of them had a lot of positive messages." In the evening, she would go through her camera roll and select images to edit before posting. The case of *inspiremydesire* is an example of how spatial missions can encourage one to go out, explore, and positively transform one's perception and relationship with one's surroundings.

For *Damenson_wheredue_findthat* and *Pxeppermint*, the "My Neighbourhood" mission was particularly inspiring because it got them to photograph their neighbourhood, for which they felt a strong connection. *Damson_wheredue_findthat* talked about photographs he took in a place in which he had lived for 12 years prior to moving to his current home. He described his former residence as his "actual neighbourhood." *Pxeppermint* talked about being excited about the "My Neighbourhood" mission because she really liked her neighbourhood. Both described being motivated to respond to the missions "Buildings" and "Landmarks" to represent and show off their neighbourhood.

The "My Surroundings" and "My Neighbourhood" missions were effective in motivating some to explore their city and take pride in representing their neighbourhoods. There were some, however, who felt unmotivated and uninspired by these missions and expressed various reasons for their preference for other missions. One common sentiment among detractors is that they felt their surroundings and neighbourhoods were not as interesting to photograph. *Trvnscxndxnt's* response to the question "what was your least favourite mission" sums to this sentiment:

> The neighbourhood one, because I had done it, and I found that the pictures weren't as nice as my other ones, like, the pictures were cool but they weren't unique. I had taken a picture of the sky and edited it, but I found this a really basic thing, it was a picture of this big park and then there was the sky, but that one was, I would say, my least favourite because it wasn't as cool as my other ones.

For *Trvnscxndxnt*, the everyday surroundings of school and neighbourhood did not provide opportunities for unique photography in comparison to other missions. *Cxrly4* also found photographing in response to the neighbourhood mission to be challenging because "the surroundings weren't particularly perfect for the types of pictures" she liked to take. In spite of not feeling inspired by the missions during the project, *Cxrly4* mentioned one outcome of the project is that she would post "more pictures related to my surroundings, instead of just my friends, and just me."

These two cases show some of the limitation of the project in general and the spatial mission in particular. First of all, to what extent someone is willing to engage with and pay attention to different aspects of their surroundings depends in part on how one feels about these places and in part on how one feels about what is photograph-worthy. One of the potential challenges and possible positive outcomes of using missions to encourage youth to attend to their everyday surroundings is in convincing them that everyday places are indeed worthy of photography. When using spatial missions in classrooms, this factor should be considered in planning and implementing the project.

Nature

Description of Mission: The human-made environment (e.g. urban/city) is full of nature. Humans are not the only inhabitants. Where does nature take over? Where is it subdued? Where is the natural world changing? Adapting? Thriving? What are your favourite aspects of the natural world in your neighbourhood? What needs to be protected? #micromission_nature.
Total Posts: 106 Post
Student Comments: 3 Positive Comments; 0 Negative Comments

The micro-mission "Nature" was the second most popular among all micro-missions only after "What I eat" with 106 and 119 total student responses, respectively. In the description of the "Nature" micro-mission, students were asked to look for nature within the urban spaces in which the project took place. Both Hill Academy and Elm Secondary are situated on the Island of Montreal and surrounded by a concrete jungle with some parks and green spaces scattered here and there. Students were encouraged to look for and seek nature in these urban environments. This theme resonated with some students. For others, a key motivating factor for sharing photographs and using the hashtag was that "nature" is a familiar and recognized genre on Instagram. For many students we interviewed, their usual online presence on Instagram involved posting selfies and pictures of friends. For some, posting images of food was quite common, and this in part explains the popularity of the micro-mission "What I eat," which is an accessible and familiar theme. For some students, posting images of nature was also a familiar part of their existing practice and online presence. The ease of association between the word "nature" and existing practices online made this one of the more accessible and popular micro-missions.

A number of students discussed viewing and posting "nature" photography on Instagram. *Magenta.a* talked about her admiration for her friend, who had a separate account from her "actual account" where she posted "pictures of nature and murals." *Magenta.a* saw this practice as standing in contrast to her generation, for whom "it's trendy to just post pictures of themselves." One outcome of the project for *Magenta.a* was to set up the Instagram account for our project, which she said she intended to keep to post pictures of nature just like her friend. Another student named Tara talked about having various Instagram accounts, "one for my dog, and an account where I post pictures of nature." In these instances, posting and viewing "nature" photographs on Instagram were already part of the students' practice, and some students associated the private Instagram that they set up for our project with this practice of posting pictures of nature and murals.

While students often used the word "nature" to describe their photography practice during and prior to the project, this word was not often used in relation to this micro-mission. In some cases, it was used as synonym of surroundings, neighbourhood, city, and landscape photography. *Drizzy_savage6*, for instance, talked about images in her camera roll using this word:

> I don't tend to take a lot of pictures of myself...my camera roll does not have a lot of images, if anything it's my vacation to Cuba and the trees outside, like the fall leaves, or I take pictures of my friends. (Interviewer: Do you share these images?)...The pictures of nature, I tend to keep that to myself.

Cloudytreefrog also described the "nature" photographs he took on his phone as pictures of "mostly just things that I like around me, like usually it's trees and stuff, and like the sky." In these cases, one can observe that the spatial missions, which encouraged students to attend to various aspects of their surroundings, were readily associated with taking pictures of nature, which was an existing part of some students' practice.

This association likely had some influence on the nature of images students posted in response to this micro-mission. There were, however, some instances of deep engagement and connection to this micro-mission. One such example is *Illogic_13*, who had recently moved from the West Coast of Canada to Montreal. *Illogic_13* described how the micro-mission "nature" influenced her transition to a new city by getting her to seek nature to photograph in the urban jungle of Montreal. This was her response to why "nature" was her favourite mission:

> (I'm from) Vancouver area. So there's a lot more forest than there is here but being able to sort of see that there is more than a just apartment buildings and the more you can find that here in Montreal that's definitely what contributed to being my favourite.

We can see that the micro-mission influenced *Illogic_13* to look for and find something specific in her surroundings that she valued. In doing so, she was able to develop and deepen her connection to the place where she had just moved. Overall, while the theme seems to have been accessible, the depth of engagement with the theme of nature varied. For some, "nature" elicited stereotyped notions of landscape photography, and for others, "nature" encouraged exploring and seeing their environment in a different way. The case of *Illogic_13* shows that there were instances in which this theme resonated deeply with some students and motivated their engagement in the project.

Notice

Description of Mission: Look carefully and closely at your surroundings. Do you notice anything that you would not have noticed if you weren't looking carefully? For this micro-mission seek out and photograph the little things that you might encounter in your everyday surroundings that generally go unnoticed. #micromission_notice.
Total Posts: 64 Post
Student Comments: 0 Positive Comments; 0 Negative Comments

This micro-mission most explicitly asked students to notice, pay attention to, and be aware of their everyday surroundings. Similarly to the "nature" micro-mission, a lexical search of transcripts revealed students often used the word "notice" to describe their experience with the project, but not always in relation to the micro-mission. Some talked about noticing in relation to peer-learning. *Beyonce33*, for example, talked about a comment left online by *who_isthis_guy* about a nice reflection in the pond *Beyonce33* had photographed, which made her notice the reflection for the first time.

Noticing was also identified by a number of students as a learning outcome of doing photography during this project. For instance, *iscreamforicecream* described how the project taught her to look at things differently: "When I go home, I really started taking pictures of everything, because I didn't notice any of these things before… I didn't really think I could take a picture, edit it, and it would turn out completely different." For this student, photography and editing were key motivators for noticing and looking at familiar spaces anew. Similarly, *Rainy_dayz* described how she learned to look closely at her environment because of doing photography for this project.

> I learned I like taking photos. It made me look at things differently because I was like just looking at this (is referring to the recorder), instead of just looking at it as a recorder, now I'm like 'oh, this has really cool like checker pattern. What if I took a close-up photo of it?' So, it's making me look at things in detail now, so I found that really cool.

This statement offers the interesting insight that one can be encouraged and develop the habit of looking at things in detail by taking close-up photographs. Taking close-up photographs of various details of surroundings was a strategy that was used by many students in response to the micro-mission "Notice." Many of the students replied to this micro-mission by observing small details to various aspects of their surroundings and taking close-up photos of their subject matter, which included patterns of leaves and flowers, a peephole on a bright cobalt blue door, and morning dew on glass. These responses were in part inspired by the prompt to "look carefully and closely at your surroundings," which was included in the mission description.

However, taking close-up shots of details was not the only strategy used by student to respond to this mission. One theme that is also present is students observing and commenting on negative aspects of their surroundings. One such example is *inspiremydesire's* image of an overflowing garbage can in her neighbourhood. This elicited *Beyonce33* to leave the comment that the image "represents our reality and it's very sad, and this picture is very beautiful but is also horrible at the same time." In this case, the conversations that emerged in response to the "notice" micro-mission related closely to issues of civic responsibility, which is the theme addressed by the next micro-mission "change."

Change

Description of Mission: Is there something you would change about your surroundings? What would it be? Why would you want to change it? Only show things that realistically can be changed with your positive contributions. #micromission_change
Total Posts: 29 Post
Student Comments: 2 Positive Comments; 1 Negative Comments

This micro-mission relates to the theme of civic engagement, which has been a key component of MonCoin from its inception. In earlier iterations, Pariser, Castro, and Lalonde (2016) found that "civic engagement grew out of participants' initial interest in, and concern for the formal, technical and aesthetic aspects of their images" (p. 211). When conducting research at Hill Academy and Elm Secondary, formal, technical, and aesthetic aspects of photography were addressed as a central part of our curriculum. Many students quoted in this chapter expressed how important it was for them to learn to take good pictures for engaging them in the project and various missions and micro-missions. This micro-mission asked students to apply their photography skills to express how they could make positive contributions to their community and everyday surroundings.

The micro-mission "change" generated 29 responses, which is fewer than most micro-missions. A few interpreted the theme of change literally by responding with images of changing tires (*sceema16*) or leaves changing colour (*angel.ofthebeach*). There were also a number of responses that addressed the theme of engaging in civic space and conversations. Examples include *kienaqcca*, who took a photo of a caged monkey to raise awareness of animal rights, and *blankpov*, who photographed garbage and recycling bins to critique waste collection in the city. These examples show that some put thought and effort into expressing their views on issues they care about. This generally did not translate into generating in-depth conversation online about the specific issues. One challenge in using the micro-mission "change" is finding ways to facilitate and encourage conversation about how one can make positive contributions to civic space. The connection between the "notice" and "change" micro-missions may be relevant here. In response to "notice," a few students responded with things in their environment they would like to change, and in some instances, this started an online dialogue. Noticing may be a useful first step to elicit themes and issues that students feel strongly about in their civic spaces. This could be used to have conversations with students about how one can change and make positive contributions to their everyday environments. As such, it might be a good idea to scaffold the micro-mission to begin with noticing, then talking about making positive contribution, and then photographing to respond to "Change."

Another factor in the low quantity of responses to this micro-mission that should be considered is the complexity of the mission. *Shama16*, who had posted an image of changing tires in response to "Change," expressed her frustration at the difficulty of the mission. *Dawn_times* also talked about how difficult this mission was, but he saw this as a positive. When asked how we could improve the MonCoin curriculum, he suggested we incorporate more diversity in the theme of the missions, and particularly including more "missions that involve exploring, and really having to think about what you're going to post, instead of knowing immediately, like "oh, I'm going to post this." *Dawn_times* mentioned enjoying the micro-mission "Change" because you "had to really think about what it is that you want to improve." The responses from *Shama16* and *Dawn_times* show that some of the diverse and contradictory ways in which students respond to the same prompt. For some, complicated missions are obstacles to engagement, while for others, they motivate thoughtfulness and engagement. This diversity in preferences for levels of complexity should be considered in designing and dispensing missions. It is advisable to incorporate easy and hard missions, and "Change" represents a more complex micro-mission requiring time and thought. The next micro-mission represents an easier mission in this spectrum.

Paths I Take

Description of Mission: What paths do you take every day? #micromission_paths

Total Posts: 86

Student Comments: 2 Positive Comments; 0 Negative Comments

"Paths I Take" provided easy access points for students to photograph their surroundings, and this is reflected in the high number of responses at 86. There is great variation in the quality of responses and the amount of effort put into taking the photograph. This variation can be observed with most student visual responses, but is more pronounced for this micro-mission. It seems taking a quick snapshot of the sidewalk and posting it is an easy way of fulfilling minimum requirements to get the grade. There is also evidence that some students put effort and deployed a variety of techniques such as using odd angles, blurring the background, or using muted colours to visually communicate their subjective connection to their everyday paths. Also, most students interpreted the concept of path literally as a path one walks on, but there are instances where students interpreted this micro-mission metaphorically. *Johnbook* described why this was his favourite micro-mission:

> It shows that we are still young and that specific mission is kind of helping us, saying 'what path do you want to take?', like there's a bad road, a good road, it all depends on what you want to choose, and it also kind of, in a way, affects with your life, because it's all about where you're going and what you're doing. So, if you take a picture of an endless hallway, that means that you're going to have an endless journey, and if you take a picture of quotes or anything, those quotes affect your journey, because that means you're strong, you won't give up or anything, so that could mean anything.

For *Johnbook*, this micro-mission provided a chance to reflect on the paths she can take in life and photograph her surroundings to express how she feels about this process. In the case of "Path I Take," simplicity of the prompt led to great variation in the quality of responses, technical strategies, and conceptual interpretations.

Another striking aspect of this micro-mission, which become visible when compiling all student responses to this micro-mission, is the variation of where and when the photographs were taken and posted online. Some images were taken in summer, winter, or fall. In other images, one can make out from the long shadows that the picture was taken late evening, while others chronicled their morning commute. Responses to this micro-mission show how spatial missions can connect students across different points in space and time. This micro-mission prompts students to take a picture while taking a particular path at any time or place.

A student might be reminded of this task at any point on a daily commute or leisurely walk and share their visual response with others in the class.

Overall, "Paths I Take" is a good micro-mission because it is simple and it connects students across time and space. Its strength is in providing a very easy access point for photographing one's surroundings, which can lead to complex variations in how students interpret and respond to the micro-mission. A potential issue to be mindful of is that the simplicity of this micro-mission may lead some to respond without putting in much effort. One way to encourage deeper engagement is to address technical photography skills in the classroom and motivate students to apply these skills to respond to this micro-mission. Taking photographs of paths can be good for practicing perspective and converging lines. The simplicity of this micro-mission is its strength and a potential limitation.

My School

Description of Mission: The third mission involves visually communicating what your school means to you. Please do not interrupt classes while taking photos. #mission3_myschool
Total Posts: 128 posts (2 iterations at Elm Secondary)
Student Responses to Mission: 1 Positive Comments; 8 Negative Comments

Based on the low numbers of posts and student responses in the interviews, the overwhelmingly clear observation that can be made about the "My School" mission and its related micro-missions is that many students did not particularly enjoy photographing their school. The response of *Dawn_times* to why "My School" was his least favourite mission sums up how some students felt about this mission:

> Well, normally I like taking pictures throughout the city and there are always colors with nature and everything and then once we got this project, just to take pictures in your school and either the walls or... anything... hum, like the ceiling and stuff... I really felt out of it because I really didn't know what to take pictures of because I felt like my school was dull and I was like, 'Oh no, not the school.'

The contrast between the colourful city and the dull school environment is a common sentiment among students. For some students, their apprehension to photograph the school was in part influenced by their attitude towards the space of their school. However, a key motivator for our research team to include "My School" as a major theme of the project at Elm Secondary was because it was critical for the collaborating art teacher to encourage students to notice and take pride in their school. And, there is some evidence that some students learned from it. One important piece of evidence for this is the images students posted in response to this mission and its micro-mission, which incorporated various angles, close-ups, editing, using light to create silhouettes, and a host of other sophisticated photography techniques. This shows that many students observed their school environment carefully and put in the time and effort to visually communicating their observations. *Dawn_times*, who found the school too dull to photograph, also talked about how he saw the school in a new perspective after photographing it.

> I like taking pictures of nature, but once I realized that I can edit and do certain Photoshop things on my phone and actually get close to certain areas in the school and take different angles, it really made my perspective on the school very different.

This statement is consistent with the general observation about "My School" that some students did indeed observe their school from a different perspective by photographing in response to the mission. In the previous chapter, we discussed some in-depth learning that occurred as a result of this mission by describing school walks, in which students moved together in physical space of the school to take and share photographs. Being together in the physical space of the school was a motivating factor. Here, we present two micro-missions as examples of how spatial missions can encourage students to observe and take pride in their school.

#micro_mission_What I Love About My School

For this micro-mission, students were asked to think about what makes their school special and why they look forward to coming to school every day. Our goal with this mission was to encourage students to have a positive perceptive of their school and to photograph and share positive aspects of their school. Two main themes emerged in response to the micro-mission. Many students shared sports-related images such as pictures of basketballs, badminton rackets, and several shots of the school team's logo. Another major theme was the art murals in the school. In fact, Elm Secondary has an excellent reputation for its art and music departments, and one can observe a sizable collection of murals throughout the school environment. This micro-mission prompted students to seek out these murals and other things they loved about their school, and photograph and share these with their peers.

#micro_mission_Where I Learn Best

For this micro-mission, students were asked to identify places they learned best in the school. This could include spaces in which they felt smart and more confident to apply what they know. There were 27 total responses to this micro-mission. Many of the responses related to the subject that students enjoyed most such as math, art, and biology. Visuals included a messy art sink, books in the library, and an artistic collage about Mitosis. Others included images of transitional or leisurely spaces such as the hallways or cafeteria. Some students identified spaces outside their school, which they found most conducive to learning. Students shared images of their favourite coffee shop, comfy couch at home, or a tree as ideal learning spots. This micro-mission encouraged students to reflect on the space of learning. For some, this encouraged them to depict their subject or classroom in school, while for others the learning space they depicted was a private, comfortable space. This micro-mission prompted some students to express their favourite subjects with their peer and others to reflect on the useful question as to what spaces are conducive and helpful for learning.

Reflections on My School Mission and Micro-missions

Although the "My School" mission and micro-missions were not the most popular, there is evidence that the micro-missions motivated some engagement with the educational environment. Particularly, the micro-missions "What I Love About My School" and "Where I Learn Best" got students to focus on positive aspects and share their impressions with others. Themes such as a passion for sports and the arts in the school emerged as students began posting their visual responses to these micro-missions. Using such positive micro-missions was a useful strategy to encourage students to take pride in their school. The micro-missions, along with the walks, and teaching photography skills were some of the key tools we used to encourage students' to have a positive perspective of and relation to their school environment. By using these tools in conjunction, we were able to influence some students to develop a new perspective of their school.

Conclusion: Design Principles for Spatial Missions

The images posted by students and their statements in the interviews provide evidence that the spatial missions described in this chapters influenced students' perception and interaction with their everyday surroundings in various ways. For example, "My Neighbourhood" got *inspiremydesire* to explore her city to photograph art, positive messages, and one overflowing garbage can. For others, "My Neighbourhood" was associated with a place where they have an emotional connection. And, others found taking pictures in their everyday surroundings to be less appealing than other missions. This variability in how student interpreted the themes and their levels of engagement with each mission and micro-mission is a common occurrence. The micro-missions built on the main themes of "My Surroundings" or "My Neighbourhood" to encourage students to pay attention to various aspects of their surroundings. The micro-mission "Notice" got students to observe details and, along with the micro-mission "Change," motivated some to express criticism of their city and neighbourhood.

In terms of the educational space, the mission "My School" encouraged students to look closely and find compelling and interesting things to photograph in a banal everyday space. This act of seeking and taking good photographs in the school gave some students a different perceptive of this space. The related micro-mission asked students to focus on their personal relationship to their school and other learning spaces. To respond, students looked for, photographed and shared images of things they valued about their school. These spatial missions got some students to see with attention and notice different aspects of their surroundings. They acted as interventions in the automatic and habitual interactions of individuals with their everyday surroundings and prompted them to explore, reflect on, and express how they see their surroundings.

Students' varied views on these spatial missions provide valued insights into the limitations and affordances of each mission and micro-mission. These limitations and affordances are synthesized into 5 general principles for designing spatial missions. Some of these principles are specific to spatial missions, while others apply to designing missions in general and are relevant for discussion here.

Design Principles for Spatial Missions

One's Feelings About a Space Influences Engagement with Spatial Missions

One's willingness to attend to a space through photography does in part depend on one's attitude towards the space. This pattern is evident in the "My Neighbourhood" mission, where some said their surroundings and neighbourhood around their school were not interesting enough to photograph. Several students had similar views about the "My School" mission. A common feeling among students was that the school was too dull or they already spend too much time there to want to photograph it. We found that, in some instances, students' general views and attitudes towards their school changed for the better by engaging in the act of photographing their school. In some cases, sharing and viewing images of different aspects of their neighbourhoods and school with their peers on our visual network convinced some that their everyday surroundings are indeed photo-worthy.

When designing and deploying spatial missions, the attitudes and dispositions of students towards their everyday spaces should be taken into consideration. Educators can take some steps in addressing this issue by providing examples and models of photography that explore everyday spaces through different themes. Also, one can consider going on photo walks with a group of students to exotic spaces, by which we mean places that are new, unknown, or desirable for exploring and photographing. This exploration may spark an interest in photographing places and influence students to take on more positive attitudes towards photographing everyday places.

Diversity, Diversity, Diversity

This is a basic principle of designing missions, and it is salient here. First of all, students' preferences and interpretations of the missions varied greatly. While we can generalize about the popularity of a mission, a detailed examination reveals a great deal of inconsistencies and contradictions in terms of why they preferred a particular mission. One student prefers a mission because it's simple and easy while another dislikes the same mission because it's not complex enough. The variation is also evident for preferences in themes and subject matter. Furthermore, there is also variation in the numbers of visual responses to each of the missions with some receiving lots of responses, while others received few. A close examination again reveals that although micro-missions such as "Change" and "What I Love About My School" had lower numbers of visual response, there was a deep level engagement and learning for some students. An educator should expect and, in fact, desire a degree of diversity and variation in terms of interpretation, motivation, and engagement with different missions.

Easy and Hard Missions

One factor to consider when designing diverse sets of missions and micro-mission is the complexity of the prompt. The micro-missions "Nature" and "Path I Take," for example, provided an easy access point and received many diverse responses. In the case of the former, nature is a familiar theme and is more easily associated with common practices, while "Paths I Take" offers direct and literal instruction. Some students preferred these missions because they provided an easy entry point for engagement. On the other side of the spectrum is the micro-missions "Change," which requires one to think about, identify, and actively look for something to photograph that needs improvement. Responding to this prompt might also require incorporating text with the images and/or writing a detailed description. This process takes time and thought, and some expressed preference for such complexity. Overall, educators can engage a diverse group of students by providing them with simple and complex missions that provide a group of student easy access points and also challenge them to use photography to communicate complex ideas and issues.

Scaffolding of Missions and Micro-missions

Another factor to consider is the order in which the missions and micro-missions are deployed. In our research, we began with the overall theme of self, then explored the spatial themes, and ended with "Post your own Missions." This structure gave students a chance to explore and express their identity through photography first, and after use this tool to explore their environment. We also thought carefully about the ordering of the micro-missions within each theme. It turned out to be a sensible decision to release the micro-mission "Notice" before "Change," for example, because of how these themes relate to each other. In other situations, an educator can think about whether they prefer to start with a simple prompt to engage a novice group or a complex prompt to challenge an expert group. Another factor that may influence the order of the micro-missions is the day of the week. For example, "Paths I Take" might be a good one for a weekday, while "Unique" or "Notice" might be good micro-mission for the weekend to inspire students to go out and explore.

Teaching and Reinforcement

The effectiveness of the spatial missions does, to some degree, depend on the teaching, classrooms activities, and instructions that are provided in concurrence with the missions. For instance, we have found that teaching compositional elements for photography to be critical for getting students excited about responding to our missions. Also, we took time during classes to get students to look at their peers' images and offer constructive comments. In some cases, we displayed and discussed specific photographs by the students or established artists to provide models and inspiration. These classroom instructions and activities, and others, were critical to motivating and guiding students' engagement with the missions. When designing missions, educators should consider incorporating instructions and classroom activities that deepen students' engagement with the missions.

References

Bateson, M., Nettle, D., & Roberts, G. (2006). Cues of being watched enhance cooperation in a real-world setting. *Biology Letters, 2,* 412–414. https://doi.org/10.1098/rsbl.2006.0509.
Kahneman, D. (2013). *Thinking, fast and slow.* Toronto, ON: Anchor Canada.
Norretranders, T. (1999). *The user illusion: Cutting consciousness down to size.* New York: Penguin Press Science.
Pariser, D., Castro, J. C., & Lalonde, M. (2016). Investigating at-risk youth visually examining their communities through mobilities, aesthetics and civic engagement. *International Journal of Education Through Art, 12*(2), 211–225.
Rose, G. (2016). *Visual methodologies: An introduction to researching with visual materials.* London, UK: Sage.

CHAPTER 7

Integrating Traditional Art Making Processes and New Technology in the High School Curriculum

Anne Pilon

In the past eighteen years since I have taught at Villa Maria High School. Our school has gone through major changes including educational reform, changing from an all-girls school to coed, and the integration of iPads in the classroom. In 2014, our high school introduced Apple iPads as a tool intended to enhance teaching and learning in all subject areas. The rationale for this decision was to encourage students and teachers to use technology for class work, to have students connect with their peers and teachers in collaborative projects, and to study topics including responsible digital citizenship. The integration of mobile technology in the art classroom posed significant challenges with regard to managing the technology and student behavior. At first, I was skeptical that a digital device such as the iPad would prove to be useful in the art curriculum. I asked "How could digital technology enhance learning about and creating art without sacrificing meaning, creativity, and artistic skill? Would the use of digital technology

A. Pilon (✉)
Villa Maria High School, Montreal, QC, Canada

take away time and opportunities to develop technical, artistic skills? How would student performance be evaluated and how would the distractions that are inherent in such devices be managed?"

In this chapter, I outline how I address classroom management and adapt my art curriculum to integrate digital technology—in addition to using traditional methods for teaching visual arts. For example, to teach still life drawing from observation, I have students use digital photography and photo-editing tools to zoom in on a section of a still life setup that they later draw by hand. Photo-editing transforms their compositions from color to black and white to help them understand gray scale. They later draw their compositions using a pencil or charcoal. Another way I use the iPad as a learning tool is to have students walk around the school and photograph hallways from one- or two-point perspective. Using the Notability app, students import their photographs and use digital tools to draw lines on their images to situate the horizon line, vanishing points, and diagonal lines to prepare a study of linear perspective. These two examples illustrate how I use the iPad as a tool to learn visual art concepts. To use the iPad this way not only saves time it also provides a means for learners to be creative in the process. While I discovered that, the iPad is a useful tool I had yet to find ways to use it as a medium for making art. My participation in the MonCoin project inspired me to explore its possibilities as a creative medium.

The first section of this chapter is about my experience of the MonCoin project. It describes how I saw the study unfold and my reflections. In the second section, I discuss how I dealt with classroom management after the iPad was introduced and address my concerns over student's privacy with regard to online activities. In the third section, I explain how mobile technology was adapted for students with special needs, and in the fourth section, I provide suggestions for art projects that use the iPad—especially the camera and editing applications. Finally, I conclude with a reflection on how the implementation of digital technology in the art classroom is changing the way I teach.

MonCoin at Villa Maria High School

In the first year the iPad was introduced in our school, I only felt comfortable teaching students to do quick online image searches, fine art photography, documentation of finished work, and to create of an electronic portfolio. However, I knew the iPad had to potential to be a creative tool and was eager to learn about it. In 2015 and 2016, I welcomed the MonCoin project into my classroom. The research project aimed to design and test strategies to integrate technology for creative and collaborative learning in the art classroom. I participated by helping the team facilitate learning activities and managing the interview process with my secondary three students. By participating in the study, I hoped to gain new skills and strategies to implement digital technology that would enable me to find practical and creative ways to use it for teaching art.

The study was conducted in two phases. Each phase lasted approximately six weeks. Every week, a member of the research team gave lessons on the elements and principles of photography such as elements of good composition and the effects of lighting. Additionally, students were introduced to a myriad of photo-editing applications to enhance their images. The students were also provided with rules of conduct as well as guidelines regarding ethics and responsibility when taking photographs, especially when those included people as subjects.

In the first phase, one group of 32 students participated in the study. They used only their iPad camera to take photographs and all of the activities took place at school. With their newly acquired photography skills, the students responded to prompts or missions provided by the researchers by photographing and posting their work on the school's educational iPad platform, Haiku. During the activities, students shared their knowledge about art and their personal, informal creative practices with the researchers and each other. In this collaboration, they learned both photographic techniques and positive ways to give constructive feedback. At the end of the project, the students had a series of images that demonstrated the skills they had gained from the learning activities. Students participated in classroom discussions concerning the common elements found through the images they produced. They also debated some contentious points about creativity and called into question aspects about how art is made. Some students shared the view that they did not consider photography to be art while others stated that they did not realize they were creating art images through photography. While the project activities were inspiring, using Haiku as a way to share images and comments proved difficult. The research team suggested using social media to share images and comments.

The second phase of the research consisted of two groups of secondary three students for a total of 72 participants. The researchers proposed the creation of a private Instagram account to allow students could post, share, and comment on each other's images more easily. We first met with the school principal to obtain approval to use Instagram for the project. We explained that the Haiku platform made it difficult to share and comment because the setup did not allow for an easy flow and exchange of content. The principal agreed; however, the students were reluctant to use Instagram for school work. Since many already had personal Instagram accounts, they expressed their apprehension that their activity on it would be exposed to their teachers and parents. Furthermore, the fact that our school did not allow students to use social media apps while in school added to their concern. These issues were resolved by reassuring students that the school had agreed to allow the use of a private Instagram account and that the sharing of images would occur only among each other and the researchers and not publicly. This discussion gave us an opportunity to address issues around types of images that should be posted and shared online and how they may be received by others, in social contexts.

During the second phase of the project, the researchers gave students homework, which obliged them to post their work outside of school hours and allowed them to use own devices if they wished. As students posted their responses to the missions, they shared more quickly and easily than they could with the Haiku platform. The interaction between them through shares, comments, and "likes" created a bridge to each other and to me and allowed students a space to be creative outside of school. In this way, collaborative learning was facilitated. While students shared their work, it was evident that not only were they making inspired artistic choices but were also influencing each other.

I was excited to see students' engagement outside of school hours through their posts. Because I wanted to learn to use my iPad as a way to make art. I decided to participate along with the students by interpreting each mission set out by the research team. When I posted my photographs, the students saw me as an artist as well as an art teacher. By providing them with feedback through Instagram, I connected with them in a different albeit superficial way. However, by simply looking at their image sharing activity, I realized that I lacked the opportunity to have a conversation about their creative intentions and struggles and to gain insight into their artistic process. Once during a parent–teacher interview, I shared a student's portfolio with her parents while the student was present. I asked the student about one of the photographs she took, and she told me how, when, and why she took that particular photograph. Having had that conversation was enlightening and made me realize that an important element of teaching and learning requires face-to-face discussion. I was not as aware of the students' artistic intentions by only observing their activity on Instagram. While using Instagram was a great way to share images and to connect with students, it cut out the crucial dialogue between my students and I and limited my understanding of their creative process.

Additionally, I could not manage and keep track of everyone's progress given the volume of photographs students took and posted, and I could not easily evaluate what they had learned. To solve the problem, I created an assignment that asked students to present a collection of their best images and write an artist's statement about them. I developed a rubric that identified specific benchmarks I wanted the students to reach in terms of artistic creation and appreciation. Their learning process was evaluated based on their ability to effectively use the photography techniques, acquired technology skills, effective artistic choices, level of engagement, and the ability to provide useful feedback to their peers. I also evaluated their ability to write about their art process, inspiration, struggles, and successes.

Classroom Management

The use of digital mobile devices in the classroom raises concerns about social and educational responsibility. Most students in our school already own a smartphone or other mobile device and are accustomed to using them for personal purposes. Our school has strict rules about when, where, and how students can use their mobile devices while in school. For example, students are not allowed to have social media apps on their school iPads and are not allowed to use their cell phones except at lunchtime. Among the many issues with using mobile devices, one of the most complicated is how to encourage students to remain on task. With an iPad always available, the temptation to play games, listen to music, watch videos, and use social media apps throughout the day is stronger than ever.

In addition to distractions, there are issues concerning social media misuse, cyber-bullying, and the tension between private and public online space. Our students purchase the iPad for school work; however, some students also use it for entertainment, gaming, and maintaining social connections while at school. This creates tension concerning when and how the iPad is used. Teachers and administrators at our school struggle to negotiate between these boundaries. During the research project, one student posted a photograph that was in violation of the parameters set out by the team. The team alerted me, and the photograph was taken off the site. The student expressed her frustration at being forced to follow the rules and, using a pseudonym, protested in subsequent posts with negative comments. It was a tense situation that was eventually resolved with an honest conversation about responsible digital citizenship and the impact of posting certain types of images online.

Classroom management is an important issue, and thus, I tell the students that they are being held accountable for how they use their iPad in class. I use Apple Classroom and Mosyle Manager to increase the iPad's effectiveness as an educational tool. Apple Classroom allows me to temporarily disable the iPad and is helpful to get the attention of the students, especially at the beginning of class. Additionally, I can view students' screens while they are working. Often times I have shared ideas with the students by projecting the screen view of a given student to the entire class. Moreover, using Mosyle Manager I can lock the iPads so that students can view a specific site or participate in a particular activity. I let students know when I use these apps to reduce the tension around the notion that I am trying to catch them in the act of using their iPads inappropriately. I always strive to reinforce the notion that the students are held responsible to use the iPads for school work during class time.

ADAPTATIONS FOR STUDENTS WITH SPECIAL NEEDS

In my class, students use their iPads when, for one reason or another, they are unable to use traditional art materials. For example, a student with a strong aversion to the feeling of dry pastels used the Notability app to draw a face in proportion. By using his finger and the different tools in the app, he was able to achieve similar results to the others. In another instance, a student who had their arm in a cast was able to explore an art topic through photographic images they took, instead of creating collages like the other students. Finally, in a case where a student with Asperger's syndrome who had great difficulty accepting classroom project proposals, digital technology proved very practical to help her bring ideas to life. I discovered that the student had an active informal art practice outside the classroom; she was creating stories through drawings and animations on her iPad and was sharing them on social media sites. The stories featured a character that represented her alter ego. I adapted the art program to allow the student to continue using the drawing and animations as inspiration to develop a body of artwork based on her interests. This work included a series of digital images, drawings on paper, a clay sculpture of her character, a life-size pair of wings and a mask, all inspired by her character. This integration of technology provided me with a way to better understand the kind of subjects that interested the student. The fact that she was allowed to explore a topic that interested her kept her engaged for the entire school year. At the end of the year, we created a video together that features her explaining her artwork, and how she made them. These examples demonstrate practical ways that technology was incorporated in my classroom to engage diverse learners. The following section describes other ideas for artistic exploration through art projects.

Art Projects

This series of activities features mobile technology for art creation. They feature many artistic skills that are similar to traditional skills taught in the art curriculum only these are digital, these include the use of layers, collage techniques, as well as concepts such as juxtaposition, appropriation, and manipulation of existing images, to name only a few.

Exploring Scale and Forced Perspective

Invite students to use the camera feature of their device to play with scale and perspective by positioning an object or themselves in the foreground and another object in the background to create an optical illusion that renders the skewed perception of forced perspective. For example: introduce the concept of positive and negative space in abstract sculpture. Ask students to create small-scale, colorful paper or cardboard sculpture with forms and openings. The students then find a place in the school where they could imagine their sculpture could be installed in a large scale. Ask the students to collaborate with their peers to photograph the sculpture using the concept of forced perspective to play with scale. They can include themselves in the photograph (see Fig. 7.1).

158   A. PILON

Fig. 7.1 Amalia Iliacopoulos and Alysson Valery-Archambault: Paper sculpture and forced perspective

ONE-POINT PERSPECTIVE AND SELF-PORTRAIT

Invite students to photograph a hallway in the school in one-point perspective. Then ask students to draw the hallway on a separate piece of paper using linear perspective and shading pencils to render the drawing. Students then photograph themselves in the same corridor and use the Pic Collage application to integrate themselves into their drawing (see Fig. 7.2).

SITE-SPECIFIC PUBLIC ART INSTALLATIONS

Invite students to imagine public monuments to be installed on the school grounds. Discuss the process of proposals and funding for site-specific public art and the purpose of public art monuments. Students make small-scale monuments with plasticine, paper, and paint. They photograph these in class and then photograph the proposed site. Finally, students can use the Pic Collage app to integrate the images (see Fig. 7.3).

7 INTEGRATING TRADITIONAL ART MAKING ...   159

Fig. 7.2 Myah Argento: One-point perspective drawing and selfie

Still Life Compositions

Set up a variety of objects on a table and shine spotlights on them to accentuate highlights and shadows. Invite the students to re-arrange the objects and lighting in their own style to emphasize a particular object and dramatic effect with the lighting scheme. Next, have the students take photographs of their arrangement and convert them to black and

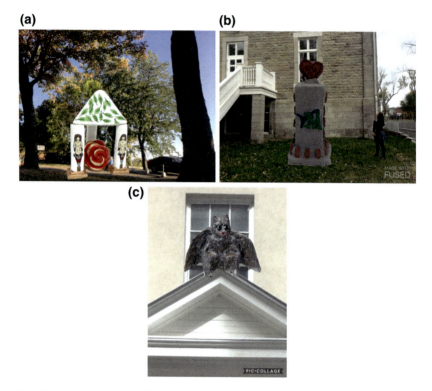

Fig. 7.3 Adrianna Paris Fumai: Monument to mother nature (**a**), Sofia Tiseo: Monument to mark the last year our school would be an all-girls school (**b**), Sofia Melatti: Gargoyle (**c**)

white using the editing tools on their iPad cameras. Finally, have the students create drawings inspired by their own photographs using charcoal and white pastels on gray paper. The advantage of using the iPad camera is that students can more easily see gray scale, shadows, and shading. They can also crop in on the objects of their choice and observe details more closely by zooming in on their photographs. This project worked particularly well at Halloween when I used scary masks and props with dramatic lighting.

Creative Advertising for Stylized Chairs

Students create stylized models of chairs with cardboard, found objects, and recyclable materials. They then photograph the models and create an advertisement using a background image appropriated from the Internet. They can add a slogan and use an app like Pic Collage or Phonto to integrate all the elements. The example below shows a student's hybrid artist's chair made with small canvases for the seat and back, and pencils for the legs and armrests. She created a product name and slogan then used an image of an art gallery as the setting for the chair. She chose a font style, color scheme, and composition techniques to create her advertisement (Fig. 7.4).

Photo-Essays, Thematic Images

Invite students to take photographs and create a photo-essay to represent their likes, dislikes, friends, places, or images of things they see that they think others might not notice. Have students explore unusual angles, create abstractions by cropping images, or use filters and tools

Fig. 7.4 Kristina Nahas: Hybrid chair advertisement

to alter colors. Next, ask students to organize their images stylistically to give an overall sense of unity. Ask students to explain their artistic choices and technical processes in a written text. This project is particularly effective for students who have great ideas and want to express them, but struggle with drawing skills. As an example, one such student skillfully represented his idea of certain aspects of the school by photographing hallways and close-ups of objects he found. He arranged them by selecting images with similarities and juxtaposing them in a grid. In this way, he was able to represent a unique expression of how he saw his school.

Electronic Art Portfolio

Invite students to create an electronic portfolio that allows them to document their work. Ask students to photograph their exercises and projects, to record the date, materials, subject, and art concepts that were explored. Ask them to include an artist's statement at the end of the year. This helps them to use art vocabulary and to identify and articulate what inspires them to make art. The electronic portfolio integrated into the school platform, PowerSchool Learning, continues to be one of the most useful tools I use in my teaching practice today. It is a great way to share their work with parents and to document their progress over time.

Reflection: What Does the iPad Do that Traditional Tools Don't?

Digital mobile devices can be used to complement traditional art making tools and media. The wide variety of online tools available to students makes it possible for art teachers to adapt standard art methods to such platforms. Mobility enables students to view and respond to each other's artwork anywhere at any time. When students use their favorite devices and apps and share their work with their peers, they become participants in a learning community. Digital platforms facilitate the adaptation of projects for students with special needs. While I continue to explore the positive aspects of teaching and learning with mobile technology, the fact is that digital mobile devices have benefits and drawbacks that continue to pose challenges.

An important benefit of digital technology is the way it quickens the pace of certain activities such as searching images for inspiration.

However, it changes how students use the school's resources. For example, in the past when students were asked to search for images in art books it might have required a trip to the library; now, a quick Internet search opens up the world of art images in an instant. This not only saves time and it also provides opportunities to learn to distinguish between good Internet sources and unreliable ones. Another way students use online resources is for ideas and inspiration. However, I have found that students sometimes use and imitate the first image they find on Google images. In doing so I wonder if students are less likely to use their own imaginations and discoveries to inspire them. Additionally, I find it difficult to observe their process as they work. In my opinion, it is necessary to encourage students to learn how to access inspiration from within in addition using of images from the Internet to inspire them. While I encourage students to draw from their imagination and observation, I also allow them to use online drawing tutorials. Finally, creating my own tutorials and demonstrations and posting them online is a strategy I use to give students access to content outside the classroom.

As an art teacher, I need to be adaptable when incorporating new digital technologies into their art classroom. To be adaptable is to remain open to an ever-shifting range of possibilities within the realm of digital mobile technology. I believe that digital mobile devices should emphasize the mobility aspect and should be exploited as such. Mobile technology can be used for creativity and collaborative practices. Social media applications can provide a space that will allow students to share art images and ideas with each other and develop a sense of responsibility in what they share publicly. Thus, art education can become an integral part of an online learning community, enabling students to build their artistic identities and to explore and share ideas with others.

Although I first saw the mobile device as a nuisance and a distraction, I now have a new appreciation for what it can do as a creative medium. My learning experience has taken me from a position of resistance to the acceptance of digital technology as a classroom tool, while remaining aware of its inherent challenges. The experience is an ongoing process as the curriculum evolves through trial and error toward what works best in my classroom. For any given project, I must assess whether there is value added in using mobile devices and digital technology rather than traditional methods to achieve the desired creative goals and learning objectives of the project.

CHAPTER 8

The New Point and Shoot: Photography Lessons Using Phones and Scanners

Sabrina Bejba

Photography is one of the most universal forms of visual expression. Yet, many schools do not have the funds to purchase equipment for a traditional photography program, which would include wet-lab darkrooms or digital SLR cameras. The purpose of this chapter is to share how to develop photography lessons using digital technology that is already available within most secondary schools—smartphones and scanners.

The goal of these lessons is to encourage students to see their smartphone as an art tool. By including technology that is more accessible to students, the art lessons become more approachable. This chapter will describe art lessons that use photography and showcase various examples of student work. For example, I will write about a lesson where students photograph objects that are important to them while focusing on symbolism, lighting, and composition. Another example is a lesson where students learn about perspective and angles by creating surreal scenes and photo illusions. I will also share a lesson about how students experiment with composition, texture, layers, and depth when digitally scanning arrangements of objects. Finally, I will share how students learn

S. Bejba (✉)
Educational Consultant, Mikʷ Chiyâm Arts Concentration Program, Montreal, QC, Canada

about framing, angles, and pacing by creating short stop-motion videos with varied materials and their smartphones.

Many students in secondary school are naturally drawn to photography—whether they are uploading selfies or following fashion trends on Instagram. Through the pedagogical projects presented in this chapter, I share how art teachers can use everyday practices to transform the way students view and use their devices to share, curate, and communicate.

FACILITATION NOTES

Access—Survey your students before beginning these projects—do not assume they have access to a mobile device. Ask students in advance to make sure their devices are charged and have enough memory space. If a student does not have a device consider group work or have a spare point and shoot camera or iPads that students can borrow.

Group Work—Many of these lessons favor group work to promote collaboration and to ensure that there is enough access to mobile devices. Each group should have at least one to two members with a functioning mobile device with a camera feature.

All of these projects can be adapted for students who prefer to work individually. If a student is regularly absent, I usually ask them to do their own project and adjust the guidelines.

Timing—Each lesson is adaptable and the order of the activities can be switched. Each lesson can be expanded into a full unit of study or shortened to be more of a skill-building activity.

Uploading Photos—Set up a system that works best for your class. Students can use Apple AirDrop, USB drives, upload their digital photos onto Google Classroom or even e-mail them to you. Students should never leave the class without uploading their photos just in case the files are deleted or lost.

Smartphone Applications (Apps)—Many of these lessons can be further enhanced by the use of mobile Apps. Since my students had a wide range of devices and operating systems, I decided not to prescribe specific apps. However, if you are requiring students to use a certain app, make sure it is easy to use on all devices, it should be free and does not take up much storage space on their smartphones.

Prints—I have noticed that some students have a hard time engaging with photography for an entire unit because they miss the tactile quality of more traditional art-making materials. Printing the students' photographs helps to make the process more tangible and shows evidence of what they have been doing in class. Set up a display area to hang the prints. Students can work on mounting the photos and even creating a booklet. You can even design a lesson around drawing, painting, or sewing on the prints. Printing images from a colored printer that allows you to print on various sizes of photo paper is the most convenient way since students can select the sizes themselves. You can also get them printed at a local photo printing center.

Photo Walks—Bringing students outdoors is a great way to engage students to see their environments differently and also provide them with fresh ideas. Taking photos in class can get old fast, so even a field trip to the school's science lab or library can open up a new realm of possibilities.

Lessons

Still-Life Self-Portraits (*4–5 class periods—75 minutes each period*)

Secondary level students are often asked to create self-portraits in art classes. Identity is a popular theme in art education, but I have found that sometimes students are weary of creating representations of their faces. This lesson asks students to explore the intricacies that make them who they are by asking them to think of the objects that best symbolize their unique characters and backgrounds.

Materials to Prepare

- Set up a buffet of miscellaneous objects on a large table or shelf area—should be in a spot where students can linger around while they choose their objects (shells, stuffed animals, hats, skull, mirrors, glass containers, etc.—consider including objects with reflective surfaces)

- A selection of fabric, bristol board paper, cellophane rolls, or large sheets of tissue paper for students to use as backdrops.
- Flashlights—if not available, students can use the flashlight function available on their phones—if the class has windows or lamps, turning off the overhead lights can allow the flashlights to create interesting shadows.

1. **Introductory Activity** *Miscellaneous Object Buffet*
   - Divide the class into groups of 3–4 students.
   - Each student takes turns choosing an object from the table.
   - Ask students to combine their objects into an interesting photograph—they must take at least 8–10 photographs—challenge them to change the *framing*, *lighting*, and *arrangement* of the objects slightly with each photograph.
   - Encourage students to change roles (photographer, lighting crew, object placing, background adjusting).
   - Each group selects the top 5 photographs and uploads them to the class computer or online platform.

2. **Inspiration**:
   Slideshow of still-life images: Show images that contain a variety of objects in one composition (e.g., Vanitas Paintings—often have a mixture of objects that are used to symbolize different aspects of life and death).

   At each image of the slideshow—ask students to imagine:
   - What kind of person would collect these types of objects?
   - What occupation might they have?
   - What type of personality would they have?
   - Does the background give us any hints about this person?
   - Which objects act as clues—symbols?
   - Does the placement influence us? Does the lighting affect how we read the image?

   Vocabulary: symbolism, lighting, composition, framing, angles, background—write these words on a poster or handout and review their meaning. Ask students to use at least one of these words in their responses to the images.

3. **Group Reflection: Group Still-Life Images (from introduction activity)**
   - As a class review the images from each group and ask the students to select which of the five images is the most striking—talk about why this image stands out using the vocabulary words.
   - List 3 characteristics that would describe the owner of these objects—ask students to point out which clues lead them to these characteristics.

   Example: "I think this person is serious because the lighting is dim and there is a dictionary with a pair of glasses on top."

4. **Brainstorm**
   - Students can create a mind map exploring what aspects of themselves they would like to include and list objects that could symbolize those characteristics. Mind maps are a great way to write ideas in a diagram structure where lines/branches are drawn to connect ideas and inspire new ones. Aspects students can explore: culture, interests, fears, inspirations, goals, wishes, personality, etc.
   - Ask students to bring in a few objects to the next class so that they can make their own still-life portraits that reflect different aspects of themselves.

   Note: Safety and appropriateness of objects—discuss what kind of objects are allowed in class. This is based on the rules, regulations, and cultural norms of your school.
   If students forget to bring in an object they can search their pockets, bags, or lockers for inspiration or use the objects from the Miscellaneous Object Buffet. Objects as simple as shoes and a sweater can be arranged in interesting ways.

5. **Project**: <u>Self-Portrait Still-Life</u>
   Once students have selected their objects, they should photograph the arrangement. Encourage students to circulate and help each other, by holding backdrops and flashlights, and offering advice. It is a great way for students to see what others are creating and provides instant peer feedback during the process.

Review Project Guidelines:
- Objects—at least five, should be varied and connect to different aspects of the student
- Placement—challenge students to arrange the objects in a few different formations
- Angles—experiment with birds-eye view, worms-eye view, close-ups, etc.
- Lighting—use flashlights or natural light effects to highlight certain areas/objects
- Background—ask students to experiment with at least 2 different backgrounds
- Practice photos—student should submit all the photos they took to show how they experimented with the different elements—at least 10
- Final Photo—select 1 final photo that best represents themselves

6. **Individual Reflection**
Each student can answer these questions in writing or verbally during a one-on-one check-in with the teacher. I usually ask students to answer at least 4 questions.

- Describe how each object connects to a different aspect of you.
- Does the placement of the objects connect to you in some way? How?
- Why did you choose that background?
- How did you use lighting to emphasize or hide objects?
- What is your favorite part of your photograph?
- What did you find most challenging? What helped you work through that?

Stop-Motion Animation (*7–10 class periods—75 minutes each period*)

The magic of stop-motion animation can be highly engaging for students. It is a technique that combines series of photographed objects being moved in incremental amounts between each frame. When the stills are combined, the object appears to be moving independently. This technique is rewarding but it takes practice and patience. Since stop-motion animation has many

> technical elements to consider, I usually ask students to use ready-made objects to animate rather than clay or drawings so that the focus is on the photography and motion—not on their drawing or sculptural skills. This approach makes this lesson accessible for many ages.
>
> To facilitate the experience, I usually ask students to animate letters and or words. This helps students understand how to properly sequence images and helps the group to have some natural structure without needing to go over plot outlines and create characters. Students can incorporate these elements if they wish, but it does not become the focus.
>
> *Of all the lessons, this is the most challenging to complete individually because the objects need to be moved between each photograph. However, I have had some students complete them independently—they are asked to compete fewer words.*

Hook Activity: Alphamation (2 classes)

This is a short lesson that asks the entire class to work in small groups to animate multiple letters of the alphabet to create one video edited by the teacher.

TO PREPARE

- Create a prototype example of a 30–60-second stop-motion animation using still photographs.
- Baskets of materials available in multiples (markers, beads, feathers, buttons, etc.).
- Bristol board paper, large sheets of tissue paper, or fabric for backgrounds.
- Tripods—students can make their own using chairs, thick wire, and rubber bands.

There are many free stop-motion apps available. If you would like students to use an app give them time to download these in advance and ensure the app is available for different mobile devices that the students have (e.g., Android, iOS).

Inspiration

Share the 30–60 second-stop-motion video that you made and ask students:

- Why do the objects appear to be moving on their own?
- How do you think this was made?
- How many photos do you think it took?

Share with the students the photos you took to create the animation to explain the process.

Hook Activity-Alphamation

- Divide the class into groups of two to three
- Write the alphabet on the board and assign each group a range of letters example: *Group 1: A–C, Group 2: D–F, Group 3: G–I, and so on.*

The number of letters each group gets will depend on the number of groups in the class.

If 26 letters are too many, consider spelling out a word or a short phrase instead and divide the words amongst the class.

- Each group chooses a set of objects for each letter—students can use drawing as well if they wish—the goal is that each letter is created with different materials.
- Students animate the letter by making it appear and/or disappear in 10 or more photos.

Teaching Tips

I try not to give them too much direction for this activity because I want to encourage them to experiment and see what works best for them. All I emphasize is that they move their objects in small increments between each photo. What I share with students:

- More photos = smoother movements in the animation.
- The photographer should stay still as much as possible, especially if they are not using a tripod.

- Make sure you can finish a letter before starting to photograph. [I find that if they continue the same letter the next class the lighting and positioning will most likely be different.]

Reserve time for students to upload photos to the class computer or to the online shared class folder. E-mailing this many photos is challenging as it can overwhelm your school's e-mail server. Students can upload photos after each letter/word.

Project: Inspiration Animation (6–8 classes)

Building off the hook activity, students work in small groups to animate a positive phrase. The materials/movements used to animate each word should connect to the theme of the phrase or meaning of the word. (Example: Friendship can be painted on two hands that join together in a handshake.)

Preparation

Compile the students' photos from the class Alphamation and create a stop-motion animation of the alphabet in order. Include upbeat music and credits.

***Note: Some of the letters might be missing due to late arrivals but it's important to still show the Alphamation at the beginning of the next class so students can reflect on what they accomplished. Students who did not submit their work will still be able to learn by watching and reflecting with the class.

Reflection

View the class's Alphamation at the beginning of the class.

Ask Students

- Which letters stood out the most?
  (You can replay and pause each group's section so the class has time to highlight 1 letter per group so each group feels accomplished.)

- What made these letters stand out?
  (Creativity of the movements, use of materials, transitions, etc.) Playing the video multiple times is helpful for students to notice details.

Inspiration

At the end of each class (while students are wrapping up), show a stop-motion animation video that uses objects paired with sound to offer students different examples of how to animate.

Project Steps

- Divide students in groups of 2–4 students (can be the same groups as the Alphamation if they worked well together)
- Ask students to choose a positive phrase—around 5 words.
- Brainstorm—Students write each word from the phrase and select a material that connects with the meaning of the word or the theme of the phrase, for example, Reach for the Stars
  1. Reach = hands reaching each hand could have a letter on it
  2. For = made up of cotton balls on a blue background to look like a sky and clouds
  3. The = gems or paper stars
  4. Stars = a string of lights that spell out the word stars

Note: Words like "for" and "the" can be written with materials that connect with the theme of the video/phrase since they aren't associated with a more specific meaning.

If students are having a hard time choosing a phrase, they can choose a song that they like and think of a short phrase from that song—should still be inspirational/motivational.

Project Guidelines

- <u>positive phrase</u>—approximately 5 words
- <u>30 photos per word</u> minimum
- <u>Materials</u>—each word should be made using a different material that connects to the words/theme of the phrase
- <u>framing</u>—including only essential elements in the background, using bristol board, fabric or tissue paper on flat surfaces

- focus—photos should be clear and sharp
- movement—smooth incremental movements—use tripod for steadier shots

Once students have most of their words planned out, they can start photographing them. The goal should be to photograph 1–2 words per class minimum.

Early Finishers

- can animate their names to create animated credits for the end
- research inspiring animation videos and list them on the board for the class to watch later (teacher should approve the videos first).

Editing

Preparation

- Reserve the computer lab for at least 3 classes to do the editing.
- Make sure all the computers have the software required.
- Save the images on the school server or an interface like Google Drive. You can also save their images on USB keys (if possible have 1 USB key per group)—make sure to collect the USB keys at the end of each class—students should be saving their files on the key and the computer server as backup.
- Label the USB keys with the name of the group (can be the title of their video).

Demonstrate

Class 1
Demonstrate:

- How to import the files into the editing software—I used Windows Movie Maker because that was what came standard on the computers at our school but there is other software such as iMovie which is great and sometimes more intuitive.
- How to change the timing of the photographs.

- How to rotate, delete, and duplicate photos.
- How to SAVE (show this at the beginning and the end of the class).

Note: I avoid getting students to crop or edit their photos because it is very time consuming and the cropping is hard to keep consistent, so the movement becomes choppy.

Class 2
Demonstrate:

- How to import sound/music—Note: Encourage students to use creative commons licensed music on SoundCloud if they wish to share their video beyond the classroom. Students should write the artist's name in their credits.
- How to include credits.

Students should edit their video and make decisions as a group. It can go faster if each student has their own computer and edits a word each and combines the videos later.

REFLECTION

I often have students complete a written reflection after this project. It's helpful for the early finishers to have something individual to work on. I ask students to respond to the following questions:

1. Why did your group choose this phrase?
2. How do the materials connect to your phrase?
3. What would you like viewers to feel or think when they see your video?
4. What were the **challenges** of working as a group and what were the **successful parts** about working with others?
5. Which word was your favorite? Why?

Video Screening

Reserve a period where the entire class gets to see all the videos from each group. If the students have done well working in groups and staying on task, I will make them popcorn!

Before the screening, talk with your students about how to give positive feedback. Ask some of the groups to review some of the challenges and successes they had so that students are reminded that each group had to work through to find solutions.

Students can fill in a review card for each animation they view:

Student Reviewer: _____

Title of Animation: _____

Most Successful Word: _____

Explain Why: _____

Adaptation: If you have access to multiple viewing devices, you can upload the videos on computers, iPads, or even on YouTube and students can watch the videos in small groups and fill out their reflection cards. This can be helpful if students are uncomfortable with the entire class viewing the project at once.

Scanography (*1–2 Classes*)

This technique allows students to put down their phones and learn how to use a scanner to capture unique still-life photos. Scanography is very similar to the traditional photogram—where students, in traditional wet darkrooms, would lay objects on photo paper under the enlarger and expose the paper with light creating a graphic shape and transparency-based composition. In this modern adaptation, students use a scanner to create their compositions. This project can be a short activity to introduce students to using objects to create compositions or even expanded to a larger unit where students can create a series of still-life self-portraits. It is also great for students who finish their other project early and need a new tool to experiment with.

The benefit of using scanners is that students can experiment with placement in a real-time way. When the objects are scanned,

> they are instantly turned into a 2D image on the computer. Since students do not have to consider different angles, close-ups, etc. the focus becomes about composition, framing, and layering. This allows students to reflect and move the objects slightly to create new arrangements.

To Prepare

- If possible, bring in a few scanners. I was usually able to get a maximum of three scanners in a class at a time. Any flatbed scanner should work—even the ones on the top of printers.

Note: If you are only able to get 1 scanner you can use this activity in conjunction with another project so that not all the students need to wait to use the scanner. If possible, place the scanner in a large closet where students can turn off the lights intermittently without disrupting the other students working. Or use cardboard dividers to block out the light.

- Make sure that each scanner is connected to a computer so that students can see their scan immediately after they press the button.
- Set up the scanners away from areas with too much light.
- Set up a buffet of materials that have no sharp edges that could scratch the glass of the scanner—can also try to use a clear plastic or clear film over the glass.
- Slideshow of scanography examples. Some scanography Artists: Maitha Demithan, Hercilia Lopes, Thomas W. McDonnell, Diane Kaye, Christian Staebler www.scanography.org or search #scanography on Instagram.

Inspiration

- Show examples of scanography—ask students how these images were made.
- Ask each student to hand you a small object from their bag—no larger than the palm of your hand—as the students bring up the objects have them sit it on the glass of the scanner.

- Once all the objects have been arranged, turn off the lights and press scan—do not close the scanner lid (you can do one with the light off and one with the lights on to show the difference in contrast).
- Show the students the image and discuss how the parts that have direct contact with the glass are more in focus than the other sections
- Clear the scanner—take your hand and move it slowly as the scanner is working—ask the students to predict what will happen to the image.

Steps

- Divide students into groups of 2–3 (depends on how many scanners are available)—this lesson can also be done individually—students can take turns using the scanners—while they are waiting they can be working on arranging their objects.
- Students can create a composition with the objects in the class or ones they bring from home or their pockets.
- Encourage students to take at least three different versions of each object arrangement—they should be moving the objects around after they look at the scanned image.
- Printing—ask students to print at least one of their photos and display the images in the class or hallway—other students will be curious about how these images were made and it will spark some interesting conversations.

***Note: Some examples online show faces being scanned—I would avoid this… but if you choose to allow students to do so at least ensure the student has their eyes closed.

Photo Illusions (*1–2 Classes*)

Artists, like magicians, have the power to make everyday scenes seem surreal. This activity will ask students to explore their environments and present it in a way that distorts reality. I prefer to teach this activity when there is an opportunity to bring students outdoors. Since these photos often need quite a bit of space—even moving to the gym to photograph can inspire new ideas.

To Prepare

- Buffet of materials: toy cars, dollhouse, fruit, wooden letters, basketball, etc.
- Handout with images that show photographers using scale and angles to distort our perspective (I use a handout so students can refer to this even if we are outside of the class).

Steps

- Distribute the handout and ask students how they think these images were made.
- Explain the different elements that need to be considered when creating a photo illusion (see below).
- Divide students into groups of two to three.
- Ask students to select objects from the object buffet (they can trade objects later).
- Students should create at least three to five different photo illusions.
- The first photo illusion could be done in class and then the class can move outdoors for more space.
- Circulate and help students problem-solve some of their ideas.
- Collect images—students can e-mail the top five images—consider printing them for the next class.

Tips to Making Forced Perspective Photographs (can be typed on the handout with the images).

- **Scale**—use distance to make certain objects seem smaller or larger than they really are—consider including a teammate in the photo
- **Placement**—overlap objects or make them touch to create the illusion of objects interacting
- **Environment**—consider the background and elements that might already be there—like a tree or basketball net
- **Humor**—create images that are silly and have fun!

Joiners (*1–2 Classes*)

It is very common for a student to take one photo and say, "I'm done!" The following project is great to encourage students to take multiple photos of the same subject and experiment with different angles and distances. It is also a great way to ask students to manipulate prints and see photography as a more tactile medium. For this activity, I often ask a friend to photograph me for the example I print out for the students. The reason I use myself as a subject is that I am someone the students are familiar with, which helps them to imagine remixing a familiar subject while also giving them control over an image of me that lightens the mood of the class instantly. Showing that you can be vulnerable by having your picture taken and manipulated makes students more open to doing the same.

To Prepare

- Take multiple photos of a subject (at least 15)—can be a person, object, or scene (take photos from multiple angles and varying distances (e.g. for a portrait of a person—photograph close-ups of eyes, hands, hair, shoulders, T-shirt logos, then back up to get shots of legs, arms, entire face, etc.).
- Print multiple sets of each photo—can vary sizes of the prints—4×6 to 8×10
- Divide sets of the photos into ziplock bags or folders—include some doubles of the same images.

Steps

- Show a few images of joiners/photo collages (Artist Reference: David Hockney)
- Ask students how they think they were made—it is fun to try to count how many photos there are
- Hand out a set of the printed photos prepared in advance
- In groups of 2–3 students overlap and arrange the photos together to create a large collage—students can fold the printouts if they

want—having doubles of the same photo allows students to repeat images they like or flip them to make them appear new
- Gluing these images can take a while so if you have a limited amount of time photograph the final layout to preserve the collage—this also makes it easier to repeat this lesson for multiple class groups.
- Students can walk around and see how different each collage is even though the photos that were taken were all the same.
- Students choose a subject—a person in the class, objects or the environment around them.
- Encourage them to take at least 10–15 photos from a variety of angles and distances—encourage them to crop the image into different close-ups and move around the subject to get a range of perspectives.
- Print the photos for next class and ask students to assemble their own photo collages.

Conclusion

Many students use mobile technology for communication on a daily basis. Sometimes the attachment to these devices are seen as distracting. I do not think the solution is to ignore or ban phones in classrooms. We need to teach students how to manage these devices to work best for them and enhance their education. These lessons encourage students to take a break from seeing their phone as only a way to update their status. The goal is to encourage students to see their phones as mobile art tools. Having your phone in your pocket can be the equivalent to walking around with a paintbrush. Art in my opinion, is mostly about communication. So, it is only fitting that we teach students how to use their primary tool for communication as an artistic tool for creation.

CHAPTER 9

Visual Mapping Workshop: Materializing Networks of Meaning

Lina Maria Moreno

There are multiple ways to understand how images and their meanings are interconnected. For instance, most high school students who have participated in MonCoin use hashtags to link different images in their social networks; it is a way of making connections. However, there might be other possible ways that could help them to expand their ideas. This chapter describes a visual mapping workshop that took place during the first iteration of the MonCoin project where students were invited to look at the connections between their pictures by creating a visual map with their pictures rather than by scrolling down their feed or using hashtags. Building this map helped them visualize their interpretations, their peer's interpretations, and the connections that emerged in between them. This workshop is helpful for teachers implementing a project like MonCoin in their classrooms and more broadly seeking to engage their students in reflections and conversations beyond the screen (Fig. 9.1).

L. M. Moreno (✉)
Research and Development, Mikʷ Chiyâm Arts Concentration Program, Montreal, QC, Canada

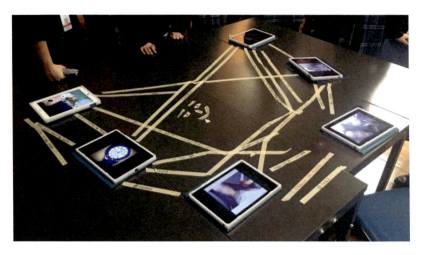

Fig. 9.1 Students create a map and look at each other's connections

TALKING ABOUT IMAGES

Visual mapping stems from "Talking About Images," a master's thesis in art education at Concordia University where I researched visual mapping as a tool for making connections, facilitating conversation, and fostering thinking in art classrooms, all of which enable groups of students to build complex interpretations around images. The workshop begins with quiet and individual reflection and then transitions into a group exercise. Visual mapping allows students to find new meanings with a set of images, in this case, images from their MonCoin feed. These meanings come from seeing their peer's interpretations and how they connect to their own. Thus, students build meaning beyond their interpretations of an image.

This workshop was structured on work by several art education scholars who advocate for teaching practices where students can build personal and embodied interpretations of artworks (Barrett, 2000; Hubard, 2007; White, 2011), rather than learning prescribed ideas or methodologies to think and talk about art. In this workshop, students have a chance to build their interpretations and to do so in a peer-connected environment where they can extend those interpretations further. Rather than striving for unanimity and a single prescribed way of understanding, they map the abundance of ideas—visually—that their pictures generate making visible the many different voices in the room. The map helps students to see their peers' ideas and how those ideas link to their own. While doing this, the group can arrive at new interpretations that no individual student would have thought possible. A networked map of interpretations like this one allows for multiple ideas, all valid, to be held in equal importance rather than centralizing one image or way of understanding, which allows multiple students to bring their knowledge to bear on an image and to see their knowledge in relation to each other's.

Drawing Connections

The workshop also builds on the idea that mapping is a performative exercise where knowledge is not just being represented but is also constructed as the map comes to be (Ruitenberg, 2007). The materiality of this map helps students to visualize their thoughts as they take shape, comment on other people's ideas, see how someone's thoughts affect someone else's. Since maps are free from the inherent linearity of text or narration, it allows viewing all the multiple perspectives at once generating a decentralized structure (Davis, Sumara, & Luce-Kapler, 2007). In this case, they are a tool to dislocate the chronological linearity of posts on social media platforms like Instagram or Facebook.

The workshop took place after the second session of the MonCoin project in a private school in Montreal. All the students in the school had an iPad that they used as their agenda and calendar, to communicate with teachers, and to view and submit homework through a platform called Haiku. Since students already had mobile devices and used them in their school work, it was advantageous to our project as it allowed us to give instructions to everyone at the same time. Additionally, they were all familiar with the Haiku platform that we were using to post pictures for the MonCoin project.

The students had already experienced the advantages of using Haiku content management system. However, Haiku's design emphasized communication between students and teachers but did not necessarily create a peer network where students could easily see the work that their classmates were posting. Unlike Instagram where users regularly see what other users post, in Haiku each student had a separate folder to save their work; their classmates' work was several clicks away. Thus, the visual mapping workshop was a useful tool to generate opportunities for students to explore a networked form of viewing and allow them to see each other's images in a nonlinear way. In other words, the lack of peer-to-peer communication on Haiku created the need for a networked and embodied viewing experience in the classroom (Fig. 9.2).

The previous week, during the first MonCoin workshop in their school, the students had explored the mission "Identity" and learned how different formal elements of photography could help to express different aspects of someone's identity. They were invited to post images during the week responding to the micro-missions "With myself," "Valued Possession," and "Origin," which were all concerning the larger mission "Identity." The day of the visual mapping workshop, the students came to class with pictures responding to these three micro-missions.

The workshop was about 45 minutes long, and the students worked in groups by the tables they were at. To begin, each student selected

Fig. 9.2 Students map the formal, emotional, and conceptual connections they find between the pictures

one picture from the micro-missions on "Identity." They displayed their chosen picture on their screen and followed the instructions to lock the screen (to prevent it from turning off or changing the image). They each left their iPad on top of the table for everyone in their group to see. Each iPad displayed the picture they had chosen to share with the group.

With their images displayed on a table, we encouraged them to quietly begin looking at their peers' images and thinking about the formal, emotional, and conceptual connections they found between the pictures. Once someone thought of a connection, they would take a piece of masking tape, paste it on the table making a line between the two images, and write a keyword on the tape to show what connections they had made. These connections could be based on common shapes, colors, ideas, and feelings that they found between the pictures. We guided students with questions like What do these images make you think of? How do they make you feel? What do they seem to be narrating? Most of the ideas that initially emerged when the students were working by themselves were detailed observations on the pictures' formal qualities: "Both are made of gold," "Both are smiling," "they are blue," "black and white," "strings and flowers" (Fig. 9.3).

When each group was ready, they gathered around the table with one of the MonCoin facilitators to talk about the connections they had made and think about what they noticed in what others did. As students talked, we "taped" to the table any other connections they mentioned to make all the thoughts visible as they discuss. For example, if a student was describing two photographs that seem to be divided into two opposite parts, like showing duality, we placed a line of tape on the table connecting the two images and wrote the word "duality" on the tape.

We also encouraged the groups to find new connections between their connections. First, they had been looking at each other's images, and then, they had moved on to looking at each other's interpretations, trying to find connections between them. As the group began discussing what they had seen, different symbolic or metaphorical meanings emerged as well. For instance, the link "They are blue" that they had made between a blue rubber watch and a bed with a blue duvet became "blue I wake up." They found a connection between the blue color of the watch, the sound of its alarm, and the feeling of waking up blue. Although the interpretation involves two pictures from different students, it is relevant that the connection written on the tape is written in first-person singular, "Blue I wake up," almost like a poetic statement

Fig. 9.3 The first connections are observations on the pictures' formal qualities with notes like "Gold" or "String + Flower"

about a shared experience. It was essential to allow the space for students to collect concrete, seemingly meaningless, interpretations and to allow the time for these interpretations to be revisited, which invited more voices, that gave rise to more complex ideas. This progression enabled the possibility of finding richness and depth within the formal elements in the pictures and the life stories they represented (Fig. 9.4).

Afterward, the students were invited to walk around the tables noticing similarities and differences between the maps each group of students created. They used bright green yarn to create a new kind of link, this time marking the connections between each table. They stood in a

Fig. 9.4 Links become more complex as students look at each other's interpretations. The link "they are blue" that the students made between a blue rubber watch and a bed with a blue duvet became "blue I wake up"

circle around the classroom and passed the green thread around creating a web around the room that linked their interpretations in different ways. For instance, they noticed that one of the tables had a map full of connections around the theme of family history while another table was also talking about heritage but from a global perspective by bringing in symbols from their family's place of origin.

Visual and Material Layers of Meaning

The visual mapping workshop brought in the intentional unfolding of the virtual space of the screens onto the physical space of the classroom in a nonlinear configuration. The pictures were no longer displayed chronologically one after the other or grouped with a hashtag. The mobile qualities of the devices the students used allowed them to take and post pictures from different places and at different times. The mapping workshop, on the other hand, allowed them to translate this mobility into movement and connection in the classroom and a material relationship with their images, ideas, and the classroom's space. Seeing each other, which was already at the core of their social media practices, became then a material and intentional exercise that helped them to understand what they saw tangibly, become aware of their interpretations, visualize how different ideas were related and arrive at new and more complex interpretations bringing to the surface layers of meaning that were underneath. The map was a materialization of the peer thinking and learning that is at work when students see each other's images.

Emphasizing spatiality rather than temporality resulted in a less hierarchical organization of ideas. In this way, the map did not fix on any one student's perspective, nor the teacher's perspective, and nor a single artwork but the relationships between them all. Besides, students were allowed to make meaningful choices in terms of what images they would like to take and to share with the group on and offline (Fig. 9.5).

This visual mapping workshop could have been pertinent at any point during the MonCoin project. As an icebreaker exercise, it could have been helpful to get students comfortable with seeing and commenting on each other's posts. It could have been used as a tool for reflection midway through the project. It could also be a meaningful wrap-up exercise where the students look back at the work they have done during the project, hear responses from their peers, and find possible connections between their posts at the beginning and toward the end of their participation. Teachers can always adapt this workshop to emphasize different aspects of the project; for instance, they can create a map using only images from a specific mission or pictures that respond to a question or theme. Even more, this wrap-up exercise could be a point of departure to begin brainstorming for art projects following MonCoin.

Fig. 9.5 Each map's configuration reflects the peer-thinking and learning that is at work when students see each other's images

References

Barrett, T. (2000). About art interpretation for art education. *Studies in Art Education, 42*(1), 5–19. https://doi.org/10.2307/1320749.

Davis, B., Sumara, D., & Luce-Kapler, R. (2007). *Engaging minds: Changing teaching in complex times* (2nd ed.). New York: Routledge.

Hubard, O. M. (2007). Complete engagement: Embodied response in art museum education. *Art Education, 60*(6), 46–53.

Ruitenberg, C. W. (2007). Here be dragons: Exploring cartography in educational theory and research. *Complicity: An International Journal of Complexity and Education, 4*(1). Retrieved from https://ejournals.library.ualberta.ca/index.php/complicity/article/view/8758.

White, B. (2011). Embodied aesthetics, evocative art criticism: Aesthetically based research. *Studies in Art Education: A Journal of Issues and Research in Art Education, 52*(2), 142–154.

CHAPTER 10

Conclusion: Heeding Enchantments and Disconnecting Dots—A Sociomaterialist Pedagogy of Things

G. H. Greer

INTRODUCTION

A group of students participating in the MonCoin project began a walk around their school to take photographs, initially with very little enthusiasm. Lina Moreno, educator and research assistant, was familiar with the high-quality photography previously produced by one of the students and was surprised by the general lack of engagement in the group. At one point, that student stopped at an unexpected spot, looking at some letters on a door. Moreno encouraged the group to stay in the area instead of moving on, in order to allow the student to engage with the door. The student noticed that a close-up shot of some of the letters formed an image of her name. There was a small moment of excitement that passed from the engaged student to the others in the group, who came over to look at the letters themselves. Each then began to take pictures of the letters, first the same close-up shot and then trying different combinations.

G. H. Greer (✉)
Concordia University, Montreal, QC, Canada
e-mail: gia.greer@concordia.ca

© The Author(s) 2019
J. C. Castro (ed.), *Mobile Media In and Outside of the Art Classroom*,
https://doi.org/10.1007/978-3-030-25316-5_10

Moreno reported this experience as one of transformation: "Frustration that becomes something else; that's a moment of learning. There are two things: the frustration becoming not frustration and the group becoming more cohesive." First, one student moved from boredom to interest and began to produce images, and then this engagement spread through the group. Moreno was also affected as an educator. She moved from prompting a reluctant group, to intentionally holding the group in a space to wait for student engagement, and then stepping back to allow a single student's interest to take a fuller form that became involving for the entire group. The group moved through an encounter together, and transformed from an assembly of disinterested individuals to a cohesive learning collective.

The goal of this chapter is to achieve a theoretically and experientially informed understanding of the kind of learning in the anecdote above. Conversation with MonCoin educators and researchers is a method here for reading educational theory and teaching experiences through each other. The experiential, or practical, component of this endeavor is informed by dialogue with the art educators of MonCoin. The chapter is structured around quotes that arose in conversation with the MonCoin research team. These quotes are used after each heading to give an anecdotal sense of the concepts in each section. The theoretical portion grows out of the sociomaterialist theories of political theorist Jane Bennett (2010) and sociologist Bruno Latour (1991, 1999, 2014, 2016) and is informed by the previous scholarship of MonCoin's principal investigator Juan Carlos Castro (2007, 2012, 2013, 2014, 2015). The remainder of this introduction will provide definitions for "sociomaterialism" and "learning", and outline the structure of this chapter.

Sociomaterialism is the broad theoretical basis of this chapter, and the work of MonCoin. To review, the definition of sociomaterialism here is the capacity to acknowledge the ways that both humans and non-humans (such as places, things, and ideas) affect and are affected by social processes (like learning). Sociomaterialism represents a shift away from what education scholars Tara Fenwick, Richard Edwards, and Peter Sawchuk (2011) refer to as "the centring of human processes in learning" (p. vi), toward a fuller account of the effects of materiality, including "tools, technologies, bodies, actions and objects… texts and discourses" (p. vi). Complexity theory, actor–network theory, and vibrant materialism are a few of the more specific systems of ideas referenced in this chapter that fall roughly under the umbrella of sociomaterialism. Sociomaterialism is characterized by the following views of reality: bodies emerge in relation to one another (rather than existing prior to relationships); networks of relationships form assemblages that operate collectively rather than (or as well as) individually; and nonliving materials are active rather than inert in social processes (Fenwick et al., 2011; Fenwick & Landri, 2012). Thus, emergence, collectivity, and materiality are hallmarks of sociomaterialism.

Fenwick et al. (2011) treat learning as: "transformation that expands the system's potential range of action" (p. 29) and "the contradictory yet relationally patterned ways (the form) in which a relational configuration of actors and artifacts mediate interaction with the world" (p. 67). According to complexity and curriculum theorists Brent Davis and Dennis Sumara (2006): "learning can be understood more explicitly in terms of the continuous process through [which] knower and knowledge are simultaneously redefined in relation to one another" (p. 155). These definitions have in common the aspects of change or transformation and encounter or relation. Form-shifting that arises from the meeting of bodies and things is also a major theme of Jane Bennett's vital materialism. Bennett (2010) describes a vital or generative force of nature: "a process of morphing, of formation and deformation, that is to say, of the becoming otherwise of things in motion as they enter into strange conjunctions with one another" (p. 118). Transformation and encounter are also apparent in this account. Although Bennett is not intentionally referring to learning processes, this description serves here to frame learning as a generative force that is not necessarily confined to human experience.

A synthesis of the above explanations brings us to the working definition of learning in this essay, which is the process of becoming otherwise through encounter. Put differently, when people, or things, change because they meet another person or thing, that change can be called learning. Where all changes that come from meetings or relationships are considered learning, it is important to remember that not all learning is inherently good. For example, a child who develops a fear of dogs after being bitten has learned something that may be useful in some circumstances, and unhelpful in others.

This chapter is organized around these two components of learning processes: *encounter* and *becoming otherwise*. The next section, *a vocabulary of learning encounters*, explores some ways that bodies can come into relation with each other in three subsections, focused on: *attraction*, *arrangement*, and *disconnection*. The following section, *becoming otherwise*, addresses transformation. This change from one state to another is the factor that determines whether or not an encounter can be called learning, while particular qualities of this change dictate whether a given instance of learning is productive. I conclude with a discussion of pedagogy or teaching methods. How can teachers support our students to learn in a transformational sense? This final section relates: first Watson and Plymale's (2011) previously developed constructivist *pedagogy of things*, and a sociomaterialist iteration of the same phrase. The practices of MonCoin educators, discussed throughout this writing, are examples of, what I call here, a sociomaterialist pedagogy of things.

A Vocabulary of Learning Encounters

It is a complex phenomenon: the sights, the sounds, the smells, the whispered conversations, the prior history of interactions between students. All of those conditions give rise to certain movements and adaptations, which I would say in the language of complexity, is learning.—Juan Carlos Castro, principal investigator

A vocabulary of learning as a material encounter can be formed from the three points explored in this section: the drawing together of forms through enchantment or thing-power (Bennett, 2010); the various network formations that such encounters might take (Castro, 2013, 2015); and the importance of disconnecting particular formations of encounter (Latour, 2016). The subsections below outline these theoretical approaches to encounter, supported by relevant selections from conversations with MonCoin researchers.

Enchantment and Attraction

The students kind of discovered something and became a group. They were all taking the exact same picture. Everyone felt like they needed to take it themselves. Everyone had to try it and then after that they were trying other things.—Lina Moreno, research assistant

As reflected in the common phrase "learning material," the use of objects and artifacts to prompt pedagogical engagement and attract learner attention is not new. In conversation, Castro recalled the work of art education scholars June King McFee and Rogena Degge (1977), and curriculum theorist William Doll Jr. (1989) as a reminder that sociomateriality has always played an important role in theories of education. Similarly, MonCoin researcher, David Pariser, discussed the nineteenth-century Swiss educator Johann Froebel, who created a series of geometric wooden solids as educational gifts for children. Modern classrooms are full of educational manipulatives, like tangrams and base ten blocks, intended to attract students toward physical experiences that give rise to learning. Teachers have been employing the enchanting power of things since the time of slate and chalk, if not well before.

What, then, might be "new" about the "new materialisms" that have prompted a renewed focus on sociomaterialism in academia and other educational settings? In answer to this question, Castro refers to the onset of the Anthropocene, an epoch defined by the effects of human-made materials such as plastics. A large-scale re-evaluation of the feedback loop between human action and the material world is underway. The majority of the world's scientists concur that humans have irreversibly impacted the natural environment. In turn, the environment has been impacting humans for some time with poisoned air and soil, and the onset of global climate change. This context emphasizes the relevance of a number of theories, or ways of thinking, including complexity theory, deep ecology, and indigenous ways of knowing. Among these, Bennett's (2010) vibrant materialism is an attempt "to counter the narcissism of humans in charge of the world" (p. xvi). Bennett's work builds on the critical idea that humans must adjust our ways of co-existing with non-humans in order to ensure our mutual survival. Beyond this important message, Bennett's focus on the attractiveness of things is useful and accessible in educational contexts.

Enchantment, according to Bennett (2010), is a drawing together of bodies in processes of affecting one another. "Body" is a word used by Bennett and other scholars to talk about humans and non-humans that affect each other. Affect theorists Melissa Gregg and Gregory Seigworth (2010) define bodies "not by an outer skin-envelope or other surface boundary but by their potential to reciprocate or co-participate" (p. 2) in exchanges of feeling or affectedness. Encounter is prompted by enchantment when things produce a "strange combination of delight and disturbance… [which]… might augment the motivational energy needed to move selves from the endorsement of ethical principles to the actual practice of ethical behaviors"

(Bennett, 2010, p. xi). In an educational context, enchantment can be related to a willingness to learn. Enchantment, or the way that people and things are drawn to other people and things, may move students from disengaged states toward readiness and from readiness toward transformation. An otherwise mathematically unengaged student who demonstrates numeracy skills during hobby activities, like role-playing games or knitting, is an example of enchantment or attraction that motivates learning.

The enchanting power of objects was used by an art teacher in the MonCoin project in an activity involving a prop box. Students were divided into six groups, each with access to a different set of objects from the box. The groups were instructed as a team to make one arrangement of things and take three different images, which should vary by scope, angle, and lighting. The objects set a mood, which in turn affected the composition and lighting. For example, the group with the skull produced black and white images in a dramatic noir style, while another group created brighter photographs affected by the presence of flowers. Unique networks of students, props, lighting, and cameras gave rise to unique creations. Research assistant, Moreno, reported that the class who took part in this activity seemed to get to a better quality of image faster than other groups. This learning appeared to be more immediately impactful than the same information conveyed, without objects, to individuals rather than groups.

MonCoin educators reported many ways that students and their photography were affected by surrounding spaces and materials. Pariser described the ways that students shifted in the presence of gym equipment:

> The gym was interesting because it was a familiar place associated in their minds with physical activity. I remember that the mood sort of changed. The vibe was different than elsewhere. The students did this whole thing with a goalie net. They just sort of had some fun with it and they took some pictures related to that.

Similarly, research assistant Bettina Forget noted particularly abstract and artful images that came from a group of students responding to broken windows. In the context of art education, there seem to be endless possibilities for student learning in response to enchantment or thing-power (Bennett, 2010).

The relations or spaces in between things, including human things, are at risk of being overlooked as relevant learning conditions when they are left unexamined. Enchantment is one way of describing such relations. Bennett calls for humans, "to find a more horizontal representation of the relation between human and non-human actants in order to be more faithful to the style of action pursued by each" (p. 98). According to Latour (1999), an actant is a human or non-human that is part of a network or collective because it affects the things around it. In the above quote, Bennett reflects that materiality cannot be contained by language, and so coming to know enchantment requires attention to the non-linguistic calls of reality. Observing the ways that students learn from objects, in and outside of art rooms, is an endeavor toward such attention. Just as Castro observed: "*In that mix, in that network if you will, of individuals, their writing, and their images, that's where learning registers.*" Noting that there is a connection or enchantment between things is the beginning of observing this relationship.

Materialist pedagogy, or teaching methods that account for the agency of things, is to a large degree a matter of curating enchantments. In conversation, Castro recalled his high school teaching experience, and the way that students who sit next to each other in art class produce similar work. The students' attentions are drawn to each other. A powerful teaching tool is the ability to direct student attention in this way and to some degree affect the enchantments formed. Examples of attention curation in teaching include seating particular students near helpful peers (or away from unhelpful ones) and selecting art to be included (or excluded) from classroom displays.

Teachers cannot control all the factors that enchant student attention. We can only create conditions that may give rise to enchanting encounters. In offline educational settings, Castro noted that the direction of attention is a function of power and circumstance. Teachers hold authority, although power also operates through policies and curriculum that dictate which learning materials students may or may not access. Restrictions on sexual health curricula are a common example of power affecting the possibilities of student attention. Circumstantial factors that direct student focus include: weather, noise from nearby construction, a bee in the classroom, student hunger or lack of sleep, and so on. Teachers negotiate these interconnected relationships of potential enchantments in order to direct learning processes.

This complex web of relations and nodes is referred to in this writing, as a "learning network." Drawing on Latour's (1999) definition of the term "collective" (p. 304), a learning network here is an association of humans and non-humans, organized around the process by which bodies become otherwise through encounter. Such networks are present in all instances of learning, although this writing focuses mainly on those within schools and school-related mobile learning contexts.

The MonCoin project used social media platforms to register and record the encounters and connections that gave rise to learning. Examining the nuances, in real time, of the encounters that arise from enchanted attention could include transcripts of classroom dialogue, maps of educational displays, curriculum documents, records of weather conditions, and endless documentation of various factors depending on how broadly the network is defined. This wide view of relations becomes an information problem. The use of educational social media can filter this potential glut of data. Instagram and the similar Haiku platform used in MonCoin serve to both define and record encounters or enchantments between students, other students, and student work. This narrower bandwidth of information around learning, enabled by social media interactions, is a constraint that makes it easier to record and visualize learning networks. The following section relates the forms and shifts of some of these networks.

Network Formations and Arrangements

> You have the dynamics between friends, and you have the table dynamics, and the classroom dynamics, and all of these are different bodies that are learning in different ways, and creating new connections. Also, culture and all of that is bleeding into it. So, when you ask a student how they learned something, definitely there are individual instances of transformation, but the collective is also a huge part.—Ehsan Akbari, research assistant

The context of mobile learning makes the delineation of networks apparent in particular ways, some of which are explored below, along with lessons learned about the impact of algorithms on learning networks in mobile media research.

In previous work, Castro (2013, 2015) has described a method for visualizing the decentralized networks of online art education spaces. Using an educational social media platform to track view counts and responses to images, Castro developed visual representations of online interactions between art teachers and their students. Individuals, their images, and image themes were represented by points or nodes.

Interactions formed links between these points. In this way, nodes with many links became easily recognizable as hubs of interest and activity. Graphic representations, called sociograms, illustrated these networks of attention in various formations.

Sociograms of learning interactions enable educators to identify major sources of enchantment or hubs of attention. Factors such as "likes," views, and comment exchanges can be represented visually, by scale, numbers, or lines. According to Castro (2015), attending to hubs in learning networks allows researchers to understand the "organization and structure of how attention and learning happens not only among individuals, but also as a collective" (p. 26). In this way, we can observe what is attracting student attention and what is being ignored. For example, in Chapter 3, Pariser and Forget use sociograms to indicate classroom social hierarchies and to illustrate the degree to which networks in the physical world and in the digital world mirror each other. Mapping these interactions also enables discussions of the impact of student-produced images, regardless of the student maker's social status. Recording online and mobile interactions allows researchers to tabulate specific and measurable observations of learning. It can also be a useful exercise for educators to consider, or estimate, network formations of learning based on offline interactions. Online or off, using sociograms to visualize the collective learner, enables foci and omissions of attention to become visible.

All measuring instruments must be accounted for in the results they produce (Barad, 2007). Similarly, the mobile media-based sociograms used in the MonCoin project yield particular kinds of observations about learning. In previous work, Castro (2013, 2014) has noted the unique character of social media interactions, related to the timing of communication, increased audience, and geographic reach, as well as the tendency toward homogeneity in the content conveyed. Research assistant, Bettina Forget noted: "*It was interesting to see the 'alternative group' reach out to another 'dynamic duo' that they don't usually associate with, but online there were other associations forming.*" Learning as observed through mobile media requires a different engagement with time and space and offers uniquely context independent insights. Learners interact online differently than they might in a strictly physical classroom.

Investigations of sociograms enabled Castro's (2015) in-depth discussion of the difference between centralized, distributed, and decentralized networks. A classroom where the teacher stands at the front and mediates all other interactions would be an attempt to create a centralized learning network. The teacher represents a central hub, and the students are each individual nodes connected primarily to the teacher. Most teachers can attest that, even in classes that are planned as centralized networks, the actual form of interactions is more distributed, involving at least some student to student interactions. Distributed networks have very few to no hubs. Information passes more independently from node to node. A classroom that is organized to operate as a distributed network would involve a lot of group work and peer-evaluation. Over time, the nodes of distributed networks often become favored or avoided. Students become attractive and unattractive connection points for each other in a variety of ways; some are more entertaining, or know the right answers reliably, or have some other form of social or literal capital. As multiple hubs form, networks cease to be distributed and become decentralized. In short, a centralized network has one hub, a distributed network has none or few hubs, and a decentralized network has several hubs.

Art education research has at times presented a dichotomy between centralized and decentralized learning networks (May, 2011; Sweeny, 2008). This binary frames teacher-centered, centralized classes as hierarchical with passive learners, while student-centered, decentralized classes are seen as active and democratic. With good humor, Akbari states of this binary that in classrooms *"reality disproves such things."* According to Castro (2015):

> a decentralized art education is called for to address oppressive pedagogy by essentially creating a space for open reciprocal relationships between learners, teachers, and content. However, decentralization, especially when it involves the Internet, does not promise a more democratic classroom. (p. 2)

Learning networks that are planned to be either centralized or distributed often become decentralized in practice. For planned centralized networks, this can lead to a lack of anticipated control, and for classrooms planned as distributed networks, the result can be an unexpected emergence of hierarchy and hegemony.

An example of an attempt at control by way of centralized network occurred during the MonCoin project, when school board information technology professionals refused to allow students access to school

Wi-Fi. This example shows that learning networks are not solely bound to exist within classrooms. Wherever individuals seek access to information, there are networks of connection that enable, disable, and affect the form of learning possibilities. The school board attempted to create a centralized learning network, whereby students might access the Internet strictly through authority figures who held Wi-Fi passwords. Educational activities, including the MonCoin project, were no exception to the student Wi-Fi ban.

This attempt at centralized control was thwarted as most students owned phones and maintained access to cellular service within the school, as well as surreptitiously obtaining the password and sharing it among themselves. The main effect of the school board's refusal to provide Internet access was not to stop students from using the Internet, but to ensure that the Internet was used by students mainly to access information that was not school related. With the permission of school administration, the MonCoin research team was obliged to fund hotspots for students to access the Internet during class time.

Another example of a shifting network in the MonCoin project involves a distributed network that was made less accessible by the creation of decentralized hubs. This occurred when Instagram changed its algorithm in the middle of one of the MonCoin iterations. Students' images had initially been posted chronologically and were thus easy for other students to locate and interact with. When the proprietary algorithm changed its programming of photo streams, Instagram began to organize images around predictions about which pictures would best capture individual student attention based on the student's online behavior. This change meant that some students' work was no longer accessible to the group.

The examples related above complicate the binary view that frames centralization as hegemonic and distribution as democratic. The school board's attempt at centralized control did not stop the students from accessing the Internet in a distributed fashion, and yet this distributed access was not particularly productive or democratic. Use of the Internet was mainly not educational. Neither was it distributed equitably. Students attained covert access through unsanctioned use of the Wi-Fi password, by being able to afford a phone, and having the skills to avoid getting caught. Decentralizing the network did not create equity or democracy.

In the second example, researchers relied on the Instagram algorithm to enable a distributed network. Algorithms, and other factors which may at first appear to be neutral or benign, can affect learning networks in unexpected ways. It is important to note that this change was made visible by the happenstance of occurring mid-iteration. The hubs created by algorithm-predicted interests may have gone unnoticed, or been misinterpreted, if they had not emerged while the photo streams were being observed. Unforeseen factors, like dominant personalities or barriers to task completion, can shift the shape of learning networks on and offline. However, proprietary algorithms, the operations of which are determined by undisclosed, trademarked programming, have particular potential to convolute online research.

Where learning is defined as becoming otherwise through encounter, an algorithm that tailors content toward students' existing taste may prevent the transformative engagement with difference required for desirable learning. Further, algorithms have the potential to reproduce and amplify bias. According to mathematician and data scientist Cathy O'Neil (2017), "algorithms are opinions embedded in code" (11:28–11:30). Similarly, Akbari states that "*these programs have the capacity to imitate humans but not the capacity to examine the holistic effects and consequences of the processes they perform.*" Castro (2014) has drawn particular attention to the lack of diversity and homogeneity that arises from computer-coded presentations of content. Attention-curating algorithms direct Internet users toward highly trafficked sites without necessarily judging the quality or accuracy of the content they promote.

Algorithms greatly affect the presence and absence of hubs in online learning networks. Castro explained the method by which algorithms exacerbate patterns of dominance and marginalization online:

> Likes beget likes, views beget views and so hegemony is constructed through social attention. It's a compounding effect that amplifies; actually, it's a mathematical concept in decentralized networks. If a lot of people are clicking on this link, it must be important. That doesn't mean it's correct or of value, but it must be important.

As described above in the section on *enchantment*, teachers curate learning by directing student attention toward information that we hope will give rise to learning. Algorithms, on the other hand, are often designed to monetize user attention through advertisements. Skillful teachers present content and relationships that enable skill acquisition, critical thinking, or exposure to diverse perspectives; algorithms, on the other hand, frequently direct attention in ways that will prolong the time a user spends online, regardless of the content consumed or connections formed.

Akbari noted with some concern that despite being labeled as "digital natives":

> Students don't know how their data is being used or how the algorithms work. Students are being used and manipulated in significant ways. And that's getting worse. That's getting codified... I don't think the use of technology in schools is something that empowers students automatically on its own.

Teachers play a very important part in guiding students to navigate the Internet, according to Akbari, by *"creating a space where adults, and youth, and youth culture can meet and have a conversation."* Educators can be guides during such conversations, regardless of whether it is the teacher or the student who possesses more proficient skills with technology.

Dialogue between youth, youth culture, and adults, as Akbari mentioned, can positively impact the content and relations of learning networks. Teachers can benefit from understanding student strategies for subverting centralized networks to evade control on the Internet. This information is not only useful for reinforcing centralized control where it may be needed, but can also reveal student needs and skills in ways that may encourage teachers to reconsider when and whether centralized networks are appropriate. In turn, students can be made less vulnerable online by understanding the goals of algorithms that curate their attention. Binary approaches to digital and mobile media, which frame the Internet, and other decentralized networks, strictly as a source of danger or liberation, can interfere with these positive outcomes.

The experiences of the MonCoin project show that learning networks, which are planned as either centralized or distributed, may shift inadvertently to become decentralized or take on other forms. Unexpected actors like algorithms, access to cellular service, and individual personalities can prompt these shifts. It is important to attend to the context of network formations in order to adapt to unanticipated developments. In the end, it is the nature of networks to shift, and so centralization and distribution on their own are not reliable teaching strategies. Accounting for learning materials, content, relationships, and individuals within networks are also important factors for impacting student development.

This subsection has discussed the arrangement of learning networks: sociograms as a way of recording and observing learning relationships; variations of network forms; and the curation of attention by educators and algorithms. Equally important to the arrangements and curation of learning networks is the ability to acknowledge the absence of a network. The following subsection discusses the stakes of misconstruing networked relations. How can teachers enable learning by discerning between networked connections that yield insight and those connections which are best left unmade?

Dots Disconnected

When we look at the view counts and likes and the images by students that are being attributed as influential. I'm always, always surprised that what they pick is vastly different from what I would say is quality. At first, I thought, "this is just a function of the fact that they don't know what good work is. You know, I have a BFA in photography, I've been a practicing artist for blablabla," and then that got me thinking that, well, no, maybe they know something that I don't. Maybe I've been enculturated into a way of thinking and knowing that comes out of a certain power-relation structure. They have to be enculturated in order to value what you value. I think that's one of the biggest changes for me, going from being an art teacher to a researcher. Just to take a step back and say, "okay, the students are really excited about this." So I have to value that first and foremost, you know, I can't squash that because that kind of excitement is important, more than what you think is "good art" or "bad art." Always, that is always happening.—Juan Carlos Castro, principal investigator

I include the above longer quote here, because it reflects a powerful example of learning that can occur when points that may appear at first to be part of the same network are examined further and allowed to remain disconnected. This chapter subsection attends to the possibilities of learning that can arise from strategically non-networked relations.

In the anecdote above, Castro unmakes the connection that automatically attributes a mentor-mentee relation to teacher-student interactions. Rather than viewing himself as an expert that is a central point of reference to naive student learners, Castro acknowledged that art educators and our students meet each other from within our own separate learning networks. In so doing, he makes space for student strengths and insights and enables a critical view of the extent to which his own expertise may arise, at least in part, from unexamined acceptance of cultural norms. Productively, this disconnection led Castro to further reflect on his own enculturation. By abstaining from imposing his own understandings onto student preferences, Castro exercised a tolerance for cognitive dissonance and gained new understandings as a result. Resistance to connection in this learning network supported Castro's own ability to become otherwise.

In the terms of actor–network theory, Latour (2016) states that "the problem is precisely to try to not connect the dots, that is to not immediately think an ecosystem is part and whole" (1:17:28–1:17:37). The perception of networks of causation can be obscured by the false characterization of interactions. Latour (2014) gives an example of misleading network connections made as part of a discovery narrative. Where one body is said to have discovered another, the network that actually gave rise to the discovered body becomes difficult to perceive. A large-scale example of this is the distortion of indigenous histories and peoples of North America as a result of the discovery narrative involving Christopher Columbus. Many textbooks distort histories of North America by beginning at the time of colonization, despite the cultural traditions and organizing governments that have existed here for millennia. The discovery narrative interferes with the perception of networks of causation.

Small-scale examples of distorting discovery narratives occur in classrooms when teachers treat students as "blank slates" or claim to "discover" student potential. In Castro's anecdote above, the ordering principles of student aesthetic values could have been obscured by a dismissive characterization of their poor taste. When it acts as a convoluting force, the concept of discovery is posed as spontaneous emergence within a single network. Reframing discovery as an encounter event between two networks leaves space for the networks of personal histories and experiences that students bring to their own learning. Rather than *discovering* student deficits, Castro *encounters* an alternative set of values.

As observed by research assistant, Bettina Forget, teachers are not the only ones who make unproductive connections within learning networks:

> You know with students in the classroom, they look at you [the educator], trying with X-ray vision to look inside your head and anticipate what you

want. I think the [MonCoin] missions are designed to counteract that a little bit. Trying to make it as much about them as possible, so that they can come up with material that we could not have sketched out for them.

In school settings, student learning is often determined by outcomes. The skills required to achieve these goals are intended to arise from learning. In this way, outcomes are often framed as proof of learning. However, if there is more than one way to reach achievement, students will surely choose the most convenient route. When education is delivered as a series of outcomes without context, desirable learning is jeopardized. If it is easier for students to determine teachers' preconceptions of creativity, students may abandon the inventions that lead to learning. Thus, the precise design of learning outcomes is essential.

According to Castro, the missions given to students during the MonCoin curriculum are designed so that:

> individuals can reference prior histories of experience, but also evaluate those prior histories as an experience, and engage with what's in front of them in order to re-evaluate and look at it. It's a lot about making the familiar strange. Taking the reflexive response to a stimulus and troubling that by taking the really familiar and expanding outward.

In one mission, for example, students were asked to take selfies, a familiar activity, but given the instruction that they must not show their faces. Compared to typical selfies, this activity prompted a variety of more complex expressions of self.

Castro referred to this method of directing student attention in Chapter 1, and it arose repeatedly in conversations with MonCoin educators, as "constraints that enable." In previous work, Castro (2007, 2012, 2013) has discussed constraints that enable as the conditions which help students to be productive versus those which do not. Castro resists the term "enabling constraint" in order to acknowledge the variability of student responses. The constraint itself is not enabling, but holds the potential to enable within specific interactions with particular students. Effective constraints must create tension for students between structure and openness, and familiarity and unfamiliarity, much like Vygotsky's (1978) proximal zone of learning. As was the case in the faceless selfie assignment, constraints in curricular design can involve removing the most direct routes between students and outcomes. A missing connection within a learning network could serve as a constraint. The absence of an easy answer may enable students to activate creative thinking.

Each of the MonCoin researchers discussed methods of leaving space for students to form their own learning relationships. Moreno and Forget both relayed experiences of waiting in different locations with student photographers in order to allow students to become engaged with their environment and to make their own connections as part of creative processes. Of such moments Forget recounted: "*I want to step out of the way and be invisible as much as possible. I want to get out of the students' way,*" and Moreno stated that "*there was openness as to what the results were going to be.*" Similarly, Pariser talked about engagement with students as curiosity and allowing students to act as guides.

Reflecting on the MonCoin project, and the need to allow students to make their own learning connections, Castro recalled that space and flexibility around student engagement are structured into mobile media art education practices by asynchronicity and ubiquity; possibilities for student engagement are literally outside of linear time constraints and available everywhere. In the context of mobile learning, time and space are made explicit as material factors in the formation of learning networks. Students can interact when they are ready, at any time and from any location. Castro frames the time between classroom instruction and online student responses as a productive increase in what teachers often refer to as "wait time," the silent moment that allows students to think after a question is asked. Opportunities for student engagement are increased in this way, by enabling a unique combination of student readiness with the omnipresent accessibility of devices, like mobile phones, that register learning.

The preceding three subsections have explored encounter as a component of learning, addressing the impacts of learning bodies that draw together and form networks, and the possibilities of curating learning through the enchantment of attention and network disconnections. The goal of this discussion has been to initiate a vocabulary of learning encounters. Continuing with the concept of learning as encounter that enables transformation, the next pertinent concept is on the result of learning encounters: becoming otherwise. The following section discusses the distinction between more or less desirable cases of becoming otherwise, and employs sociomaterialism as a lens for registering changes.

Becoming Otherwise

> What was more sort of nebulous was when you have a mission like "what I make," or "take a self-portrait without showing your face," you also have some sort of idea of what could come out, but the beauty is that you don't know. You're looking for the instances where students will come up with something you could not even have conceived of. That is so awesome, because then you know that they've learned something.—Bettina Forget, research assistant

This section begins with an illustration of a learning process in the MonCoin project through a sociomaterialist lens and concludes with a discussion of the distinction between desirable and unproductive learning. The concepts of emergence, collectivity, and materiality, which characterize sociomaterialism (Fenwick et al., 2011; Fenwick & Landri, 2012), are used here to enable recognition of learning as a transformation.

Emergence is a term in complexity theory that references the continual adaptation that occurs within self-organized systems. According to Fenwick et al. (2011) "Knowledge (e.g. new possibilities, innovations, practices) emerges along with identities and environments when the system affords sufficient diversity, redundancy and multiple feedback loops" (p. 12). There are many approaches to the concept of emergence among education scholars. Some pose "emergent and enacted" against "represented and acquired" (p. 18) knowledges. The purpose of this distinction might be very roughly translated as similar to Freire's (2005) critique of the banking concept of education, in which students are treated as receptacles for pre-formed ideas. When knowledge is emergent and enacted teachers learn with students, their learning is unpredictable, and their relationships come into being along with a distinct dynamic as a learning collective. Discussing emergent learning, Castro stated that *"learning and expressions of such give rise to a collective learner."* He has explored this idea in depth in Chapter 1.

Emergence can be used to describe the ways that Moreno's group of students, in the anecdote at the start of this chapter, moved from an unmotivated collection of individuals to an engaged collective. The group began their walk with an assignment or mission, but without any other set criteria. A process of adaptation began when one student in particular became interested in the letters on the door, and Moreno gave this student time to investigate her interest. The instigating student experimented with different angles and image frames which enabled emerging possibilities, innovations, and practices. As the engagement spread throughout the collective the environment shifted, for the group, from boring to interesting, and the student's identities changed from cool and disinterested teenagers to engaged novice photographers.

During this activity, the students' energy adjusted as a collective. The student, who was known to Moreno as an engaged photographer, initially conformed to the lack of enthusiasm in the group. Collectivity is evident again when the interest sparked between this student and the letters on the door spreads through the group. Educators, who have managed behavior concerns by arranging which students sit where, are intuitively aware of collective potentials. For better or worse, the dynamics that arise between students are as powerful in the learning process as those that originate within individuals. Accounting for collectivity in learning enables educators to direct these potentials productively.

Materiality also plays a powerful role in learning. Educators who have students who work better or worse when listening to music, and whose concentration is affected by noise or lighting or the proximity of holidays, all have experience with the effects of material on learning processes. How would Moreno's walk have worked without the letters on the door? As Edwards (2012) says: "to make things happen humans are entangled with the non-human or things" (p. 528). Materials play vital roles in learner engagement. Learning collectives include non-humans; emergence includes the unpredictability of materials. In this case, materiality became apparent through the unforeseen affinity between the letters on the door and a particular student's name. The artificial intelligence of algorithms, discussed above, is another example of material actors in learning processes. The renaissance of materialism, as Castro calls it, is relevant here not as a return to modernist illusions of objectivity, or an emphasis on measurable evidence, but rather as a call to attend mindfully to the expressions of non-linguistic realities.

It is important to make some distinctions between the many degrees and multiple modes of becoming otherwise that may be registered as learning by applying sociomaterialist lenses. This entire array of transformations is included here under the umbrella of learning, with the important caveat that not all learning is impactful, productive, or without harm. In schools, teachers aim to enable particular kinds of transformations. We want students to develop skills and hopefully to more broadly enable a general good. It is important to distinguish between learning networks that lead to desired outcomes and those which do not. In this writing, desirable learning enables bodies to adapt to contexts that are not harmful, and increases the likelihood of students being able to adapt again when needed. Unproductive learning involves transformations that adapt learners to harmful contexts, inhibit possibilities for further adaptation, or create a transformation that fails to create a meaningful impact. Learning may be productive within particular contexts, and not within others, or there may be aspects of an experience that are unproductive while other facets of the experience hold value.

An example of learning with an unproductive aspect occurred during one of the project iterations. Akbari recalled that the team gave too much information during one of the missions. Specifically, students were asked to create "comfortable" and "uncomfortable" images. Akbari noted that framing this mission as a binary was the first issue that limited student creativity. Further, students were given an example image of "comfortable" and "uncomfortable" photographs. In their own images, many students used the same photographic filters as the examples, rather than reflecting for themselves on other ways that the concepts "comfortable" and "uncomfortable" might be expressed. The research team had been aiming for more diversity and variation in student responses. However, the examples drew a connection for students between comfort and sepia tones, and between discomfort and cold, blue light. These connections allowed students to copy a formula, and foreclosed the need for deeper conceptual engagement. In this way, students were able to follow instructions and meet the set learning outcome, without thinking for themselves about unique solutions to the challenge.

Most teachers have developed an array of tools in order to meet the needs of individual learners in varied curricular contexts. In some cases, meeting an outcome is important, no matter the route or the student's retained understanding. This might be the case when a particular outcome is interfering with the more global learning experience of the student, where high stakes testing determines an underfunded school's budget, or if inflexible outcomes have been prescribed to a group of students with a diverse range of abilities. Individualizing programming for gifted or struggling students may involve connecting or disconnecting different sets of knowledge and skills for different students—Tomlinson (2000) outlines some effective differentiation strategies. Learning happens for students as a result of both: the connections teachers make and those that we choose not to make. Barriers to learning occur in the same way. There is no universal formula; however, a harmony can be reached between student needs and the supports that teachers provide. This attunement must also account for whether we want students to deeply and creatively engage with the subject at hand, or just do the thing. For this reason, unproductive learning is defined above as context dependent rather than meeting or missing particular outcomes.

In the "comfortable"/"uncomfortable" example, recalled by Akbari, the research team was aiming for critical engagement that would result in varied student responses. However, students were reaching what was intended to be a creative outcome with overly uniform and conventional images. This lack of diversity may have resulted from student mimicry of the examples or of peers' work, or from predicting teacher preference. The students may have learned, or become otherwise, during this activity; however, the images that students posted were not as diverse as the team had hoped. This aspect of uniformity may be said to represent the undesirable learning, in this context, of reproducing sameness. In terms of the definition of unproductive learning, in this one aspect, the students may have become adapted to the harmful context that teacher approval or task completion is more important than self-expression or experimenting with diverse skills. This understanding could also deter students from further creative adaptations. Most teachers experience some instances when we have to prioritize outcomes over student engagement or creativity. A few incidents of teachers making too many connections for students will probably not make a lasting negative impact. The repeated and sole emphasis on outcomes or teacher preferences over the course of a students' educational career would be greater cause for concern, particularly in contexts where the goal is to develop creative and critical thought.

The capacity of teachers to enable the desirable learning of students is greatly impacted by the ability of those same teachers themselves to learn. The anecdote at the start of the previous section recalled Castro's experience of learning about his own enculturation. Disconnecting students' engagement from his own assumptions about poor taste enabled Castro to adapt to the (harm-free) context of students as experts on their own tastes and experiences. This adaptation set the stage for the further learning that arose from a critical examination of Castro's own tastes. Thus, the transformation Castro described fits the criteria for desirable learning, and furthers Castro's curiosity about the ordering principles of student tastes. Where such curiosity exists, a teacher is less likely to overprescribe set routes for students to meet learning outcomes, leaving space for the students to create their own learning experiences. Similarly, Akbari described the learning of the research team in relation to framing the "comfortable"/"uncomfortable" mission too narrowly as a binary, and in relation to giving example work that the students copied. As noted in his Chapter 6, Akbari reported that through these experiences, the research team realized the value of creating more open-ended prompts to encourage more diverse and personal responses to missions.

MonCoin's curriculum was part of a design-based research methodology, meaning that it was developed over a number of iterations with reflection and adaptation taking place between and throughout this process. Researchers were able to identify areas in need of improvement in the first phases and address these needs later on. In this sense, the project itself became otherwise and, by the definitions of this chapter, the project learned.

For Bennett (2010), the enchanted bodies which become otherwise are never necessarily human. The letters on the door in the opening anecdote of this chapter drew the attention of an otherwise disinterested student and became something other than the name of a room. The horizontal view which enables Bennett to equate the behaviors of humans with the transformations of things is similar to the principle of symmetry in actor–network theory (Latour, 1991) which acknowledges the influential power of both humans and non-humans in processes of becoming. In Moreno's walk with the students, the enchantment of the letters on the door was a form of "non-human agency" (Bennett, 2010, p. 98) that presented "the condition of possibility of human agency" (p. 98). The letters became something other to the student; this in turn supported the transformation of the student from disinterested to engaged, which in turn once again transformed the group dynamic and the art that the students produced.

This section completes the portion of this chapter that is structured around encounters and transformation as components of the learning process. The following section reviews the concept of the pedagogy of things: the history of this idea, a push toward sociomaterialism, and a summary of the ways that MonCoin's educational practices align with these ideas.

Pedagogies of Things

> What moved me along, or my engagement, was very basic curiosity to see what the students would do when this material was presented or when challenges or topics were given. The students were sort of my guides and I got them to articulate what was special about something.—David Pariser, researcher

The pedagogy of things, in this writing, is a way of teaching that attends to the participation of non-humans in the social process of learning. Acknowledging materials in this way draws attention to useful factors that may otherwise be overlooked or underestimated. Sociomaterialism is used here to push beyond surface-level perceptions that treat learners as active agents and the environment as a passive container of observable things. The stories of MonCoin educators draw attention to the ways that shifting non-human presences is reciprocal with the activities of humans. Algorithms are one example of non-human actors that is currently specific to mobile learning contexts. However, such artificial intelligence is becoming increasingly pervasive in everyday life. There are ways in which the involvement of non-humans in social processes is new; however, seeing artificial intelligence as one of many non-human vibrant materials (Bennett, 2010) can help humans to transfer our intuitive and age-old understandings of the non-human world, to mobile media and online contexts.

C. Edward Watson and William Plymale (2011) originally coined the term "pedagogy of things" as a play on the "Internet of things," which refers to the Internet connectivity of non-human devices, appliances, and vehicles. This reference gestures to the potential of technology in educational settings to provide not only student-to-student connectivity, but also to connect students more directly to their environment. The field work of Watson and Ogle (2013) uses a constructivist framework to illustrate the ways that Internet connectivity enables experiential learning.

This chapter adds to, and shifts the focus of, Watson, Plymale, and Ogle's work on the pedagogy of things. To describe this shift, it is helpful to outline four key ways of bracketing learning: first, the individual human experience; second, the social interaction between humans; third, the experience of encounter between humans and non-humans; and finally, an environmental level at which non-humans become otherwise in relation to each other. A constructivist pedagogy of things is concerned with the third category as a way of enabling the first; however, the current writing employs a sociomaterialist approach which emphasizes the fourth. Davis and Sumara (2006) characterize this fourth category as interobjectivity:

> It is not just about the object, not just about the subject, and not just about social agreement. It is about holding all of these in dynamic, co-specifying, conversational relationships while locating them in a grander, more-than-human context. It is about emergent possibility as a learner/knower … engages with some aspect of its world in an always-evolving, ever-elaborative structural dance. (pp. 15–16)

A sociomaterialist pedagogy of things entails the appreciation of interobjectivity in educational contexts. This conceptual move creates space for learners to engage reciprocally with the objects around them, acknowledging that both humans and our environment have the capacity to be active. In this way, sociomaterialism supports open-ended pedagogy which explicitly enables a horizontal relationship, not only between those whom Freire (2005) refers to as teacher-students and student-teachers, but also between people and the world around us.

Any educational setting might be described using constructivist or sociomaterialist terms without a fundamental shift in actual pedagogical practices. The goal of the current writing is not to interpret effective pedagogy through a sociomaterialist lens, with the pretense of linking sociomaterialism to effectiveness. Rather, I hope to have isolated, from the broad range of effective teaching strategies, pedagogies which, like vital materialism, encourage "a polity with more channels of communication between members" (Bennett, 2010, p. 104). Engagement with sociomaterialist theories has enabled MonCoin researchers to identify factors which develop or obscure "a perceptual comportment… [that is] unusually aware of or susceptible to the enchantment power of things" (Bennett, 2011, 15:46–15:54). The MonCoin curriculum is a collection of strategies for engaging productively with these factors.

Like the work of Watson and Ogle (2013), much of North American public school pedagogy is influenced by constructivism. This approach frames learning as an individual construction that arises through individual human experience. In practice, this looks like setting predetermined learning outcomes and enabling experiences that draw students toward conclusions that are already known to educators. This outcomes-focused, or backward design, approach has become dominant for many reasons, which there is not space to explore here. The goal of the current project is not to detract from the variety of valid teaching styles that includes constructivism, but to open a dialogue that encourages the constant growth and revision of the tools teachers employ to support our students. Following Barad (2007), who encourages a move "beyond the well-worn debates that pit constructivism against realism, agency against structure, and idealism against materialism" (p. 26), learning theories are not posed against each other here but build upon each other in dialogue. Sociomaterialism can productively apply constructivist understandings of individuals to broader discussions of networks. This shift does not pose resistance to constructivism, but places the focus elsewhere. Where many constructivist educators advocate for student-centered, experiential learning, sociomaterialism broadens the focus on individual learners, to include learning relationships and collectives.

The pedagogy of things is described throughout this chapter as an emergent, collective, and material approach to learning that attends to enchantments, networks, and productive disconnections. Every day, teachers curate educational spaces by enabling the conditions that are likely to give rise to learning, navigating a plethora of unreliable factors, from passing police sirens to unanticipated student life circumstances. In real life classrooms and mobile learning contexts, the creation of completely predictable educational scenarios is not possible and is therefore not a realistic hallmark of quality teaching. A more sustainable approach to pedagogy includes exercising modes of attention that enable teachers to respond to student circumstances. Such mindful responsiveness can enable the facilitation of flexible learning networks that adjust to ever-evolving student needs. Attending to emergence, collectivity, and materiality is a move toward this kind of flexibility, and also toward the kind of open-ended curriculum that leaves the position of mastery available to students. When educators guide learning in this way, rather than merely serving as sources of information, we become free to wonder along with our students.

References

Barad, K. (2007). *Meeting the universe halfway: Quantum physics and the entanglement of matter and meaning.* Durham and London, UK: Duke University Press.
Bennett, J. (2010). *Vibrant matter: A political ecology of things.* Durham and London, UK: Duke University Press.
Bennett, J. (2011, September 27). Artistry and agency in a world of vibrant matter (recorded lecture for The New School). Retrieved from: https://www.youtube.com/watch?v=q607Ni23QjA.
Castro, J. C. (2007). Enabling artistic inquiry. *Canadian Art Teacher, 6*(1), 6–16.
Castro, J. C. (2012). Learning and teaching art through social media. *Studies in Art Education, 53*(2), 152–169.
Castro, J. C. (2013). Teaching art in a networked world. *Trends, the Journal of the Texas Art Education Association, 2013,* 87–92.
Castro, J. C. (2014). Conclusion: The code we learn with. In V. Venkatesh, J. Wallin, J. C. Castro, & J. E. Lewis (Eds.), *Educational, psychological, and behavioral considerations in Niche Online Communities* (pp. 402–409). Hershey, PA: IGI Global.
Castro, J. C. (2015). Visualizing the collective learner through decentralized networks. *International Journal of Education & the Arts, 16*(4). Retrieved from: http://www.ijea.org/v16n4/.
Davis, B., & Sumara, D. (2006). *Complexity and education: Inquiries into learning, teaching, and research.* Mahwah, NJ: Lawrence Erlbaum Associates.
Doll, W. E. (1989). Complexity in the classroom. *Educational Leadership, 7,* 65–70.
Edwards, R. (2012). Theory matters: Representation and experimentation in education. *Educational Philosophy & Theory, 44*(5), 522–534. https://doi.org/10.1111/j.1469-5812.2010.00719.x.
Fenwick, T., Edwards, R., & Sawchuk, P. (2011). *Emerging approaches to educational research: Tracing the sociomaterial.* New York, NY: Routledge.
Fenwick, T., & Landri, P. (2012). Materialities, textures and pedagogies: Sociomaterial assemblages in education. *Pedagogy, Culture & Society, 20*(1), 1–7. https://doi.org/10.1080/14681366.2012.649421.
Freire, P. (2005). *Pedagogy of the oppressed.* New York: Continuum.
Gregg, M., & Seigworth, G. (2010). *The affect theory reader.* Durham, UK: Duke University Press.
Latour, B. (1991). *We have never been modern.* Cambridge, MA: Harvard University Press.
Latour, B. (1999). *Pandora's hope: Essays on the reality of science studies.* Cambridge, MA: Harvard University Press.

Latour, B. (2014, May 27). *How to better register the agency of things: Semiotics.* The Tanner Lectures in Human Values (recorded lecture for Yale University). Retrieved from: https://www.youtube.com/watch?v=18pYfcbBRL8.

Latour, B. (2016, November 22). *On not joining the dots: Radcliffe Institute* (recorded lecture for Harvard University). Retrieved from: https://www.youtube.com/watch?v=wTvbK10ABPI&t=4582s.

May, H. (2011). Shifting the curriculum: Decentralization in the art education experience. *Art Education, 64*(3), 33–40.

McFee, J. K., & Degge, R. M. (1977). *Art, culture, and environment: A catalyst for teaching.* Belmont, CA: Wadsworth.

O'Neil, C. (2017, April). *The era of blind faith in big data must end.* TED Talks 2017. Retrieved from: https://www.ted.com/talks/cathy_o_neil_the_era_of_blind_faith_in_big_data_must_end?language=en#t-98010.

Sweeny, R. (2008). Unthinkable complexity: Art education in networked times. In M. Alexenberg (Ed.), *Educating artists for the future: Learning at the intersections of art, science, technology and culture.* Bristol, UK: Intellect Books.

Tomlinson, C. A. (2000). *The differentiated classroom: Responding to the needs of all learners.* Alexandria, VA: Association for Supervision and Curriculum Development.

Vygotsky, L. S. (1978). *Mind in society.* Cambridge, MA: Harvard University Press.

Watson, C. E., & Ogle, J. T. (2013). The pedagogy of things: Emerging models of experiential learning. *Bulletin of the IEEE Technical Committee on Learning Technology, 15*(1), 3–6.

Watson, C. E., & Plymale, W. O. (2011). The pedagogy of things: Ubiquitous learning, student culture, and constructivist pedagogy. In T. T. Kidd & I. Chen (Eds.), *Ubiquitous learning: Strategies for pedagogy, course design and technology* (pp. 3–16). Charlotte, NC: Information Age Publishing.

Index

A
Abstract sculpture, 157
Actant, 199
Actor, 9, 36, 37, 49, 50, 104, 111, 112, 205, 211, 215
Actor–network theory (ANT), 8, 9, 194, 207, 214
Adaptable, 163, 166
Addictive Apps, 83
Adolescent's identity formation, 28
Advertisement, 161, 204
Affect, 19, 28–37, 40–44, 84, 109, 117, 130, 143, 168, 185, 194, 197, 199, 203, 204
Affecting bodies, 40, 43
Affection idea, 33, 40, 42
Affective sciences, 30
Affect pedagogy, 36
Affect theory, 20, 28, 29, 36, 38
Algorithms, 9, 200, 204–206, 211, 215
Anonymity, 59, 67, 69, 71, 73, 86
Anthropocene, 197
App-dependent, 84, 85, 91, 92
App—enabling, 84
Arrangement, 111, 159, 165, 168, 169, 178, 179, 196, 198, 206
Art apps, 87, 88, 94
Artificial intelligence, 22, 129, 211, 215
Asperger, 156
Asynchronicity, 114, 209
Asynchronous online connectivity, 106, 111
At-risk youth, 2–4
Attention-curating, 204
Attraction, 30, 195, 198
Autistic, 61
Autonomous ideas, 32

B
Becoming otherwise, 195, 196, 204, 209, 211
Behaviorism, 85
Blended learning, 103, 104, 106–109
Boys, 55, 63–66, 79, 80, 84

C

Centralized learning network, 202, 203
Centralized network model, 17
Civic engagement, 2, 3, 141
Civic spaces, 133, 141, 142
Classroom management, 152, 155, 156
Classrooms, 1, 2, 17, 18, 54, 60, 87, 109, 111, 137, 150, 183, 184, 197, 202, 203, 207, 217
Classroom social connections, 55
Classroom's space, 190
Collaborative learning, 78, 86, 107, 153, 154
Complex interpretations, 184, 190
Complexity thinking, 8, 9, 77, 86
Conatus, 32, 33, 43
Constraints that enable, 10, 11, 22, 77, 78, 86, 208
Constructivism, 85, 216, 217
Constructivist framework, 215
Conversation, 22, 43, 85, 90, 91, 107, 125, 141, 142, 154, 156, 179, 183, 184, 194, 196, 199, 205, 208
Creative arts apps, 85
Creative choices, 69
Critical pedagogy of place, 108, 109
Curator, 50

D

Decentralized model, 17
Decentralized networks, 17, 200–202, 205
Deleuze, Gilles, 29, 31–34, 37, 40, 42, 44
Design-based research (DBR), 18–20, 112, 214
Dialogue, 63, 74, 95, 97, 142, 155, 194, 200, 205, 217
Digital images, 1, 28, 42, 157
Disconnection, 196, 207, 209, 217
Distorting discovery, 207
Distributed networks, 202–204
Drawings, 63, 64, 94, 157, 160, 171

E

Educational space, 104, 105, 128, 131, 147, 217
Electronic portfolio, 152, 162
Embodied interpretations, 184
Emergence, 10, 18, 35, 117, 195, 202, 207, 210, 211, 217
Enchantment, 196–201, 204, 209, 214, 216, 217
Encounter(s), 9, 33, 35, 42, 44, 45, 108, 129, 139, 194–197, 199, 200, 204, 207, 209, 214, 215
Engaging for girls, 81
Essence idea, 33

F

FaceTime, 88, 93
Face-to-face discussion, 155
Fear of Missing Something Important (FOMSI), 83, 84
Food shots, 64
Forced perspective, 157, 158, 180
Framing, 116, 166, 168, 174, 178, 212, 214
Fundamental emotions, 32

G

Game, 10, 41, 67, 77, 80, 82–84, 87–90, 92, 94, 97, 155, 198
Gamer Boys, 50, 65, 67–69
Gender, 63–67, 79, 80, 84, 86, 98

Gender differences, 79, 84
Gender identity, 63
Gender socialization, 80
Gender stereotypes, 78, 79
Girls, 21, 55, 63–65, 67, 68, 77–80
Goffman, E., 20, 48–51, 74
Google images, 1, 12, 163

H
Haiku, 112–114, 153, 154, 185, 186, 200
Hockney, David, 181
Hogan, Bernie, 48, 50, 51, 53
Hogan, Patrick C., 28–31

I
Idealized bodies, 43
Identity, 3, 4, 10, 18–21, 28, 29, 36, 38, 39, 43, 44, 48, 50, 52–54, 59, 65, 67, 68, 73, 78, 79, 82, 85, 86, 111, 149, 163, 167, 186, 187, 210, 211
Identity online, 3
(Im)mobilities, 10
In-class status, 72
Informal and formal learning, 6, 7, 107
Instagram, 3, 6, 38–42, 60, 64, 74, 84, 86, 88, 90, 91, 94, 95, 106, 107, 114, 137, 138, 153–155, 166, 178, 185, 200, 203, 204
Interobjectivity, 216
iPad(s), 21, 87, 90, 96, 112–114, 116, 117, 151–157, 160, 166, 177, 185, 187

J
Joiners, 181

K
Knowledge, 5–8, 10, 11, 19–21, 33, 34, 40, 54, 59, 73, 79, 82, 98, 109, 134, 153, 185, 195, 210, 212

L
Land-based pedagogy, 109
Learning, 2, 3, 5–11, 16–22, 28, 37, 38, 45, 49, 72, 77, 78, 80, 81, 83, 85–87, 93–95, 98, 99, 103, 105–113, 115–117, 120–124, 132–134, 140, 145–147, 149, 151–153, 155, 162, 163, 184, 190, 194–201, 203–217
Learning network, 199–207, 209, 212, 217
Learning styles, 77, 78, 81, 98
Learning to Love You More, 11
Lighting, 116, 117, 123, 153, 159, 160, 165, 168, 170, 173, 198, 211

M
Making visible, 185
Mapping, 7, 20, 34, 110, 185, 190, 201
Massumi, B., 29, 31, 32, 34, 35, 42
Material encounter, 196
Material relationship, 190
Mental well-being of adolescents, 54
Methods of research, 132
Micro-missions, 12, 13, 50, 118, 121, 123, 127, 128, 130–134, 137–147, 149, 150, 186, 187
Mind maps, 169
Missions, 2, 3, 10–13, 21, 63, 78, 81, 85, 87, 103, 108, 112, 115, 118, 123, 124, 127, 128, 130–134,

136, 137, 141, 142, 147–150, 153, 154, 208, 212, 214
Mobile learning (mLearning), 9, 10, 200, 209, 215, 217
Mobility, 4, 5, 8, 9, 19, 31, 54, 113, 162, 163, 190
Mobility studies, 8, 9
MonCoin curriculum, 2–5, 9, 10, 12, 13, 16, 18–20, 22, 29, 48, 50, 53, 54, 72, 103–105, 111, 112, 114, 115, 118, 125, 128, 142, 208, 214, 216
MonCoin research, 18, 20, 48, 194, 203
Motifs, 60, 63, 65–67
Multifunctional, 94, 97–99
My Neighbourhood, 12, 63, 121, 127, 131–133, 136, 147, 148
My School, 12, 63, 118, 120, 127, 132, 133, 144–148
My Surroundings, 114, 127, 131–133, 136, 137, 147

N
Nature, 63, 121, 127, 132, 134, 137–139, 149
Negative affects, 32, 33, 40, 44
Neighborhood walks, 111, 114, 115, 119, 121, 122, 124
Neo-tribal, 51–53
Neo-tribalism, 52
Neo-tribe/neo-tribes, 67
Netflix, 89, 90, 92, 96–98
Networked map of interpretations, 185
Networked photography, 38
New materialisms, 197
Non-linear, 186, 190
Notability app, 152, 156
Notice, 121, 127, 132, 139–142, 147, 149, 150

Notion idea, 33, 42

O
Ocursus, 33
One-point perspective, 158, 159
Online learning, 17, 103–107, 111, 124, 163, 204
Online persona, 73, 74
Online spaces, 27, 103, 104, 107, 108, 112, 116, 118, 124, 155
Online status, 72
Outcomes, 85, 98, 107, 117, 122, 123, 134, 137, 205, 208, 212–214, 217

P
Participatory culture, 6
Paths I Take, 142
Pedagogy of things, 196, 214–217
Peer-learning, 2, 9, 16, 140
Perception, 21, 31, 35, 38, 80, 108, 116, 123, 124, 127, 128, 130, 132, 133, 136, 147, 157, 207, 215
Performance, 20, 48–51, 67, 72, 73, 79, 91, 109, 152
Personalized teaching approach, 74
Phonto, 161
Photo essay, A, 161
Photography, 6, 13, 21, 43, 69, 87, 103, 104, 111, 112, 115, 116, 118, 120, 122–124, 131, 132, 134, 136–141, 144–146, 148–150, 152, 153, 155, 165–167, 171, 181, 186, 193, 198
Photo Illusions, 179, 180
Photo walks, 148, 167
Physical bodies, 27, 33, 43, 44

Physical spaces, 103, 104, 106, 108, 110, 112, 115, 116, 118, 120–124, 145, 190
Pic-Collage app, 158
Place-based education (PBE), 108–110
Positive affects, 32, 33, 40
Post/Respond to a Mission, 12
Post-subcultural, 52, 53
Power School Learning, 162
Preparation, 173, 175
Prints, 167, 181
Pseudonyms, 59, 65, 66, 71, 104
Psychic tax, 84
Psychoanalysis, 29, 31
Publishing, 39

R
Reciprocity, 36, 37, 61, 83, 84, 91, 93
Recognition acts, 37
Reflection(s), 21, 28, 29, 140, 152, 162, 169, 170, 173, 176, 177, 183, 184, 190, 214
Relational space, 110, 111
Ridiculed online, 40
Role of the teacher, 17, 36, 37

S
Scanography, 177, 178
School policy, 111, 115, 124
School walks, 114, 116, 118, 120, 121, 123, 145
Science, Technology, Engineering, and Math (STEM), 78, 80, 86, 96
Self, 12, 63, 133
Self-esteem, 33, 41
Selfies, 1, 4, 39, 41, 137, 159, 166, 208

Sharing, 2, 5, 6, 29, 41, 87, 92, 93, 97, 117, 123, 137, 148, 154, 157, 203
Site-specific public art, 158
Smartphone applications (Smartphone apps), 77, 98, 166
Smartphone(s), 1, 2, 4–7, 9, 10, 20–22, 38, 43, 54, 77, 78, 81–84, 87, 93, 106, 134, 155, 165, 166
Snapchat, 84, 88–94
Social associations, 51, 52
Social interaction, 6, 45, 48–50, 95, 105, 107, 108, 215
Social media, 2, 3, 5, 6, 8–10, 12, 16, 17, 20–22, 28, 29, 36, 38–45, 50, 54, 60, 83, 84, 86, 89, 95, 97, 103, 118, 153, 155, 157, 185, 190, 200, 201
Social media apps, 78, 81, 82, 87, 88, 93, 94, 154, 155, 163
Social practice art, 11
Social reciprocity factories, 84, 91
Social science, 31, 36
Sociograms, 20, 55, 63, 74, 201, 206
Sociomaterial frameworks, 8
Sociomaterialism, 19, 194, 195, 197, 209, 210, 214–217
Sociomaterialist, 194, 196, 210, 211, 216
Space of emergence, 82, 84, 86
Space-time, 110, 111
Spatiality, 21, 103
Spatial missions, 21, 127, 128, 130, 131, 133–138, 143, 145, 147, 148, 150
Special needs, 152, 162
Spinoza's Ethics, 31
Still life drawing, 152
Still-life Self-Portraits, 167, 177
Stopmotion, 94
Stop-motion animation, 170, 171, 173, 174

Subcultures, 52
Symbolic Interactionists School, 49
Synchronous online connectivity, 106, 109

T
Technology, 4, 5, 8, 10, 19, 21, 22, 28, 36, 38, 39, 45, 54, 77, 78, 80–83, 86, 87, 98, 99, 103, 105, 109, 110, 151–153, 155–157, 162, 163, 165, 182, 194, 202, 205, 215
Theory of affect, 29–31
Thing-power, 196, 198
Third-space pedagogy, 10
Traditional photography, 165
Transformation, 9, 134, 194–196, 198, 209–214

U
Ubiquity, 2, 10, 44, 209
Undesirable learning, 213

Unifunctional, 97
Uploading Photos, 166
Utility apps, 94, 96

V
Virtual, 35, 40, 43, 48, 52, 84, 87, 92, 94, 107, 190
Virtualities, 28, 29, 34, 35, 39, 42–44
Visual mapping, 183–186, 190
Visual representations, 200

W
Worked-example approach, 5

Y
YouTube, 92, 95–98, 177

Z
Zones of proximal development, 11

Printed in the United States
By Bookmasters